METHUEN LIBRARY REPRINTS

SBN/416 13350 9

ON THE WRITING OF HISTORY

ON THE
WRITING OF HISTORY

by

Sir CHARLES OMAN

K.B.E., Hon. D.C.L. Oxford, Hon. LL.D.
Cambridge and Edinburgh, F.B.A.

CHICHELE PROFESSOR OF MODERN HISTORY
IN THE UNIVERSITY OF OXFORD

BARNES & NOBLE, Inc.
New York

METHUEN & CO. Ltd
London

First Published, 1939

Reprinted, 1969
by
Barnes & Noble, Inc., New York
and
Methuen & Co. Ltd, London

Printed in the United States of America

PREFACE

HISTORY, I conceive, may be best defined as man's effort to record the doings of man. And since men differ infinitely in their characters, positions, and opportunities, the records will present the most varying aspects, ranging from the autolatrous narrative of his own exploits by an ancient Eastern king, to a propagandic attempt to represent (or misrepresent) the whole of the annals of mankind as a logical process, tending to justify an author's personal opinions—philosophical, religious, political, or economic. 'Il n'y a pas d'Histoire, mais seulement des histoires,' wrote the French critic. This devastating epigram goes too far. For while it is true that all written history bears the impress of the writer's personality—even when he is trying to be impersonal —there are certain crude facts which cannot be denied. Julius Cæsar was certainly murdered, Alaric sacked Rome, Charlemagne was crowned on Christmas Day A.D. 800, Napoleon lost the battle of Waterloo. But as to precisely why and precisely how these events took place, historians may have the most divergent views according to their predispositions. It is sometimes possible for the patient researcher to come to definite conclusions which satisfy not only himself but all other reasonable persons. But adequate and complete evidence is not accessible in all cases, and when it is not, the researcher—call him historian or historiographer or what you please—must be content to submit his reconstruction of a crisis, a period, a course of centuries, or his conception of a human personality, as the nearest thing to truth that he can attain. Another historian may come to different conclusions, and each will regard the other as misguided, perhaps as maliciously perverse. Perchance the exhilarating clash of controversy may follow—an exercise not so habitual with historians as with philosophers—but still not infrequent, and always satisfying. For every historian—like every philosopher—thinks at the end of a controversy that he has defeated his opponent. And even if the balance of learned opinion leans in favour of one controversialist, the other will be placidly content. 'Populus me sibilat; at mihi plaudo '—or to use a modern tongue, ' il n'y a que moi qui aie toujours raison '.

Recognizing, then, that even in what is generally called ' accepted history ' there may be room for doubts, I have ventured in this book to make certain suggestions as to the way in which those who wish to study it, and still more those who intend to commit their views to paper, should start upon their way. It is above all necessary to ' try the sources '. The sources may sometimes be thin, obviously poisoned at the fount, when all the available evidence is *ex parte*. Or they may be so numerous, and coming from so many spring-heads, that the stream of history grows turbid, and those who gaze into it may see very different reflections. It is easy to note the whirls and eddies which correspond to one's own expectations, and to ignore those which do not. This, as I have stated further on, is the main danger to all honest historians. The secondary danger is that of getting so much absorbed in research that the student may lose himself in hypotheses—like a German advocate of *Quellen forschung* sniffing round the New Testament— and produce not readable narrative but spiders' webs of controversy. Above all, we should be comprehensible, and this is possible without having to adopt the ruthless methods of the *vulgarisateur*, who tells his story with blatant self-confidence, and ignores all facts that fail to fit into his version. This sometimes comes from mere ignorance—there are those who rush into print to serve their own propagandic ends, without having mastered all the evidence, preferring to leave unread what tells against them.

I hold, then, that the historian must submit the results of his research with a frank acknowledgment that his work bears the impress of his personality, and that he makes no claim to omniscience or infallibility. He has made an honest attempt to grapple with all the accessible material, and has not neglected to take into consideration the evidence that seems to clash with some of his conclusions. To do otherwise would reduce him to the moral level of the *vulgarisateur*. Above all, he must not 'pontificate', and denounce all who differ from him as ignorant, or malevolent, and worthy of condign chastisement. To use such language is merely unmannerly. One may correct without being abusive.

A book must bear the impress of the author's personality, and inevitably of his moral judgment of men and things. The attempt of certain worthy people to push self-restraint so far that they merely record events without commenting on them, leads to the production of unreadable books. One feels sometimes that one might as well settle down to peruse Haydn's *Dictionary of Dates*. It is far more stimulating to the mind to come upon the effusions of a fanatic, or an acknowledged liar. Then, at least, one's attention will not falter.

It has often been the fashion to censure authors who are accused of holding that historical writing is a department of *belles-lettres*. There may, in some cases, be a foundation for the charge. To drag in epigrams and paradoxes, and to wander off into irrelevant rhapsodies, or picturesque imaginings of the motives which may have swayed a man or a mob, is no doubt reprehensible. Not less so, however, is the fault of crushing out all colour, and of treating events as merely episodes in some process of inevitable evolution, and personalities as merely typical developments of their age or their surroundings. This tendency is at its worst when an author composes a sort of pseudo-scientific vocabulary of his own, and makes matters darker by using words in senses not appreciated by the common man—the usual fault of philosophers, but one that need not affect the historian. I have made some humble remarks later on in this book on the abuse of the word ' progress '.

If I have any messages to deliver which are not mere glimpses of the obvious, they may be summed up in two phrases. The first is that the writing of history is a matter for individuals, and that joint-stock history is a mistake—despite of Lord Acton's eloquent pleading in its favour. The second is that in my conception history is a series of interesting happenings, often illogical and cataclysmic, not a logical and orderly development from causes to inevitable results. In short, history is full of ' might-have-beens', and these sometimes deserve as much attention as the actual, but by no means necessary, course of events.

C. OMAN

OXFORD, *September* 1939

CONTENTS

I

WHAT IS HISTORY?

AFTER having been for fifty-three years occupied in the writing and teaching of history, it is not unnatural that one should have endeavoured to arrive at the exact meaning of that almost too familiar word. The conclusion is not so easy to reach as might have been expected, for on careful investigation, it is found that different people attach very different connotations to it.

I have heard it asserted, by those who take the widest possible views, that 'History' is the record of all that has ever happened, so far as it can be ascertained. Most of these people would limit the inquiry to what has happened in this terrestrial globe of ours. But logically the term might be expanded to embrace the record of what has happened in the solar system or the universe. The idea is not so surprising as might at first be thought—for many universal histories of the ancient sort go back to the formation of the round world from chaos as a preliminary excursus—certainly the Greeks, the Hindus, and the Hebrews started from this point. I am not sure that Mr. Wells to-day does not do the same. In this sense history would include the origins of the universe, not merely of the world.

But most writers would be content to restrict the meaning of the word History to the record of what has happened since *homo sapiens* appeared and began to leave traces of himself in his flint or stone tools and weapons. They may leave the ichthyosaurus and the pterodactyl out of the scope of their inquiry. The word History, coming from the original Greek verb ἱστορεῖν, means primarily inquiry and investigation, and *might* undoubtedly be extended to mean inquiry into everything that can be investigated—such as geography and geology, the development of plant and animal life, no less than of human life. Herodotus, the father of ' history ' as we all call him, thought it quite within the scope of his inquiry to make hypotheses as to the geological origin of the defile of Tempe— with the wise corollary that ' perhaps anything might happen in a very long space of time '. But clearly a historian of to-day may make inquiries, quite legiti- mately, as to the desiccation of those wide tracts of Central Asia where Marc Aurèle Stein digs up temples and documents from the rolling sand, or as to the formation of the Zuider Zee, or the erosion of the east coast of England, or the apparently radical change in the climate of Greenland, which seems to have been a main cause of the extinction of the ancient Norse settlement in that Arctic region. One cannot eradicate physical phenomena in the world from the sphere of historical inquiry, though man is not responsible for earthquakes, or volcanic explosions, or tidal waves.

But I think that in the main History must be held to be concerned with man, and that his records rather than those of the world's surface must be the chief object of our research. There was a time when one might have almost said his written records or perhaps his oral traditions to a certain extent. But to

parody an ancient epigram, ' the spade is mightier than
the pen,' and of recent years, since Archæology superseded Antiquarianism, the spade has not only supple-
mented the evidence of the pen, but in many cases
controverted it, so that early tradition has to be swept
aside by reconstruction of ancient happenings—often,
unhappily enough, rather hypothetical reconstruction.
Look at any history of the Eastern Mediterranean
lands as told by an eighteenth- or early nineteenth-
century historian, compared with the latest attempts
to arrive at a consecutive story. What would Rollin
or even Grote have made of Minoan, Sumerian, or
Hittite paragraphs in the learned volumes of to-day ?
It is one of the fascinations of historical inquiry that
there are long epochs where the inquirer may revel in
hypotheses, just as scientists have long been able to
do in their physics, chemistry, medicine, or biology.
And this not only in the epochs which we were wont
to call pre-historic—but the term has now become
antiquated—but in far more recent periods. The
enterprising historian may make for himself almost
as many explanatory hypotheses as he pleases on the
inner meaning or the inner causes of such phenomena
as folk-wanderings of many ages, the break-up of
the Roman Empire, the Anglo-Saxon settlement of
England, the Renaissance, or the French Revolution.
And if he chooses to stress some pieces of evidence,
and to attenuate others, and perhaps to invent a few
more from his inner consciousness, he may provide
delightful controversies with other historians, who
have chosen to envisage the sum of the phenomena
in another pattern. Sometimes the juxtaposition of a
sufficient number of contradictory reconstructions

of a period of history will provoke from the irreverent
man in the street the conclusion at which Benedetto
Croce's dazed pupil arrived, that the true and positive
record of any series of events is so uncertain that it is
quite unnecessary to bother about them at all. Nothing
can be known with certainty, and ' doctors disagree '.
The worthy Walter Raleigh, as an amusing, if not
quite contemporary tale relates, got a glimpse of
this attitude of mind when he made a note of that
sudden scuffle in the Tower, of which he, as an eye-
witness, and other persons present, all gave completely
contradictory accounts. Nevertheless he started to
write a Universal History, defiantly, and got as far
as Perseus and Æmilius Paullus in that extraordinary
and eloquent torso. The anecdote would have a
more convincing effect if he himself had left a record
of it—but it is only attributed to him. I am far
from being driven to this agnostic conclusion, and
am prepared in most cases to act like a Scottish jury,
and to give my verdict of ' proven ' or ' not proven '
when there is what judges call no ' reasonable doubt '
about the facts. Though what is ' proven ' in a
historical verdict may often be problematic—the
event must be conceded—e.g. the sack of Rome by
Alaric, the crowning of Charlemagne, or the Peace of
Versailles. But what were its essential causes, and
its consequential results ? This is specially difficult
when the moral judgment tries to slip in, as it so
often does. Moral conventions vary in different ages
and among different peoples—as King Darius discovered when he interrogated certain Greeks and
certain Indians as to the proper way of disposing of
deceased parents. They seem still to differ to-day,

to one brought up like myself in Victorian decades, when I contemplate happenings in Germany or Russia, and the enthusiastic comments of certain Germans and Russians upon them. But, as I shall explain presently, I am endeavouring to look upon the record of history, so far as we can recover it, as a thing not to be contemplated merely from the point of view of enforcing moral judgments by the observation of human vices or virtues. This has been a very popular conception both in ancient and in modern times among certain classes of historians. But I fear that it is only one of the many aspects of the vision called the ' Philosophy of History ', against whose acceptance as the explanation of all things I am presently about to protest.

But meanwhile I am compelled, somewhat ruefully, to confess that history, in the all-embracing conception of it which some people nourish, must show as its branches the annals of all human activities, from the discovery of the use of fire to the invention of radiotelegraphy. I suppose that it must include the detailed survey of the development of agriculture, metallurgy, navigation, medicine, music and art. The thing that I used, in my simple youth, to call history, is now labelled ' political, military, religious, and constitutional history '. This is a dire blow to the poor Victorian : with the greatest desire to avoid narrow-mindedness, I still cannot rise to the duty of acquainting myself with and mastering the history of flint-knapping, or of Chinese music. There are some people—I think Mr. Wells is one of them, who find more pleasure in contemplating the development of cereal agriculture, or telegraphy, than in following the story of Julius Cæsar, the Crusades, or Napoleon. And no doubt I ought to be mastering all the folio pages of Herbert Spencer's tabulated indices on the manners and customs of savage tribes, and following all the suggestions of *The Golden Bough* with enthusiasm, rather than reading La Noue and Montluc about the Huguenot Wars of France, or puzzling out the evidence concerning the Massacre of St. Bartholomew. From the point of view of the advocates of the 'Wider Oneness' in history, the fortunes of sixteenth-century England or France are relatively unimportant. I fear, therefore, that I must confine myself to collecting my premises and drawing my conclusions about a 'History' that is taken more or less in the old sense, and that does not include either speculations as to the formation of the terrestrial globe, or arguments as to the causes why the Blackfellows of Australia were still in the 'stone age' when Captain Cook came upon them, and had been so when the Parthenon, or the Pyramids, were being erected a few thousand years back. Still less shall I endeavour to follow those who make calculations as to the number of millennia that must have intervened between the invention of flint-knapping and that of gunpowder. The 'History' on which I am commenting will only go back to the ages in which we have documentary or monumental evidence to help us, though it will have to include what human tradition believed about those documentary or monumental pieces of evidence. For we must occasionally take notice of what later ages thought about works of which the real date or origin had been forgotten. These conceptions of the later men about the relics

left behind by the earlier men were often erroneous
and sometimes absurd. What the Hebrew thought
about the Tower of Babel, or Herodotus about the
Labyrinth, or the early Saxon invader about ' Wodens-
dyke ', or Geoffrey of Monmouth about the setting-up
of Stonehenge, is worth noting—if only to show the
development of what some people call ' ætiological
myths ', and the way in which they creep into historical record. But often there is something more
valuable than this in the traditions of the later age.

History, then, is the investigation of evidence,
written or sometimes unwritten, about series of events
concerning which we are able to make some conclusion. It is dangerous to say in many cases that
we can give the real and complete account of such a
series of events, but we can arrive at certain results
which to the inquirer are acceptable. This is not
altogether clear to the man in the street, or the beginner
in investigation, who comes to the historian with
some simple-sounding query—to ask not merely
the date of the battle of Hastings or the American
' Declaration of Independence ', but to inquire where
a succinct account of the Reformation, or the French
Revolution may be obtained. The inquirer must too
often be given not the certain and definite answer
that he wants, but a list of controversial works setting
forth different views, and coming to divergent conclusions. At the most, the honest historian can only
say that, in his own opinion such and such a work
sets forth the story best—but he must own that there
are people who consider that work biased or mis-
leading. For history is not a purely objective thing,
it is the historian's way of envisaging and correlating

a certain series of events. As the Frenchman said, ' Il n'y a pas d'Histoire—mais seulement des histoires '.

One may, perhaps, when the period is sufficiently remote, obtain a standard account of Ptolemaic Egypt, or the provincial system of Imperial Rome, or of the administrative methods of a mediæval monastery, or of the organization of the Byzantine army. But can any one conceive a standard history of the Jews or the Jesuits, of the Balkan Peninsula in the Middle Ages, or of England in the seventeenth century, which should be equally acceptable to a Jew, a Roman Catholic, a Protestant, a Greek, Serb, Bulgarian, or Turk, or a modern English Liberal and Conservative ? If there is any large section of history on which no controversy ever takes place—it must be a pretty dead section of history ! But such stagnant reaches are not too common—in early times controversy can range on the validity of evidence ; in later times on the moral or political meaning of an event or an epoch. Some writers can get excited and controversial about the Hittites or the Etruscans—others as to the real drift of Magna Carta, or the underlying motives of the Great Peasant Revolt of 1381. The evidence of the spade can sometimes be the source of controversy, no less than the evidence of autobiographies or official documents. All this wrangling keeps history alive, and is a joy to countless researchers, and to the editors of Reviews, Zeitschrifts and Journals, monthly or quarterly.

But to get to my main point—History looked at from the right point of view, is (I think) a series of happenings, not a logical process, and those who try to explain it by the popular slogans such as are inspired by the words 'Evolution' and 'Progress' are not to be trusted—least of all when they, consciously or unconsciously, slip in philosophical or moral deductions from their observation of world-annals. The fact is that History is not a tale of logical processes or necessary evolutions, but a series of happenings—some of them so startling as to deserve to be called cataclysms. One has to study these happenings with a cautious conviction that they *might* have happened otherwise, and that no word is so dangerous as the word 'inevitable', and no conception so dangerous as the idea 'progress'—unless (of course) one takes progress in the literal sense, and makes it mean no more than movement in one direction, e.g. Hogarth's 'The Rake's Progress'. For movement may mean motion towards a precipice no less than towards a paradise. When I read certain authors I am reminded of the schoolboys whom I used to examine forty years ago, and who always answered the familiar question, 'Are we better than our ancestors?' with the cheerful reply, 'Yes, certainly, for they were ignorant of steamers, railway trains, and electric lighting.'

Whenever I run upon a writer whose papers are full of abstract general terms, such as Liberty or Anarchy, Natural Man, inimitable ideas of morality, Free Thought or Free Trade, State Socialism, the rights of the Individual, Orthodoxy or Heresy, economic desiderata, constitutional or unconstitutional, I know that I have come upon a propagandist, and must go warily in accepting either his premises or his conclusions. Wherefore popular phrases about the 'Philosophy of History' leave me very cold.

And as I look through the casual historical allusions which abound in certain works, I am reminded of the wise dictum of the centenarian Doctor Routh of Magdalen to the young and enthusiastic Burgon, ' Always verify your references '. Propagandists often find it convenient to quote the phrase and to slur over the context. And you cannot expect them to give an unbiased account of the views of those with whom they are controverting—this is too much to ask of any man. This criticism, no doubt, applies to myself as well as to every one else.

Looking therefore on history as a series of happenings, sometimes apparently inconsequent, our main task is to make out what observers, contemporary or non-contemporary, have thought about them, with no *parti pris*. But, of course, we soon learn that the observer may sometimes be stupid, ill-informed, or consciously malignant, capable both of *suppressio veri* and of *suggestio falsi*. There have been not infrequent writers from John Cantacuzenus in his monastery down to Talleyrand in his old age at Valençay, and Napoleon Bonaparte at St. Helena, whose every statement must be investigated with suspicion. And occasionally one meets with historical authors who not merely falsified facts, but actually invented long screeds of deliberate lies, like Geoffrey of Monmouth and some others of his mediæval compeers. Of them more hereafter, when we are speaking of the investigation of sources. The tendencious compilation of forged annals was a development of the same mentality that led thirteenth-century abbots to manufacture forged charters, when they had some manorial gain to compass. But to invent history may be merely a method of self-advertisement, or an outbreak of megalomania, on the part of a literary man of the ' pushing ' type, who is determined to make himself known. It corresponds to the publication of false travels of a startling sort, like George Psalmanazar's account of Formosa, or de Rougemont's adventures in Northern Australia. Or again, the unscrupulous aspirant to literary renown may produce out of his brain mediæval plays and poems like poor Chatterton, or mislaid Shakespearian tragedies like Samuel William Ireland.

Some historic forgeries are not obviously propagandic for any political end, but merely intended to secure celebrity for the inventor, like Professor Bertram's wonderful account of Roman Britain in the spurious *Richard of Cirencester.* But more, perhaps, as we shall presently see, are not simply devices for self-advertisement, but attempts to falsify history in the service of some cause, national or religious, which needs a little support in the matter of fresh evidence. The sad thing, of course, is that the injudicious forger may suffer rapid exposure, and do his cause terrible harm. But there are plenty of cases where no immediate indictment and conviction has followed, and where a piece of forged history has had its influence for centuries—as was the case with Geoffrey of Monmouth—and—a much more important instance—the matter of the False Decretals, which were taken seriously and used as the most powerful political tool through all the long struggle of the Popes and Emperors in the Middle Ages. Even Bertram's *Richard of Cirencester* had about a century of acceptance.

We must, of course, distinguish between the
work of the deliberate falsifier and that of the merely
stupid repeater of obviously erroneous statements
concerning the past. He is much easier to convict of
careless or reckless driving as he speeds on his way.
Sometimes he is really ignorant of the fact that
memories of tribal legends, or of rumours that were
disproved long ago, or obvious anachronisms, should
be tested before being written down. In the Middle
Ages the reverence for the written word of a predecessor was so all-pervading, that astounding statements continued to be repeated by chronicler after
chronicler, each copying the last ; it was rather
exceptional to find the man who used his critical sense,
and disputed a generally accepted legend, because he
found impossibilities in it. Sometimes the impossibilities were very humorous ones, as I shall be showing
when I come to deal with Ralph Higden's reasons
given in his *Polychronicon* for rejecting much of early
Greek history. But very frequently a screed of false
annals continued to be repeated for generation after
generation—many survived till the Renaissance set
men's minds to the investigation of all ancient evidence,
however time-hallowed. The same impulse that led
to the testing of the validity of the False Decretals
led, in a less important sphere, to the exposure of
early screeds of British History, like the stories of
Brutus the Trojan who landed at Totnes, and colonized
the island which was to take its name from him, or
of King Lear and his daughters, or the birth of
Constantine the Great from Helena the daughter of
Old King Cole of Colchester, or of the dealings of
Merlin with Vortigern. All this stuff survived in

serious chronicles down to the end of Tudor times, and was only thrown over in the seventeenth century, though William of Newburgh—almost a contemporary of Geoffrey—had denounced it as an impudent fable very soon after it was published. It got the forger the bishopric of St. Asaph—the sort of prize, no doubt, that he was aiming at when he startled the learned world with his preposterous composition.

One must distinguish a deliberate forger like Geoffrey from less malignant falsifiers of history, who merely added folk-tales and tribal legends on to the beginning of the first periods of which they had real knowledge, such as Snorro Sturleson, Saxo Grammaticus, or the Lombard Paulus Diaconus : their pre-history is always far less obviously a deliberate compilation by a forger than Geoffrey's stuff ; it merely patches up national origins by echoes from sagas and ballads.

Attempts to bolster up legendary history, by the more ingenious method of forging monuments or inscriptions instead of chronicles, are not very common, but by no means unknown. Sometimes a false tradition was attached to an existing monument of uncertain age, and after a time some ingenious corroborator added an inscription to the already time-hallowed tomb or stones. Such was the case with King Arthur's much-visited sepulchre in Glastonbury Abbey, revered by so many pilgrims. Absolute deliberate forgery was a later development—very prevalent among eighteenth-century antiquaries, who wished to prove their private hypotheses by visible evidence. If they could not misread an existing inscription—like Sir Walter Scott's Monkbarns in *The Antiquary*—who turned a crude eighteenth-century scratching into a memorial of Agricola—they sometimes foisted a surreptitious discovery on the archæologists of a not too exacting generation. There was once a terrible example in the Edinburgh National Museum, purporting to be a contemporary record of the breaking of the Great Roman Wall. But the habit was as prevalent on the Continent as in Britain—French and Italian antiquarians were quite capable of glorifying a city or a family by a conveniently discovered inscription. This mentality still persists—as witness the elaborately forged Glozel finds, of a prehistoric alphabet among various shards, which have excited French archæologists within the last ten years—and actually found some defenders.

Such work links on with less creditable instances of misplaced ingenuity, which have crude financial gain as their impelling cause, not the mere corroboration of a theory or the self-advertisement of an ambitious excavator. I mean, of course, the forgery of coins, jewels, or statues for which Renaissance Italy had such an unenviable celebrity. The skilled engraver or sculptor found that there was a market for ancient Greek or Roman stuff, and proceeded to supply it, often with the greatest ingenuity. Cavino and the other Paduan forgers of ancient Roman coins of historic interest kept a *bottega* which supplied princely cabinets with medals of every possible historic event or hero. They would even produce coins of Tarquin or Miltiades if there was a demand for them. This was comparatively innocent, since the modern specialist knows the coins impossible. But improvisation of new interesting moneys of people who *had* struck coins was worse. A good many of us have seen the medals of Julius Cæsar with VENI VIDI VICI in a wreath, and of Nero, Titus, or Hadrian with vast edifices on their reverses. The ' Paduans,' as these falsities are generally named—though they did not all come from Padua, have long ceased to deceive. But the spiritual descendants of the Renaissance forgers still survive, and occasionally have their triumphs. The gold Roman aurei of the Hofrath Becker still survive in some collections—so do the Greek staters of Constantine Christodoulos. But the greatest of all modern achievements of the forger was the tiara of Saitaphernes, the vast Greco-Scythian gold helm which adorned the Louvre for many years in my memory, till it was deposed on the discovery of its ingenious maker still alive in Odessa. Somebody must have made a good deal of money out of it, when the specialists of the Louvre acquired it, and placed it in a position of honour. But all this sort of forgery must be carefully differentiated from the other class of forgery which has either propaganda of some sort, or the desire for self-advertisement at its back. The ' fake ' ever since the sixteenth century has normally been produced merely to make dishonest gain ; it will continue so long as there are artists who are unscrupulous, and buyers who are insufficiently expert in the lines of research in which they are interested.

But putting aside imposture, we have to consider other pitfalls for the student of any branch of history. One of the most obvious is the desire to discover corroborative evidence for one's particular conception of a period, or an individual, or of a general *weltanschauung* as the Germans call it. This is most

easily accomplished by a judicious choice of authorities
of the right tendencies, and a blind eye turned to
those which are less convenient. When vexed with
an authority whose narrative contradicts one's theories,
it is easy to decry him, to point out his untrustworthy
bias, or perhaps, applying the newest methods, to
show that there is internal evidence of his having
used poisoned sources in his compilation. For early
and ancient periods it is, of course, more profitable to
discover traces of miscellaneous borrowing in the
inconvenient author. In modern times it is always
open to use the art of ' debunking ', to show that an
author's family origins, education, political connex-
ions, or private life, make him a source unworthy of
serious confidence. And, of course, there are such
authors, as I have already explained, whose every
statement has to be tested—but sometimes their
testimony has a basis of fact, and it is unsafe to say
that a thing never happened merely because A or B
declares that it did happen. Statements of an inconvenient sort must be investigated before they are
turned down. Occasionally our evidence is contradictory enough to make one doubt whether the
' received version ' of an episode is quite convincing.
I remember this feeling coming upon me more than
once in reading ancient history. Can one trust Cicero
or Demosthenes with complete confidence about the
character and aims of Catiline or Æschines ? Political
orators defending themselves are notoriously biased,
partisan writers not less so. Hence arises a tendency
of revulsion, opposite to that of ' debunking ', which
impels some writers on history to take up the task of
' whitewashing ', to prove that the Emperor Claudius

was not a pedantic fool but a far-sighted statesman, or that Richard III was a pious and conscientious man, quite incapable of having murdered his nephews, the victim of the malice of Tudor detractors.

Personally I distrust both the ' debunker ' and the ' whitewasher ', foes equally to a sound judgment. But I am *not* content to say that the two of them, taken together, will reduce one to a sort of middle conclusion, and leave one with a feeling that no historical character is either white or black—all a sort of whitey-brown. Quite the reverse—I believe that there have been thoroughly worthy men, and thoroughly bad ones. And I am under the impression that the most insidious epigram in the world is ' tout comprendre c'est tout pardonner ', i.e. that excuses and palliations can be found for the most detestable characters. Those who plead in this fashion for Nero or Marat are, to my mind, misguided. Nevertheless, as I have said already, this is only my personal opinion, and I am undoubtedly allowing my moral sense to influence me. Moral sense being a personal affair, it is open for any one with a moral sense of a different brand to differ from me. But I shall continue to hold him a very misguided individual—he may hold the same opinion about me, if he pleases, and may set forth his theses, which will certainly not convince me. Some people adore Adolf Hitler, others Karl Marx. I am therefore of the opinion that where we have considerable evidence from both sides, we are entitled to make up our judgment and reach our conclusion, but it must only be after careful consideration of the inconvenient evidence from the defendant's witnesses. In short, the working historian must act as a jury of

2

one—he may give his ' guilty ' or ' not guilty '—
sometimes like the cautious Scot he may have to fall
back on the unsatisfactory ' not proven '.   But a
continuous series of ' not provens ' makes a dull
record.   There are people who have written history
on that line of thought, setting forth ' pros ' and
' cons ', and sitting on the hedge when the decision
ought to be given.   From the reader's point of view this
is disappointing—he prefers a verdict of some sort,
not a string of counterbalanced arguments with a
query at the end.

Occasionally one meets with history written from
the point of view of the ' superior person ', who looks
upon the antics of men and nations with the sort of
feeling with which we regard the apparently objectless
scurryings to and fro of the inhabitants of an ant-heap.
Perhaps such writers do not feel the decided contempt
and dislike for mankind in general and its habits
which Swift showed in *Gulliver's Travels*, but they
show a sort of contemptuous pity for the futile activities of their predecessors or their contemporaries.
This is the sort of attitude of survey which one can
detect in Gibbon's famous *Decline and Fall of the
Roman Empire*—a book with a curious misnomer.
The superior person studies the mentalities of the
men of past times with curiosity, but seldom with
sympathy.   There may be a sigh for the end of the
Age of the Antonines, ' the period in which the
greatest number of mortals in recorded history
enjoyed the greatest amount of peace and prosperity '.
A little deeper inquiry shows that this was not a real
Golden Age, but an age of gilded iron, when ideals
were dead, the old religion defunct, and Art and

Literature slowly sinking toward the decadence of the
third century. But what really interested Gibbon were
the absurdities of Byzantine Court ceremonial, the
eccentricities of hermits and heresiarchs, the spiritual
pride of those thirteenth-century quietist monks on
Mount Athos who could see the divine light of Mount
Tabor by putting themselves into a state of self-
hypnotization, or the delusions of Mohammedan
fanatics or early Crusaders.

Surveying the men of the Dark Ages with the
serene self-satisfaction of eighteenth-century culture,
and a wide knowledge of literature and history—not
quite so all-embracing as he thought—Gibbon produced a picture of human violence and futility, with a
conviction that all this was coming to an end in an age
of more enlightened reason. He finished the last
page of his great work on June 27, 1787, launched it
on the world in 1788, and survived just long enough
to see the development of the French Revolution.
This was a tragedy as violent as any that he had
described with such philosophic irony. He died on
January 16, 1794, in the middle of the ' Reign of
Terror ', a few months after the execution of Queen
Marie Antoinette, and a few months before those of
Danton (April 5) and Robespierre (July 28). He
had lived just long enough to hear of the ' Goddess of
Reason ' enthroned on the high altar of Notre Dame.
But what a goddess—and what Reason !

But the superior person who writes histories is still
with us—I often come upon him pontificating. A
few years ago he was explaining to us that all ancient
evils were to vanish under the happy reign of the
League of Nations. The Golden Age was once more

at hand, and old national and racial hatreds were to
die down. To-day this thesis is getting a little out of
date. Now one set of superior persons are assuming the
mantle of Cassandra and warning us of the approach-
ing end of light and liberty. While yet another set
again are proclaiming their enthusiasm for the happy
removal of all old conventions, and rejoicing in the
casting off of the burdens of intellectualism and
individualism under the régime of the totalitarian
state—which is to make them all homogeneous if
not all contented. I noted a German speech last
summer in which the actual boast was made that the
Reich had shaken off ' the nightmare of intellectualism '. Comment is superfluous—thought is to die
out, and blind obedience to authority to be the only
mental attitude permitted to the citizen—or rather
to the slave of the state. If he persists in thinking
aloud, he will find himself proclaimed a public enemy,
and must expect the doom of the traitor. I shudder
to think of the sort of faked history which will form
part of the pabulum served out to the normal individual, and wonder how far he will be able to digest it
without difficulty.

I got a glimpse of the said pabulum in a pamphlet
sent me in July, setting forth how ' true German '
history should be taught. Perhaps it was not more
surprising than some Irish popular histories which
I have glanced at—the difference was that the Gaul
and the Jew halved the part which the Englishman
has all to himself in certain manuals from across St.
George's Channel. There was a Teutonic Golden
Age, just as there was a Celtic Golden Age, when all
was romantic (if somewhat in the twilight) before

the pestilent alien intervened. Of course the primitive Teuton was essentially much more civilized than the Roman, just as the Ivernian was when compared with the Viking or the Norman. And what scoundrels were those malevolent witnesses Sidonius Apollinaris and Giraldus Cambrensis who talked about 'barbarians' and unpleasant habits, and insufficient appreciation of *meum* and *tuum* among those heroes of the Teutonic or the Celtic Golden Ages! Propagandic history is the worst of all activities—fortunately it is usually produced by people with no sense of humour, and the critic has his hour of pleasure in cutting it up. But, all the same, it may do untold harm among simple folk, who are not equipped with the power or the desire to test it. A constant repetition of biased history is dangerous when there is no opportunity given of hearing the other side—and this is possible in a totalitarian state, when the governing power suppresses free discussion of official theories. There are, I fear, millions of Germans at the present moment who have never read the confutation of the old *einkreisung* allegations of 1914, which have now been revived as an explanation of the origin of the ' Great War '. This may seem absurd to English readers, who know that Edward VII and Mr. Asquith (oddly conjoined in German imaginations) were as unlikely people to pursue an offensive policy as can be imagined. But if counter-statements are unavailable for the student, official distortion of history may pass, in a way that would be impossible in a state where free discussion is available in history as in all other things debatable.

II

ON SOURCES AND EVIDENCE

AS I have already explained, I am taking 'history'
to mean not all that has happened since the
terrestrial globe came into existence, but a consideration of the record that man has made of man's doings.
Conclusions may be made not only from written
matter, but from all manner of unwritten evidence,
from tombs and temples down to statues, reliefs,
ornaments, implements, and furniture. There are
certain sections of history for which we have no written
authority at all. Not only is this true of prehistoric
periods, but also of epochs for which documentary
material no doubt once existed, but has perished.
Yet for some of these a sort of history can be reconstructed from other sources. Take, for example,
the Greek kingdoms in India in the first and second
centuries before the Christian era. The books of
Apollodorus of Artemita and Isidore of Charax are
lost, but we have from coins not only a long list of royal
names, but sidelights as to the extent of the dominions
of these kings, the conquests that they made, the sort
of civilization in which their subjects lived, the gods
that they worshipped, and the way in which their
power came to an end. This is a case in which some
sort of annals can be compiled—as witness the ingenious book recently published by Mr. Tarn, which
is full of probable hypotheses backed by some sort
of evidence, on which the specialist must form his own

conclusions. It is less easy to deal with lost civilizations like those of the Mayas in Central America, where what we possess is not legible coins, but vast surviving ruins, with plenty of architectural detail and carved relief, but no intelligible inscriptions or certain means for fixing dates. So, too, is it with the widespreading ground-plans of Mojendra-Daro in Scinde, which appear reasonably ancient, and the far more recent-looking discoveries in South Africa, such as the 'Zimbabwe Kraals'—as inscriptionless as the ruins of Scinde—possibly the relics of a dimly remembered ' Kingdom of Monomopata ' of which early Portuguese navigators told.

But I am afraid that I must leave the Mayas and the possible Kingdom of Monomopata alone, when I am dealing with the general trend of historic inquiry, and must leave them in company with Neolithic and Bronze Age pre-history (if the word may be used), though they may be in a mere chronological way less ancient than things visible in other regions of the world, concerning which we have more definite information—e.g. the relics of the Sumerians, the Hittites, or the Etruscans. For of these last we have a certain amount of available evidence in scripts that can be read more or less, and in scraps of traditional memory preserved by other races.

Visible but enigmatic traces of the civilization of perished communities are hard to fit into a general scheme of world-history. It is difficult to refuse the name of historical memorials to things small or great which were deliberately intended to be informative to later generations by those who fashioned them. This is true not only of inscriptions on stone or metal, or in later times to records on parchment or paper. The term covers, I suppose, even cairns or mounds erected over the bones or ashes of a king or a patriarch, and destined to keep a memory alive in the tribal community. Sometimes such endeavours have been successful—and the name of an otherwise forgotten worthy survives, perhaps in a mutilated form—as 'Scutchamfly Barrow' preserves the tradition of King Cwichelm of Wessex. Sometimes a later age has attached to a burial-mound a wholly erroneous attribution to some more recent personage. East and West are full of such misattributions, from Wales to Palestine.

But it must be confessed that the sort of 'history' with which we are dealing practically begins with the invention of writing—an early monument with a legible inscription is a very different thing from a barrow or a tumulus. And when inscriptions begin to be long, and are accompanied by the adornments of sculptures or bas-reliefs, and come to have explicatory 'captions' dealing with those representations, it cannot be denied that we have got into the edge of real history. Even if we had no written records to help us, we could put together a good deal of historical information, about Seti or Rameses, Sennacherib or Assur-Bani-Pal—not to speak of Augustus or Napoleon.

But of course inscribed monuments, triumphal or funerary, whether erected by a king to commemorate his own exploits, or by his successors to do him honour after his death, are necessarily very one-sided documents, to be used with all caution when reconstructing history. They must inevitably be laudatory. I only remember one memorial which is the reverse—the space dedicated to Marino Faliero in the set of portraits in the Doge's Palace at Venice—LOCUS MARINI FALERII DECAPITATI PRO CRIMINIBUS. The insincerity of funeral epitaphs is notorious : very unworthy personages may have pompous inscriptions set over their bones, from which no reader could have guessed at their real characters. And the same is true of honorific monuments or medallic inscriptions, which are often deplorably false. Statues of Louis XV, ' le bien aimé ', may be verified, as also medals commemorating the clemency of Tiberius, the security of the rule of Otho or Vitellius, the British victories of Caracalla, and the Parthian victories of Macrinus, while (most absurd of all) Gallienus, under whom the whole Roman Empire broke up in rebellion, chose UBIQUE PAX, as one of his numerous coin-types. Some equally humorous inscriptions may be quoted from the modern English currency. King Henry VIII, of sanguinary memory, styled himself on his gold crowns, HENRICUS REX ROSA SINE SPINA—the thornless rose ! And Charles I, with most unconscious irony, placed on his pennies JUSTICIA THRONUM FIRMAT, and on his gold angels AMOR POPULI PRÆSIDIUM REGIS—the King's protection is the love of his people !

Still, however insincere their wording, monuments and inscriptions do give some sort of evidence. Events which never took place are not generally recorded, though actual events may be lamentably misrepresented. I must, however, make one or two exceptions —there are medals which must be described as a little ' previous ', e.g. those which may be obtained at a moderate price commemorating the Coronation of King Edward VIII. But the most beautiful example

is the fine medal which Napoleon, while his army lay
at Boulogne, caused to be prepared at the Paris mint,
showing the DESCENTE EN ANGLETERRE, with a figure of
Hercules strangling the giant Antæus, and FRAPPÉ A
LONDRES below. But such cases of wholly false
evidence are rare—so rare that in arriving at historical
deduction they may practically be disregarded. What
does frequently occur in monumental records is
misrepresentation by way of exaggeration — biased
versions of things that did actually happen. For
example, to use instances which I have already quoted
—Caracalla was actually in Britain, though his
' victories ' ended in the evacuation of large tracts
of British ground, and Sennacherib did invade Judæa,
as his bas-reliefs show, though he in the end went
home foiled.

In many ancient and all modern cases, monumental evidence can be tested with the aid of written
sources. We know that despite of the Vendôme
column and the bridges of Jena and Austerlitz,
Napoleon did not end as the dictator of Europe, but
as an exile grumbling and fabricating history at
St. Helena. But who can say to what extent the
figured exploits of Egyptian or Assyrian kings represent actualities ? As the lion in Æsop's fable remarked to the man, there are many statues of men
slaying lions—but if only the lions were sculptors
there might be quite a different set of statues.

But I have been lingering too long over monumental evidence, and the need for testing it. History
is to be studied from many other sources—all modern
history mainly from written sources—chronicles,
autobiographies, speeches, pamphlets, collections of

treaties, charters, statistics, codes of laws, and so forth. The task before the historiographer, of correlating diverse material, and testing every item before he arrives at the conclusion which seems to him most reasonable, is full of difficulty. But when he has made his decision, he must make it clear. Stolid impartiality, the setting forth of ' pros ' and ' cons ' with no definite final judgment, can only lead to the production of very dead stuff.

In this line of composition that admirable man, Lord Acton, went wrong, as I feel, when he put forward his conception of the historian as a passionless creature, in the famous introductory preface which he wrote for the *Cambridge Modern History*. ' Contributors must understand,' he said, ' that nobody must be able to tell, without examining the list of authors, where Bishop Stubbs laid down the pen, and whether it was Fairbairn or Gasquet, Liebermann or Frederic Harrison, who took it up. . . . Our account of Waterloo, for example, must be one that satisfies French and English, German and Dutch, readers alike.' I may remark, incidentally, that the admirable *Cambridge Modern History* has not actually reached this ideal : individualities peep out. The chapter on Waterloo, as it chanced, fell to my own charge. Though I did my best to arrive at exact truth, I cannot declare conscientiously that it would satisfy patriotic German or Dutch readers. In sober fact, it is impossible to write history, save in the most arid form of annals, which will satisfy every one, whatever his race or creed. ' Litera scripta manet ', no doubt ; but our first task is to test our authorities ; all written stuff has not the same value, and it is sometimes necessary to reject authorities as reliable material, even contemporary ones. There are chronicles, autobiographies, speeches and pamphlets composed with deliberate intention of misrepresenting the truth, if not of absolutely denying it. Less malignant, but equally tiresome to the student of history, are documents in which the author is not intentionally falsifying the progress of events, but practically doing so, owing to bad information, personal bias, or sometimes mere stupidity. To the former class of untrustworthy authorities belong many insincere autobiographies, many libellous pamphlets, and many political speeches, in all of which the perpetrator was quite aware of his own false witness, but was set either on shirking responsibility for his own acts, or on obtaining some temporary advantage by a bold assertion of untruths. To the second class we may ascribe all manner of misstatements not made from deliberate intention to lie, but coming from the heedless acceptance of rumours, unjustified suspicions, or the dislike to accept good evidence because it is unpalatable.

I have already mentioned some cases of absolute deliberate forgery, when speaking of the early British history of Geoffrey of Monmouth, and of Bertram's ingenious *Richard of Cirencester*—examples of shameless invention. These purported to be discoveries of ancient documents : Geoffrey challenged all critics to be silent, because they had not seen the Welsh chronicle of early British kings ' which Walter Archdeacon of Oxford brought out of Brittany '. Bertram copied a manuscript in the Copenhagen Library which unfortunately got burned just after he had completed his transcription !

But much more common are falsifications of autobiography, when a scoundrel tries to cover patches of his discreditable past—like Barons Kolli and Trenck —or a statesman to shuffle out of moral responsibilities, as did John Cantacuzenus (a bad specimen of a Byzantine), or both Talleyrand and Savary in the pages of their controversy which relate to the judicial murder of the Duke of Enghien. They hated each other, but each came to the conclusion that the whole burden of guilt might best be laid on the broad shoulders of Bonaparte—who did not refuse to accept it.

Deliberate falsification with intent to deceive, and the use of conscious falsehood, is perhaps less frequent than misstatement made on inadequate grounds from personal bias. Stupid repetitions of old rumours fall into this class—they go back far into the Middle Ages and were often repeated for generations. One is not too careful to test evidence which falls in with our own prepossessions—though evidence contrary to them runs the risk of being criticized or even ignored, when one has one's thesis to set forth. Orators in the law courts or the political assembly can always make out a case if they turn a blind eye to counter-pleas, and think only of the end that they have in view—the conviction of an enemy, or the discrediting of a minister. Vitriolic stuff, like Coke's indictment of Sir Walter Raleigh, Pitt's of Walpole, or Burke's of Warren Hastings provoke only exasperation in the historian, who must yet read them in order to appreciate the mental attitude of partisans at the moment. The net result may perhaps be that the reader begins to conceive doubts as to the whole picture—to wonder if Cicero's attacks on Mark Antony were wholly justified, and to smile at Mr. Gladstone's denunciations of Lord Beaconsfield. Collections of speeches are, as every one must acknowledge, the most tedious section of historical sources—their chief use is to throw light on the psychology of the speaker rather than on the course of events. Of all such collections the most irritating, to my mind, are the Panegyrics which Roman rhetoricians of the decadence used to address to their emperors. Definite facts can only be extracted from them by careful search, and are then probably smothered in adulation. Addresses by his senate to Napoleon are much the same sort of productions.

Official documents, such as proclamations, charters, financial statements of budgets or taxation, and legislative enactments, from whole codes of laws down to private acts of parliament, may be as tedious sometimes as speeches, but often contain crucial information, since they are not explosions of rhetoric but deal with practical problems of the moment. Sometimes the interest is psychological, sometimes cultural. We should know much less about Early Anglo-Saxon mentality if we had only the chroniclers to help us, and not the laws of Ethelbert or Ine. Accurate knowledge of what the Norman Conquest meant to England is best realized by a careful study of Domesday Book. Even proclamations by a ruler like Richard III, Henry VIII, Queen Elizabeth, Bonaparte, or Adolf Hitler are useful not so much for the statements contained in them, but as showing the official view of their governance, which it is wished to impress upon a nation. Often insincere and hypocritical, arrogant or dictatorial, they are no doubt *ex parte* statements, but at least show the spirit of the times, from the point of view of the governing authority. And it is the same with charters, great and small, from short original grants to tedious repetitions in an ' inspeximus '. They can be used in series to demonstrate cultural or administrative growth in a fashion which could be obtained from no mere chronicle or set history. Such details did not usually engross the attention of writers bent on producing a narrative or even an annalistic survey. Hence the real merit of those hard-working folks who wade through not only documents of some attraction, such as the *Cartæ Baronum* or the Pipe Rolls, but manorial statistics or bailiffs' accounts. The results of their labours are useful materials for history, or sidelights on history, but it is a mistake to believe that history can be written from them alone, as some people seem to think.

Alfred is much more important than Alfred's laws, or William the Conqueror than Domesday Book, or Luther than the text of the theses which he nailed up on the church door at Wittenberg. Augustus Cæsar cannot be visualized from the *Monumentum Ancyranum*—though it is an interesting record of the light in which he hoped to be remembered—nor Napoleon from a file of his *Bulletins*—though these again have to be studied in order to get at his mentality. Wherefore I hold that constitutional, institutional, or cultural history have their places, but that they are not dominant in the history of mankind. Take an example from to-day—are the Weimar Constitution, or the Nazi Constitution, if it may so be called, so worthy of note as the personality of Adolf Hitler ?

Institutions grow and perish after a longer or a shorter period. Is there any importance to-day in the constitutions of Cleisthenes or the mythical Servius Tullius ? I will even grow profane and add that little result comes from the various attempts to vamp up a constitution for England between 1649 and 1660, or for France between 1789 and 1802. The Abbe Sieyès could turn out a new constitution on any day of the week. Constitutions come and go—it is the ' cataclysms ' as I have called them which are the true turning points in human history.

For history is a series of happenings, punctuated by cataclysms, not a logical and orderly process. And the occasional cataclysm sweeps away institutions that may have lasted for a thousand years, and leaves of them only a rather meaningless record—relics to be explored by the patient eye of the researcher, or the laborious spade of the archæologist. Yet there are many who will try to reconstruct what they must needs call a ' Philosophy of History '. I can only see a series of occurrences—and fail to draw any constructive moral from them.

III

ON THE TESTING OF AUTHORITIES

(1) CHRONICLES AND NARRATIVE HISTORIES

WHEN we have left behind us those very early periods for which monumental evidence is helped out by some slight assistance from the written word—generally of a very intermittent sort—and have got well over the edge of pre-history into history proper, the task of inquiring becomes much more complicated. Annals and chronicles are followed by narrative histories cast in a literary form, and autobiographies, biographies, and—not least important—collections of letters, have to be taken into consideration, tested, and placed in correlation. The nearer that we get to modern times the more difficult does the task of arriving at certainty become, because the mass of material to be worked through becomes even greater.

Even annals and chronicles, which are generally the predecessors of set historical narratives, may contain—as I shall presently be showing—the germs of the ' historic urge ', which sets the writer to introduce some sort of comment or explanation of the events which he is recording. But true narrative history is a later development, when the historiographer sets to work to cast into more or less literary form his conceptions of the progress of events in some period short or long. Probably he does so with some guiding

3

impulse, which may be of any sort, from a desire to glorify the origin of his race or his religion, to a desire to warn his contemporaries against the danger of the present by contemplation of the disasters of the past.

The didactic purpose of history was very simply stated by the Venerable Bede in his preface : ' If history relates good things of good men, the attentive hearer is excited to imitate that which is good ; but if it mentions evil deeds of evil men, the pious reader learns to shun that which is hurtful and perverse, and is excited to do things which he knows to be good and pleasing to God.' A very different mental attitude from that of the gloomy and denunciatory Gildas who finds a general destruction of everything that is good, and a general growth of everything that is evil, so that his task is to emphasize the crimes of the misdoers rather than the exploits of the few valiant souls in a degenerate age. His mentality is the same as that of the old Hebrew prophets, from whom he borrows many a screed. Oddly enough, moral instruction as the end of history may be detected all down the ages. It certainly was at the back of the mind of Plutarch, when he wrote his invaluable Parallel Lives, not with the Christian inspiration of Bede or Gildas, but from the old heathen point of view of the philosopher, who has to judge mankind from a platform of his own, and to indicate moral decisions without reference to religion or politics. For Plutarch had got rid of the Olympian deities, and could have no politics as the citizen of a small Bœotian town in the reign of Trajan or Hadrian. Indeed, he was as well aware of the dangers of old Greek civic politics as were Thucydides or Polybius, in centuries where such unhappy civil brawls were the rule of the day. But such dangers were now out of date.

Thucydides, whom every one knows, and Polybius, who is far too little studied, were not destitute of intention when they wrote, the one to expose the errors of contemporary political thought, the other to recommend the submission of his countrymen to the inevitable Roman domination.

Propagandic instruction is, of course, not the design of all historians. Some simple souls are merely set on recording ancestral tales, lest they may perish. ' In my book,' says Snorro Sturleson, ' I have had the old stories written down, as I have heard them told by intelligent folk, concerning chiefs who have held dominion in the Northern lands. Although we cannot say exactly what truth there may be in them, yet old and wise men held them to be true.' The same yearning after the dim glories of ages where racial tradition is full of romantic legends of high improbability, or absolute impossibility, inspired the Lombard Paulus Diaconus and the Dane Saxo Grammaticus. They recorded Lombard or Danish pre-history because they loved it, bound though they were as Christian clerics to acknowledge that its mythological atmosphere was unorthodox. We owe them thanks for preserving much that might otherwise have perished, and sometimes sigh to think that we might perhaps have had an Anglo-Saxon historiographer of similar tastes, to supplement the very orthodox narrative of the Venerable Bede. But only poetical scraps, like *Beowulf*, of the old English traditional folklore have come down to us. I fancy that Livy, while he was writing the earlier books of his immense Roman history, lingered over prodigies and oracles and supernatural phenomena for much the same reasons that made Saxo or Snorro discourse on Odin.   They were quite remote from the serious thought of the Augustan age.

There are plenty of historians of whom it must be said that they are neither set on propagandic work among their contemporaries, nor on preserving ancestral tales which have no particular bearing on the politics of their own day.   A frequent impulse is the desire to give some account of events of importance of which the author has been a witness at first or at second hand, things seen or things heard of which are likely to interest the intelligent public of his own generation.   Such, I suppose, was the inspiration of Herodotus and Froissart, much-travelled men, who had visited many lands and met with many notable personalities.   They thought that their experiences, and their inquiries into things past as well as things present, were worth recording, and that there were many who would appreciate them.   It is a mistake, I believe, to conceive of Herodotus as solely set on celebrating the defeat of Persia by the Greeks—and more especially by the Athenians—or on Froissart as writing merely to please his many and various noble patrons.   On both of them there has descended the desire to write history because it was picturesque and interesting, not because it had a specially moralizing or propagandic lesson to give.

Such good folk, with a story to tell, leave no snares behind them for those who reconstruct history in a later age.   Quite otherwise is it with a certain class of writers whose narratives can never be looked at without an uneasy feeling that they are deliberately ' faking ' history, not merely telling their tale with the bias inevitable to most human beings, but actually falsifying facts. Their object is not really to detail the happenings of the age with which they are dealing from their own point of view, but to misrepresent them. The worst cases of all are, of course, those who are aiming at a *succès de scandale*, who want, apparently, to become ' best sellers '—like Suetonius, who achieved this bad pre-eminence by writing of the crimes, vices, and follies of the early emperors rather than of their reigns and administration. He had been a secretary of Hadrian, cashiered (as we are told) for affronting the Empress Sabina, and had access for many years to imperial secret archives, of which he made a lurid use when he was turned loose on the world. He is the spiritual father of all those authors of modern times who have written ' private lives ' of Charles II, Louis XV, Napoleon, or George IV. Tacitus told of many horrid things, and hinted at more ; but his tale is the result of *sæva indignatio*, a hatred of the régime of the Augustan dynasty, while Suetonius was by nature *ardelio cloacarum*, the man with the muck-rake. ' If a fact is mentioned only by Suetonius,' said a French critic, ' we are at once relieved from any necessity for believing that it ever took place.' It is a thousand pities that the curious collection of imperial biographies known as the *Historia Augusta*, often our only authority for scraps of third-century history, seems to have been written by a school of historiographers who took Suetonius as their model, and give us derogatory anecdotes about the personalities of a series of somewhat shadowy monarchs, rather than accounts of their civil and military doings. Sometimes, reading the *Historia Augusta*, we are driven to think of J. J. Rousseau's despairing remark that among several untrustworthy and contradictory tales, the only thing is to select that which seems the least unlikely. This unhappy choice lies before the historian in many ages, from Ancient Greece to Post-War Europe : and when he has made it, he checks upon the classical scholar's old dictum ' potior est difficilior lectio ', and is left doubting in the end.

This is certainly the case when we read that venomous person, Procopius, on the Emperor Justinian. Are we to believe that there is any truth in the one version of him as a malignant spirit with almost preternatural attributes, or in the other which makes him a mere pedant, dominated by an unscrupulous wife, and with few human traits save envy and jealousy ? Procopius gives authority for each view. It is fortunate that the majority of historians do not inspire us with any such distrust as Suetonius or Procopius. From Xenophon to Matthew Paris, Lord Clarendon, Macaulay, or Samuel Rawson Gardiner, we find them giving what they believe to be trustworthy narrative, though we may often recognize a bias, and sometimes a lack of complete information, but deliberate falsification is far from their intention. Every man, save the dehumanized purveyor of unprejudiced information, of whom Lord Acton dreamed, has his personal inclinations—he may be democrat or oligarch, optimate or ' popularis ', Guelf or Ghibelline, Whig or Tory, but he is trying to set forth things as they appeared to him, not to manipulate them with deliberate *suppressio veri* or *suggestio falsi*.

And here lies the difficulty of the modern historian, with all the diverse material before him. The criticism of authorities is one of the primary duties of him who would arrive at a reasoned conception of any kind of history. And critics have always existed, from the jaundiced person who wrote ' *de malignitate Herodoti* ', to Professor Firth judiciously appraising the precise reliability of Lord Macaulay. The task of determining the relative value of contradictory information is fascinating, if sometimes hazardous. Not only has the good faith of an authority to be determined, or his mentality, bias, intelligence, or simplicity, but also what opportunity he had of investigating the incidents which he is recording. A rather inferior witness on the spot may have seen something of which an authority of much greater weight got a false impression. To take a very modern example : the Duke of Wellington was undoubtedly the person best entitled to give an account of the battle of Waterloo. But as certainly, in his great dispatch of June 18–19, 1815, he is in error as to the moment at which La Haye Sainte fell into the hand of the French. There are scores of impeccable witnesses against him. Or to get back to the opposite end of history—Thucydides gives a form of words for a certain document in which he was interested—there was no reason whatever to doubt it. But unfortunately a contemporary inscription was dug up in Athens a few years ago giving another and a different set of words. With such instances before him among the highest authorities, the modern historian has to be very careful of his statements, even of quite unimportant ones. Yet he must come to some conclusion : his readers will find him intolerable if he presents them not with a continuous narrative, but with two or more divergent statements ending with a note of interrogation.

This, we may say incidentally, is one of the fascinations of the study of history to students of a certain type of mind. An episode sometimes presents all the puzzles of a good detective novel, where the reader works out the clues, and then comes to a conclusion which may turn out to be wrong. For in history, unfortunately, there is no explanatory chapter at the end, to clear up the motives and disentangle the true solution from the ' red herrings ' which have been drawn across the track. This is why the evidence about Mary Stuart's ' Casket Letters ', the identity of the Man in the Iron Mask, the details of the Popish Plot (including the death of Edmund Berry Godfrey) or the fate of the Dauphin in the Temple, has led to so many pages of interesting speculation. Some people even make mysteries where there are none. The story of the end of Edward V and his brother in the Tower of London has been raked up again as a problem more than once in recent years by perverse and devoted admirers of Richard III. It is impossible to acquit Crookback and to explain the whole tragedy as ' Tudor calumny '—even without the evidence of the pathetic bones recently investigated. I do not say that ' historical puzzles ' play any very important part in our general conception of the progress of events, but they are undoubtedly attractive to researchers with a romantic turn of mind and a love of mystery.

The modern historian has to set forth his tale

from the comparison of all available evidence, written or unwritten, which he can collect. What shape the result will take will depend largely on his own mentality—sceptical or enthusiastic, propagandic (perhaps unconsciously), or severely staid and well-balanced, in constant dread of unfairness. But ' broad-mindedness ', as has been acutely remarked, ' is often only the result of a fear of being thought narrow-minded,' and may become an obsession, and leave the reader yearning for a more free exposition of the writer's private opinions.

In its extreme form this dislike for definite conclusions and dread of committing oneself to a theory, sometimes drives students to shrinking from an attempt to write narrative history, and confining their activities to producing ' materials ', to collecting unpublished matter and printing it with little or no comment on its general application, or to putting together statistics to fling at the head of the perplexed reader, or to compiling bibliographies of all sorts of authorities, good, bad, or indifferent, relating to a special subject.

Lord Bolingbroke in his amusing *Letters on the Study of History* dismisses this sort of researcher rather contemptuously. ' They get no wiser or better by the study themselves, but may perhaps enable others to study with greater ease—making fair copies of foul manuscripts, and giving the signification of hard words. Our obligation to them would be much greater if they were in general able to do anything better, and submitted to their drudgery for the sake of the public. But they make their research an end in itself, and wish to be revered as erudite.'

This is, I suppose, an early protest against what a modern Frenchman called the *fureur de l'inédit*, the idea that newly discovered stuff *must* be more valuable than old and generally received versions of some event, more especially when one has dug up the new document oneself.

Bolingbroke—very unjustifiably from our point of view—got irritated with editions of ancient chronicles and charters, and declared that real history could only be studied from the Renaissance onward, when a conspectus of the whole political and social state of England, France, or Italy can be put together from countless sources. He rather cruelly dismissed the annals of the Dark Ages as no more worthy to be called history than the tuning-up of the instruments of an orchestra, before the overture of an opera begins, can be called concerted music. ' Such introductions are at best no more than fanciful preludes that try the instruments and precede the concert.' He would be far from insisting that a knowledge of mediæval chronicles is necessary either for the writer or the reader.[1]

The ingenious statesman refused to see that the study of the modern cultured centuries, of which he gives an outline, has its roots in mediæval facts and fictions and cannot be understood without them. In short, to the philosophic student of history in the mid eighteenth century, chronicles, mostly written by cloistered clerks, were decidedly ' Gothic '.

For my own part I find Bolingbroke's views about mediæval chroniclers not only misplaced but decidedly antipathetic. They express the mentality of the

[1] Letter III of the edition of 1752, vol. i. p. 71.

' superior person '—an individual whom I detest—
for we have no right to set up ourselves as above
common human weaknesses. But also they bear
witness to a lack of a certain perception of what is
interesting and what is not. An eighteenth-century
man of culture dismissed as ' barbarous and Gothique '
half the things that are really worth observing in
architecture, art, and literature. He had no use for
Fra Angelico or Bellini or Roger van der Weyden,
preferring the pictures of Guido Reni, of Domenichino,
or of Raphael in his more decadent later period.
Goldsmith in the *Vicar of Wakefield* got a very early
glimpse of a turn in the tide, when he made the would-
be *cognoscente* of 1766 pass on to his young
friend the ' tip ' that the last thing among art-critics
was to praise a painter called Pietro Perugino. But
for many years after that date the noble formers of
galleries preferred to buy Paul Veroneses or Tintorettos
rather than Peruginos. And they hung them up
in palaces that, when they were not of the purest
classical outlines, verged on the baroque. If they
ever condescended to the Middle Ages, it was by
building bogus ruins, sham fragments of castles or
abbeys, like that in which Shenstone lodged his
' distressed anchorite '. Bishop Percy had not yet
published the *Reliques* of the Old English ballads
which took the world by storm (1765), nor Horace
Walpole printed his half-disowned ' Gothic ' romance
of the *Castle of Otranto* (1764) when Bolingbroke
wrote his *Letters on History*.

For my own part I have never felt any distaste
for early chronicles, especially those of the anecdotic
sort, like the delightful Icelandic Heimskringla, or

Saxo Grammaticus, even when they are full of obvious ' folk tales ', or have an occasional miracle introduced (as has the usually prosaic Anglo-Saxon Chronicle under the year 797), or indulge in episodes of witch- craft, like Paul the Deacon, or give impossible screeds of genealogy or geography. To arrive at the spirit of the times is always interesting and profitable, even if that spirit may appear to us sometimes credulous and childlike, and at other times a little inhuman. It is always well to know where the lines were drawn between right and wrong, the possible and the im- possible, the known and the unknown, at any period of the development of national or individual mentality.

Early sources, of course, differ in the most divergent fashions. Some are little better than annals, ' containing nothing more than dynasties and gene- alogies and a bare mention of remarkable events in the order of time, like chronological tables '. Appar- ently the early Roman *Fasti* to which Livy alludes were something of this sort, drawn up by the Pontifex Maximus and filed. Later on some incipient historian would use them as foundation for a continuous narra- tive, probably adding to them scraps of folklore and tribal tradition. In this way all the early parts of the Anglo-Saxon Chronicle seem to be based on some sort of dry ancestral records of this kind, which only wake up into narrative from the moment when King Alfred set his writers to work. They could add genuine stuff as far as the memory of the last genera- tion could reach back, but ran dry of detailed informa- tion when they had arrived at Egbert's time. It was exceptional when they inserted a screed of ancestral heroic tragedy—like the story of the End of King

Kynewulf—or a borrowing from Bede, of whom they might have made much more use. Where the writers of the Chronicle *did* use Bede freely was in their early section concerning Britain before the coming of the English, and here they were merely repeating what Bede had got at second hand from Gildas or Orosius, so that the Chronicle from the sixth century backward has no original value at all. Alfred's inspiration, however, worked on after his death. The copies of his original compilation dispersed among many monasteries, received continuations from various local writers, who added variants of their own as the years went on, so that a Peterborough ' Anglo-Saxon Chronicle ' would differ materially in the tenth or eleventh century from a Canterbury or Abingdon one. Unfortunately the original text got interpolated in some cases by the pious frauds of monastic chroniclers, who slid into the original annals records of imaginary honours or benefactions made by kings to their own particular houses. These can generally be picked out with ease.

It is a thousand pities that Ethelweard, writing about 960, who had Bede and the Anglo-Saxon Chronicle both to hand, and might have constructed a valuable and independent work on his own tenth century, did little more than copy his authorities, and failed to give us a good narrative of events from Alfred to Edgar, which were well within his knowledge. He was much more set on displaying his Latin (which was bad) and his few scraps of Greek, than on producing a continuous historical narrative. The marvel was that being a layman and of royal descent, he could write a fluent Latin booklet for the admiration of the Continental relatives to whom he addressed it. Such a phenomenon was unique in the tenth century.

Chronicles based on annals and straying back into tribal folklore were by no means the only products of the historic urge during the early Middle Ages. The ambitious author occasionally aspired to write a General History, and went back to Adam, by means of borrowings from the Old Testament, complicated after a time by screeds from Orosius or some other late-Roman compendium. Sometimes he was content, like Gregory of Tours, to ' tell of the wars of kings with hostile peoples, of the Martyrs with the heathen, of the Church with the heretics '. But too often he insists on going back to the Deluge, and treats us not only with excerpts from the books of Moses, but with tedious inventions deriving his own race from some unrecorded descendant of Japhet. Some of the Anglo-Saxon genealogies, not content with arguing back from their own day to Woden in far too few generations (to take the Northumbrian list that misty ancestor must have lived about A.D. 250) then proceed to get back from Woden in fifteen generations more, to ' Sceaf the son of Noah who was born in the Ark ! ' This calculation, taking the usual thirty-year genera-tion, would fix Noah somewhere about the time of Alexander the Great !

For reckless and irritating genealogical inventions the Celts were, if anything, greater sinners than the Teutonic romancers. The Irish are perhaps a little wilder than the Welsh. If British genealogists falsified their origins by minimizing the Roman conquest of Britain, and turning Roman rulers into native British kings, the Irish chronologers of the seventh and eighth centuries invented five dynasties going back to the Deluge, and then wiped out Partholans and Tuatha de Danann and such like, in order to make every respectable Irishman a descendant of Eber and Eremon, the Milesians who came from Spain at some vague date. Really both Britain and Ireland were settled by no single race, but by successive tribes coming from over seas and impinging on each other with most mixed racial results. The last-comers were north-Gaulish invaders, like the Atrebates and Parisii in Britain, or the Menapii in Ireland. But no single race peopled either island. If any one hopes to get many useful historical additions to Celtic history of the early centuries after the Christian era from the lives of Welsh or Irish saints which come into the period, he will suffer much disappointment. Their legends are, indeed, more astounding than those of the comparatively tame holy men of the Frankish or Anglo-Saxon hagiology. St. Patrick turned Coroticus, King of Alcluyd, into a fox, in punishment for his molestation of Christian converts. Vortigern, as Nennius tells, was destroyed by fire from heaven, along with his castle and his harem, by the imprecations of a saint. Brandan went sailing in the Atlantic till he found not only the Earthly Paradise and angels, but Judas Iscariot, afloat on an iceberg for one day's cooling from hell-fire, in return for the one gratuitous good action of his vile life. St. Piran, if he did not go so far seaward as St. Brandan, accomplished a more surprising feat by coming from Ireland to Cornwall not on a boat but on a mill-stone. We grow weary when in lieu of useful historical anecdotes we get tales of resuscitated corpses, of lecherous kings who have monastically inclined daughters, and of those more amiable but somewhat feckless monarchs who insisted on heaping upon cenobites grants of land of fabulous extent—' sore saints for the crown ' as James VI and I would have observed.   It is true that Frankish and Anglo-Saxon kings had this foible in a certain measure : even the Venerable Bede doubts whether there are not too many monasteries.

The fascinations of the Dark Ages in the way of marvels and miracles were, as has been already said, wasted upon the cultured and sceptical historians of the eighteenth and nineteenth centuries, who treated them with contempt, and only mentioned them as shocking instances of superstition, or perhaps occasionally of pious fraud.   This was a psychological error. To understand an age one must have some notion of its foibles and its convictions, and not merely scoff at them.   Beliefs at which we now smile with condescending pity, and conceptions long since forgotten, have had practical importance in ages of greater simplicity.   Odd as it may seem to us, the old ' geocentric theory ', the notion that the terrestrial globe was the centre of the Universe, and that sun and moon and planets revolved around it, had a practical importance.   It was the base of countless centuries of folk-psychology, which placed the earth as a fixed thing, with heaven above and hell below.   Ascending, one would reach at some undetermined distance the abodes of divinity ; descending one would find central fire and the furnace of the damned.   Hence in popular belief angels might occasionally descend from above to assist in a miracle or comfort a saint. Similarly, the existence of Hell below was demonstrated by volcanoes spitting out flames and lava. Dante was echoing the universal tradition of the Middle Ages, when he made his descent to the *Inferno* through gloomy caverns ever tending downward to the abode of Satan. Was there also in the conception an echo of classical heathen tradition—Æneas in Virgil tended downward from the caves of Avernus—and Virgil himself was Dante's guide in his awe-inspiring adventures? Or was the appalling aspect of Vesuvius or Etna, or Stromboli (into which a pious hermit saw the soul of the Arian Theodoric precipitated) sufficient indication of a dread underworld?

In any case the existence of a not too distant heaven and hell pervaded all mediæval conceptions of life and death, and should never be forgotten when we are investigating them. The nearness of the supernatural, only doubted by a few premature sceptics, explains social phenomena which to an eighteenth-century historical critic appeared to be either matters of fraud, or of what we should now call mass-suggestion, the self-hypnotization of a crowd. Stories of saints seen fighting at the head of an enthusiastic army—as St. George was seen by many at the battle of Antioch in the First Crusade—lingered on even to the sixteenth century—there is a faint suggestion of ' Sant Iago ' being seen by the Spanish Conquistadores in Mexico. And the supernatural side of the mission of Joan of Arc raised no doubt among the rank and file of the French Army (whatever crafty courtiers may have thought). Meanwhile the English frankly accepted its existence, but ascribed it to

4

the diabolical influence of ' that limb and disciple
of the fiend La Pucelle, which useth sorcery and
enchantments '.

Witchcraft, indeed, had a very important part
in fourteenth and fifteenth-century politics—one could
always accuse one's enemies of using it—even the
staid Henry V proceeded in the law courts against
his stepmother Joan of Navarre for sorcery ; and the
fall of Humphrey, Duke of Gloucester, as a statesman
was marked by the condemnation of his wife Eleanor
for practising against the life of Henry VI by the
time-honoured method of melting his image in wax.
James III of Scotland burned a whole covey of wizards
and witches for conspiring along with his brother
John of Mar to cause a vacancy in the throne by
occult methods.   Even James VI and I, in the latest
sixteenth-century years, took seriously the efforts of
Dr. Fian and his crew to sink the ship that bore
him from Norway—and cremated them all.

Such being the everyday interference of the supernatural in contemporary politics, it remains to be
seen what the historians made of it.   Generally it was
accepted wholesale and utilized—to have doubted it
would have cast a shadow on all the legends of the
saints, which the orthodox must accept.   The miraculous could always be utilized by authority—even
that unlikely person Edward IV had a nice little
miracle to comfort him on his march from Ravenspur
to London—as witness the author of the ' Arrival '.
At the most an abnormally suspicious person might
try to rationalize a miracle, or (if worked for the benefit
of an enemy) to ascribe it to human fraud rather than
to diabolical arts.   Such explanations were welcomed,

of course, by the eighteenth-century reviser of mediæval history, who could understand fraud, but was less experienced in the phenomena of mass-hypnotization. And in his revision he missed the spirit of the former age.

In speaking of narrative history, we must not, of course, confine ourselves to general histories going back to Noah, or extending over a considerable range of centuries. With them must be classed a certain amount of monographs, lives of a single person, or accounts of an event or a short crisis. These are, of course, much more valuable to the modern student than the longer narratives—for a writer knows his own time and his own contemporaries, but gets progressively less useful as he recedes into antiquity. Putting aside the biographies of saints—usually worthless—though there are some which, like the lives of St. Wilfrid and St. Dunstan, contain noteworthy facts—we occasionally get a tribute by an attached dependent to his patron or patroness, like Asser's Life of King Alfred, or the *Encomium Emmæ* devoted to a much less worthy personage, or Eginhard's well-written *Vita Caroli Magni*—a testimonial to the excellent Latin taught in Charlemagne's Palatine School. His successor is the much inferior Nithard who wrote *De Dissentionibus Filiorum Ludovici Pii*—a monograph on the break up of the Carlovingian Empire under the quarrelsome grandchildren of its founder. Sometimes the clarity of a narrative from these ages is disturbed by an author's ill-judged attempt to carry it out in Latin verse—this was the case with Abbo's interesting account of the siege of Paris by the Danes in 886—and with Guy of Amiens' long poem on the battle of Hastings. The tyranny of scansion and quantities is always injurious to accurate description—as Horace says, one sometimes wants to use a word ' quod versu dicere non est '.

While the modern student is making a general survey of the historical literature of the Christian states of the West, which can be dealt with practically in one broad conspectus, he often forgets to consider parallel with it the similar products of the Christian East. Indeed Byzantine history was very much neglected down to the eighteenth century—and when Gibbon did write his great *Decline and Fall*, the purely Byzantine chapters of it were the least satisfying section of the long work. It is easy to forget, while immersed in Western problems, that in the Dark Ages there centred round Constantinople a copious supply of evidence for the historian, both in long narrative histories, monographs on limited topics, biographies (alas ! too often ecclesiastical), and illustrative side-material of all sorts, such as the military manuals of the Emperor Maurice, Leo's *Tactica*, and the shorter treatises of Cecaumenos and Nicephorus Phocas. It is natural to note that the connection between East Christian and West Christian history, attenuated enough already in the seventh century after the Lombards conquered most of Italy, and the Popes repudiated their allegiance to iconoclastic emperors, breaks off almost completely in the eighth. This was a long age of troubles in the Byzantine Empire, which barely succeeded in saving itself from the series of Mahometan invasions by the valour of Leo the Isaurian and his successors, and historical evidence runs at its lowest—just as it did contemporaneously in the West in later Merovingian days. There is a long gap in first-class contemporary authorities between the age of Justinian and the sort of Byzantine Renaissance which grew up under the Macedonian dynasty. But even here the stream never runs so feebly as in the West, though we feel it waxing very shallow between Procopius' vast works and the equally voluminous supply of miscellaneous information given by Constantine Porphyrogenitus. What would we not give for something corresponding to that imperial compiler's *De Administrando Imperio* and the rest, from any contemporary Western statesman ? The seventh and eighth centuries' bitter iconoclastic controversy poisoned the comparatively few orthodox pens that dealt with the militant Isaurian dynasty. Nevertheless, though historiography sometimes flickers, it never grows extinct, or dwindles down to mere annals, as in so many Western countries.

The most surprising thing, perhaps, in Byzantine literature is the fact that the intellectual and artistic renaissance which began with the Macedonian emperors was not stunted by the disasters of the late eleventh century, when Seljouk Turks and Frankish Crusaders proved so troublesome to the house of Comnenus. Byzantine histories go on at a high degree of literary merit right down to the end of the empire— though we may feel that personal bias is more evident than plain desire for truth when we read the interesting pages of Anna Comnena or John Cantacuzenus. This gives a sidelight on the persistent insinuation of Westerns who came into collision with Byzantines, from Liutprand onwards, as to the Greek being no friend to honest plain speaking. But as to whether the Franks were entitled to throw stones at the Byzantine glass houses, any one who reads crusading chronicles may conceive his doubts. Prejudice against the East-Roman went on for generations after the Crusades, and may certainly be detected even in Gibbon's wonderful work. It has been reserved for modern days to discover romances of Byzantine chivalry like ' Digenes Akritas', and records of hard fighting with the Saracen, which has caused a general recession from the popular view that the annals of Constantinople are a string of court intrigues and rather ridiculous theological wranglings.

Who can pardon the general destruction of still surviving classical literature which took place when the Franks sacked the great city in 1204, and consigned the long-preserved books of ancient Greece and Rome to the rubbish-basket, while the statues of the old world went to the melting-pot? The eighteenth, and even the nineteenth century used to use the word ' Byzantine ' in an opprobrious sense, conceiving that it carried with it a suggestion of stylized and hieratic art, hollow and insincere court etiquette, venomous ecclesiastical controversy, latent cruelty concealed under meticulous culture, an offensive arrogance towards external races. In fact I have seen the Byzantines compared to the Chinese of the old régime—wonderfully civilized and rather inhuman, considered from a modern European point of view. The Western writer instinctively resented seeing his French, English, German, or Italian ancestors lumped together as ' barbarians ' at Constantinople in the twelfth century as they were lumped together as ' Foreign Devils ' at Pekin in the eighteenth.

And it was easy to compare the art of Byzantine ikons with that of Chinese vases or gilded reliefs, and to compare the ceremonial of the Summer Palace with that in the *De Ceremoniis* of Constantine Porphyrogenitus. Tales of ingenious cruelty could be collected from both civilizations, and of insincere and formal politeness. The tortuous dealings of the Mandarins with Lord Macartney in 1793 were very like the slights experienced by many a Western ambassador to Constantinople between the ninth and the twelfth centuries. All this, of course, is rather unjust to the Byzantines—perhaps also to the Chinese. We are ridding ourselves of much ancient prejudice, when dealing with the great empire which was for so many generations the buffer state of Christendom against Islam. Finlay's treatment of it superseded Gibbon's sarcastic narrative, and from Finlay onward a series of more recent historians have endeavoured to do it justice.

IV

ON THE TESTING OF AUTHORITIES

(2) AUTOBIOGRAPHIES, BIOGRAPHIES, MEMOIRS,
LETTERS, ETC.

A N autobiography is a deliberate summary of
the writer's conception of his own career,
generally produced late in life, when there seems to
be little more to come that is likely to be of interest.
In this, of course, the autobiographer may occasionally
be deceived, as was the unfortunate (and mendacious)
Baron Trenck, who having published his astounding
memoirs in 1787, involved himself in the French
Revolution, and after three years of political jangling
got guillotined as a conspirator in 1794, at the age of
sixty-nine.

This sort of work needs more careful inspection by
the historian than almost any other class of evidence,
being often written with complete insincerity, and
sometimes with a failing memory, even when deliberate
misrepresentation is not intended. Autobiographies
are as a rule the product of the leisure hours of an old
man. Sometimes they are written as vindications of a
career that has been criticized, sometimes as mere
reflections of one's own doings, regarded as an interesting panorama, though there may be nothing very
exciting in them. Such screeds have been produced
by country clergy, minor artists, fourth-rate politicians, obscure propagandists, and self-conscious

psychologists, as well as by men of mark. They are often tedious, but sometimes, even when written by most unimportant people, contain useful sidelights on odd corners of social or provincial history.

Very occasionally in recent centuries an autobiography may be nothing but a ' pot-boiler '. An elderly and impecunious person thinks that he may get a useful sum from the publishers for his reminiscences. In this case the more scandalous the work the better is it for the author—or his publisher. Of such class are the memoirs of Casanova, Major Semple Lisle (from whom Thackeray got the inspiration for his famous Barry Lyndon), Moreau de Joannes (with his fabled adventures in Ireland and at the Mutiny of the Nore), Baron Kolli, Major Carleton (of whom Macaulay swallowed too much), and several others who could be named. These sort of autobiographies betray themselves by their overplus of perilous escapes, and usually of amatory adventures, destined for a public with a taste for sexual thrills. They can never be trusted as secure evidence, though their authors actually existed, and (no doubt) saw some queer things.

But autobiographies are usually inspired not by sordid gain, but (as I said above) either by the idea of self-vindication against criticism, or by the simple desire to tell of what the author considers to have been an interesting life.

But defensive propagandic autobiographies are far more rare than those whose foundation is simple self-esteem—the desire to set forth what the author considers to have been a meritorious life's career, whether in high or in obscure social circles. Outstanding examples are Sully's oddly named *Œconomies Royales,* invaluable for the study of the psychology of his master Henry IV not less than of his own. On the other side of French sixteenth-century political faction Montluc's narrative of his rather sanguinary military life is invaluable, as showing what swash-bucklers thought of Huguenots. No doubt in both cases the author keeps himself in the limelight, as is natural with an old gentleman telling his tale of adventure, but he is honestly intending to narrate lurid happenings, not romancing or shuffling off criticism : the incidents can often be verified, though the explanation of them requires the historian's reviewing eye. There is a surprising amount of autobiographical material of value in French sixteenth-century history, and the stream never ceases to run in the later generations down to this day.

In Great Britain the flow of such work commences later, and is much less copious. Omitting the hysterical religious maunderings of Margery Kempe, who was so close to heaven and plagued so many bishops, the series hardly commences before the late sixteenth century. And, oddly enough, the first really inter-esting autobiography is Scottish and not English. I mean the long tale of Sir James Melville of Halhill, who was in the thick of things from 1550 to 1600. He was present as a young man at the battle of St. Quentin, and lived as an old man to hear of Gunpowder Plot. His memoirs cover an immense space of time, and are full of incident. He was Mary Stuart's neglected adviser in her troubles, was nearly murdered by Bothwell, went on secret embassies to Queen Elizabeth, saw all the elaborate kidnapping plots which diversified the early reign of James VI, and only failed to follow his king to England because he was now too old, and set only on leaving a record of many years of strange happenings before it was too late to write.

There is unfortunately from England no autobiography parallel to that of Sir James Melville ; none of the greater political personages left behind them from the Tudor age a reasoned narrative of the experiences of a lifetime. We have plenty of material— letters, reports, arguments, state papers, narratives of an incident, but nothing continuous, only interesting scraps—though some of these, like Vere's *Commentaries*, are important, and can compare perhaps with La Noue's similar notes from the great French Wars. But no person of wide experience sat down to give at length his reminiscences of what life was like under Henry VIII—or under Elizabeth. This is rather strange, because Montluc, Tavannes, Castelnau and others did cover paper on a considerable scale in times as perilous in France as the reign of Elizabeth in England. Now is there any one in England like Brantôme, who wrote if not his own life, at any rate the notes of his personal observations on the lives of most of his contemporaries.

In England the first really interesting autobiography, ranging over a long life, does not come till the year 1600 has been well passed (I omit the much less vivid tale of Henry, Earl of Monmouth). Lord Herbert of Cherbury wrote with a delightful lack of self-consciousness, quite unable to appreciate the fact that many of the anecdotes about himself which he relates would appear to later generations comic rather than magnanimous. He was courtier, soldier, scholar, philosopher, and occasionally diplomat or duellist, but absolutely unconscious of the greater movements of his age. The Thirty Years' War seems to have passed over his head as merely a noisy phenomenon, and the political unrest of England all through the central years of Charles I only gave him the opportunity of showing personal pique. When the great civil war broke out he was not quite sure which side he ought to take, and found royalists and parliamentarians both dilapidating his castle of Montgomery, and making him a wanderer at the age of sixty-five. His garrulous reminiscences give amusing sidelights on every court from London to Rome, but entirely miss the spirit of the times. But no student of seventeenth-century history should excuse himself from perusing them. He was a long generation before Edmund Ludlow, whose memoirs I count the first really representative exposition of English political problems of the time when Lord Herbert was still lingering on with the mentality of the past.

Complete autobiographies are comparatively rare in the period which follows ; we get rather memoirs, which do not give a complete record of the author's life, but of certain portions of it, when he was involved in matters in which he considered that he had played an important part, or when he thought it worth while to commit to paper memories of events which were too little understood. King James II, oddly enough, left behind him not an autobiography but a narrative of his boyish recollections of the great Civil War. Lord Clarendon wrote no record of his adventures abroad with his exiled master from 1649 to 1660, but an account of his unlucky administration in the difficult position of first minister of the restored king from 1660 to 1667—he had the leisure to do so after his ill-deserved exile. His greater work written in his same last years was a *History of the Great Rebellion*, not of his own personal reminiscences of those troubled years. Gilbert Burnet's *History of My Own Time* is not exactly a history nor exactly a memoir—being too partial and personally biased for the one, and too much busied with matters in which the author had no part, for the other. The judicious Sir William Temple wrote not an autobiography but memoirs for 1672–78, invaluable for a knowledge of contemporary foreign affairs, and for a picture of his own appreciation of himself, but a sketch of experience during a period, not a conspectus of a whole life. The case is similar in France, where the level of memoir-writing is very high and its record invaluable, including not only the sidelights from anecdotic court-chroniclers like St. Simon, but the self-revelations of persons of high political importance such as de Retz in the early years of the period and d'Argenson in the later times of the *ancien régime*.

Autobiographies slide into memoirs—which deal not only with the author's personal reminiscences, but stray off into high matters of state. And memoirs tend to connect themselves with diaries, which are often memoirs caught before they have grown stale. Samuel Pepys's diaries, for example, are hard to classify, when he goes off from his sometimes squalid private doings into matters of high national importance. And Evelyn, normally busy with science and arts, sometimes turns off in his diary into the shrewdest political comments, for he had good opportunities of observation and utilized them.

The Golden Age in France of autobiographical memoirs commences with the Revolution. At the end of the cataclysms that raged between 1789 and 1815 there were an immense number of survivors left, who in the dull years after Waterloo set themselves to tell their life's history—sometimes for self-glorification, sometimes for self-excuse. Many of them lived to vast old age, and had ample leisure. Of Chateaubriand's *Mémoires d'outre-tombe* I have already spoken—he was a man of genius who felt that his spiritual and political divagation needed explanation. Talleyrand, also a man of genius but with a most cynical and shameless twist in his moral composition, takes probably the first class for *suppressio veri*, no less than for *suggestio falsi*. But Barras, the old director, left to fatten in obscurity by the complaisance of Bonaparte, runs Talleyrand close for misstatement as well as for malignity. Of him, as of Suetonius, it might be said that the fact that he makes an assertion sets one off at once to verify its authority, with a strong prepossession that it will be found untrue. Bourrienne, sufficiently untrustworthy on many points, makes a very poor third when compared with the two other survivors from the tempest. But almost every ex-imperialist minister or official wrote his memoirs, or had them written for him, from Savary, the Emperor's *gendarme à tout faire* down to much less busy and less compromised satellites. Generally the autobiographies are self-excusatory— sometimes the author does not seem to see that he has anything to excuse, even when he knows that he has figured in a prominent place in the *Dictionnaire des Girouettes*—that amusing catalogue of the civil and military ' Vicars of Bray ', which expressed so much hidden public contempt. Some of the memoir-writers possessed a sufficiently facile turn of con-science to permit them to look back on their careers with a humorous grimace, like Réal, whose *Indiscrétions* show that he considered the position of Minister of Police under Bonaparte as on the whole a comic business, full of absurd incidents. It is a pity that we cannot tell how much of the supposed legacy of Fouché is his own writing, and how much his editor's ; if all genuine it should surely have been more amusing.

But all these books of Revolutionary and Imperial souvenirs are as untrustworthy as they are valuable for the sidelights which they throw on the mentality of the age.

Nor are the innumerable autobiographies of the military men less interesting. Marshal Marmont's many volumes are inspired by the need of self-defence against the Napoleonic legend—he had suffered too much from the familiar insult ' Ragusade ', which must unjustly put on his shoulders the blame for the Emperor's final collapse in 1814, and he was set on exposing the blindness no less than the talents of his master. But the large majority of the military auto-biographies are regretful reminiscences of a glorious fighting time, in which the authors consider that they played their parts with credit. Most of them are full of slips when investigated by the cold test of official records. Marbot is probably the most careless of them all—but he had repeated his adventures so many times to the younger sons of Louis Philippe, to whom he served as a sort of military tutor, that by constant repetition they acquired a set form of inaccuracy. Thiébault, a more malignant swashbuckler, set on making most other soldiers fools or knaves, is less interesting to read because of his incessant carping, though he is as skilful as Marbot in discovering thrilling adventures from which he extricates himself with perfect coolness.   It is a relief to pass on to minor autobiographers who are less set on blatant self-glorification though by no means destitute of self-appreciation, such as St. Chamans, d'Espinchel, Lemonnier Delafosse, Lejeune, Gonneville, or Fantin des Odoards, who all give us accounts of a long military life.   There are even witnesses from the ranks —a thing rare in earlier ages in France no less than in England.   Altogether this is as wonderful an age for reminiscences among the fighting men as among the civilians, and every one of them gives interesting evidence—but evidence that must be severely tested.

It is curious that no English statesman of the highest class has left behind him any memoirs corresponding in importance to the best of the French ones.   We have only letters or correspondence collected by admiring relatives or secretaries, which are much inferior material for realizing a man's estimate of himself.   The only statesmen of some note who survived to write about themselves were the long-lived Brougham—who certainly had plenty of leisure in thirty years of old age, and had many errors to defend, and Junius' butt, that much maligned prime minister the Duke of Grafton.   Neither of them produced such interesting or informative stuff as might have been expected from two persons who excited such lively animosity among their contemporaries.

The available English autobiographies are mainly from much less important sources, whether in the political, military, or literary spheres, useful for side-lights, but not for a comprehension of the main inspiring tendencies of the period. Nobody in England of a position comparable to that of Talleyrand or Barras or Marmont or Chateaubriand left a set autobiography behind. We only get patchy diaries, journals, and collections of letters from our ' Great Men ' to enable us to comprehend the directing spirits of the age. And these have often been strung together and edited by third-rate literary executors. How often does one feel, when trying to master the personality of a man of real mark, ' save us from our friends and relations ' ? Those who die in harness, with no leisure of old age at their disposition—unlike Grafton and Brougham, Talleyrand and Barras—have not the time to compose an *apologia pro vita sua*, or a perspective of ' things seen '. This is a disappointment to the historian, who always likes to know what was a man's appreciation of himself, even if it is, like Lord Cochrane's, a very biased one. There is often a malicious pleasure in pointing out its little inaccuracies, and its tendencious omissions. And judgments on contemporaries are always more interesting when made by those who knew them well, and faced them on equal terms whether as friend or foe. Sometimes there are historic figures whose general reputation recorded from their acts and from public documents contrasts so strongly with the impressions which they made on those who were in

5

private and personal contact with them, that we are left in a state of puzzlement as to why they were so greatly disliked or so greatly appreciated. It is hard to make out why Charles James Fox commanded so much enthusiasm, or Lord Shelburne so little. From personal experience I know that this sort of contrast between the public and the private reputation of prominent men goes on to this day. Sometimes the journalist is responsible for it, sometimes subterraneous rivalries, sometimes an unlucky lack of humour or of tact in an otherwise attractive personality. Or, on the other hand, a happy geniality of address, and a talent for bluffing may cause many inconsistencies to be ignored or forgotten. The ' man in the street ' gets his general impressions, and does not know how fallacious they may be. Sometimes a silly epigram, or a popular caricature remains for ever, most unjustly, attached to the reputation of a man to whose personality they have no real appropriateness.

Of private letters, as opposed to letters which are no more than circulars or propagandic addresses, comparatively few, like those of Cicero or Pliny Junior, have survived from the ancient world. But only too many of them for the historian's comfort are at hand from the fifteenth century onwards. They are not such interesting material as autobiographies, but nevertheless they enable us to get personal impressions of individuals—sometimes quite notable individuals, but not infrequently dull people of very coarse clay. The enormous series of the *Paston Letters*, for example, preserved by some chance of fate, does not bring us into touch with any personage of note or great ability, sympathetic or the reverse, but does give us a picture of social life in a not very inspiring century. The weak point of collections of letters, as material for history, is that too often they have been gone through by admiring literary executors, who cut out passages that are of no credit to the writer's heart or perspicacity, or delete altogether epistles that would cause pain to his surviving friends. I fancy that Tiro, or whoever it was that edited Cicero's surviving letters, must have consigned many to the flames or the wastepaper basket, when we note how much that is unflattering to the orator's memory still survives in those that remain. Those which showed not mere political tergiversation or shuffling, but dishonourable intrigues and adulations would not bear publishing. What survives is sufficient to throw curious sidelights on many personal and political crises, because the future is unknown to the writer at the moment. Cicero was no great prophet or reader of other men's minds.

What a treat it would have been to historians if some similar proportion of Cæsar's correspondence had come down to us—probably Augustus burned it all—Divus Julius must have written many things unsuitable to a divinity! Pliny's letters have little of the interest of Cicero's—as is natural, since he collected and edited them himself, and nothing transpires which he would have wished to hide. He succeeds in leaving a picture of a liberal, cultured, and broad-minded gentleman—as he would have desired. That the modern reader would detect a disposition somewhat priggish to our taste would not have occurred to him—it was part of his pose. We owe him a debt for his lively picture of the great eruption of Vesuvius in A.D. 79, and for his descrip-

tion of the Christian community in Bithynia in A.D. 105
—which he persecuted in the mildest manner possible
consonant with legality.   What we should have really
liked from him would have been private letters written
under the tyranny of Domitian.   Unfortunately it
is certain that the unhappy memories of those years
would be precisely the things that Pliny would not
have wished to pass on to posterity.

Collections small and great of private letters—as
opposed to official correspondence—begin to be
common from the fifteenth century onwards.   Some
of them are those of unimportant persons—like the
Pastons or Cely ; there is plenty of such dull matter
in France and Italy.   Others are of notable men like
Erasmus who were not primarily concerned with
politics.   In the eighteenth and nineteenth centuries
the bulk becomes overwhelming—so much so that
the historical researcher, with the best intentions
and no lack of zeal—fails to discover the existence
of interesting batches of them, sometimes obscurely
printed and forgotten, more often unprinted and
lurking in some dusty family deed-box or bureau.
Such letters fall into three classes, two of them already
represented in the typical examples that we have
given under the names of Pliny and Cicero.

(1) Collections of letters published by the writer
himself, as were Pliny's, may be valuable, but are
the least useful of the three classes.   They will give
us some opportunity of judging of his character as it
was, or as he wished it to appear, and they will contain
his version of things that he thought worth noting at
the time when he was writing.   But undoubtedly the
redaction will not include letters in which he appears

in an unfavourable aspect, either from want of perspicacity, or as showing wrong or uncharitable judgments of other people, who have afterwards vindicated their capacity or their honesty. And he will most certainly leave out letters which would hurt a surviving friend, or provoke a surviving personage of importance, a monarch or a minister, who could revenge himself for the affront.

(2) The second class consists of posthumous publication of letters by a relative or a literary executor, who is in sympathy with the writer, and issues the collection in vindication of the reputation of his kinsman or patron. A very few of this sort have been issued by the admirer while the writer still lived in old age, reluctant to display himself, but not unwilling to let some one else discharge the task. As an example of this take Colonel Gurwood's publication of the Duke of Wellington's official correspondence— a most exasperating run of volumes, for not only have many important items been left out, but in those that do appear about one name in twenty is represented by a blank space—the editor fearing to offend people of importance who still survived, or their heirs, or to rouse the wrath of a corps, a public office, or even a foreign power, of whom scathing mention was made in the original. The old Duke had ordered him to err on the side of caution, as was generally known. Thirty years later Wellington's heir issued a supplementary series of letters—far more satisfactory to the historian, for the old generation had died out, reticences were no longer necessary, and some very queer facts came out.

But as a rule collections of letters are published by

a relative or a literary executor—a son, widow, or secretary. These are often vitiated by the same faults that exist in a series issued by the author himself. For the editor will omit, or tone down by excision, letters that put the writer in a bad light, exposing intrigues, personal vendettas, or gross instances of misjudgment. Such failings of a great man must be hushed up by his admirer. Some of the worst editing has been done by stupid or ignorant relatives, who were imperfectly acquainted with circumstances of thirty years back, and did not realize what was important or unimportant, creditable or discreditable, at a somewhat remote date for which their personal memory did not serve.

(3) Much the most valuable sort of collections of letters for the historian are those published by editors with no personal relations with the writer, who let out everything, good or bad, because they are not set on vindication or adulation of the person concerned, and are only bent on producing new historical evidence. Here we have some chance of seeing the writer as he was, not as he wished to appear, or as his heirs wished him to appear. Take, for example, the series of Napoleon's *Lettres Inédites* edited by Lecestre. The original enormous set of thirty-two volumes was published in the reign of Napoleon III, under his patronage, as a good piece of imperialist propaganda ; all the many-sided activities of his uncle were duly displayed, and the effect was undoubtedly what had been intended—to enable France to realize the greatness of the founder of the dynasty. But there were judicious omissions—letters that showed the seedy side of that genius were care-

fully omitted. But when the present Republic had been in existence for a good many years, it occurred to politicians who did not like the memory of Napoleon, that historical accuracy required a more complete exposition of his marvellous character, and Lecestre was given leave to go through the enormous file again, in search of what had been omitted in the official and propagandic early edition. Hence the two volumes of *Lettres Inédites de Napoléon*, and three later edited by La Brotonne containing all that his nephew had ordered to be suppressed—a very damaging collection. As Lecestre says in his preface, ' isolated from the main collection, they give an exaggerated impression of him. The great man disappears—we only find a being self-centred, brutal, and violent, who crushes without pity every one who appears to stand as an obstacle to his will and pleasure.' There are some very sinister orders, e.g. one hinting at the advantage of torturing prisoners in order to extract information. This sort of publication is only possible when a bulk of correspondence has fallen into the hands of an editor who has not only no wish to defend the writer of the letters, but does not object to expose his turpitudes. In English politics something of the sort happened when the Parliament in 1645 published the private correspondence of Charles I, which had fallen into their hands in his baggage after the battle of Naseby, and revealed all his intrigues with Irish rebels and foreign Catholic powers. Unfortunately it is possible to forge letters—as was shown during the Parnell case in 1888—if the forgery is detected things go badly for those who have used the documents.

Nowadays the conscientious editor publishes everything, satisfactory or unsatisfactory—the most that he can permit himself is explanatory notes, which may attenuate or emphasize, according to his bent, anything unexpected that may turn up. He must not suppress evidence—even when he thinks it is a pity that it should have come to light, as his eighteenth and often his nineteenth-century predecessors would have done.

Diaries, of course, have for the historical researcher much the same sort of advantages and disadvantages as letters. The advantage is that, if honestly reproduced, they gave the writer's impressions of the moment, before there has been time for them to be altered by subsequent happenings, which often falsify early hopes or fears. Unfortunately it is by no means rare that an author publishing his own diary cuts out entries which prove him to have been a poor prophet. And still more is this the case with diaries edited after the author's death by literary executors. The best-known case in our own recent history is that of the diaries of Charles Greville—that most cynical and disgruntled commentator. The earliest publication of it cut out long screeds of scandalous stuff which would have hurt the feelings of persons still living. A second edition inserted more paragraphs of revelations or suggestions which were considered to be growing innocuous. The third and most complete edition, only just printed, at an exceedingly high price, gives reserved scraps of ancient scandals, and hard judgments, by a man with an unpleasant mind, from Queen Victoria's early years. Each edition causes the reader to dislike more intensely the diarist, who was in such an excellent position for obtaining inside information, and set down all that he heard with sardonic satisfaction.

The letters of many self-centred people display them as they wished to appear rather than as they were. The same is the case with some diarists, who write even for themselves with the pose of an injured innocent or a misunderstood genius—one cannot but suspect them of a craving for posthumous glory for themselves, or posthumous revenge on their real or supposed enemies. This notion will not fit exactly for persons who frankly confess in cipher their small turpitudes, like Samuel Pepys, who can hardly have expected that any one would have the patience to decode from his ingenious cryptograms his very ingenuous confessions. Diaries are *not* generally kept in cipher : usually they are intended to serve as refreshers for the memory of the writer in years to come, or to minister to his self-esteem, or to be read at some distant day by appreciative eyes. Tens of thousands of people start diaries—only a few keep them up for many years—sometimes, apparently, only because they are too obstinate to confess that they have erred in beginning them.

When the modern historiographer has been through all that he can discover that relates to the subject of his research in the way of narrative histories, autobiographies, biographies, speeches, diaries, and letters, not to speak of monuments and inscriptions (which will be of importance mainly to the men whose study lies in very ancient epochs), he has yet other material which must be revised and tested. The most obvious class of documents is that including political pamphlets or treatises, which goes very far back.

They are not unknown in classical times, and are fairly common in the Middle Ages, when statesmen, or would-be statesmen, took in hand schemes for turning back Mohammedan invasions, encouraging naval development, or re-forming a constitution, like Marino Sanuto writing *de recuperatione Terræ Sanctæ*, Egidio Colonna advising *de regimine principum*, the author of the *Libel of English Policie* discoursing on commerce and navigation, or William of Ockham's *Monarchia Sancti Romani Imperii* laying down the law between Church and State. But from the sixteenth century onward such material is overwhelming, and no student of history can hope to read everything that is available, from Machiavelli's *Principe* to the showers of booklets that continue to appear about the League of Nations. ' Sufficient for the day is the evil thereof ', and each modern writer must be content to deal with the documents that concern the period in which he is specially interested. In some cases the task is absolutely maddening, since much controversy is worthless, from bias, malevolence, or sheer ignorance. It is difficult to say whether the politico-religious pamphlets of the seventeenth century, or the factious Whig-and-Tory ones of the eighteenth, produce the more depressing effect on the reader who is set on making sound and honest conclusions. Yet political pamphlets had their importance—and for many purposes discharged the functions which have now devolved on newspapers and periodical reviews. Hence came their popularity —it is surprising to note in contemporary records the number of thousands of some of them which were sold, and the effect which they obviously had on public opinion. The pamphleteer was a personage whom

statesmen could not afford to ignore, and sometimes
statesmen themselves became pamphleteers.

Often the pamphlet reaches formidable dimensions,
and develops into a serious treatise on political philosophy, turning the crisis of the moment into a typical
development of world-history. It is sometimes difficult to decide whether a well-known work should be
ranked as an overgrown brochure, or a contribution
to the study of the so-called Philosophy of History.
The student desirous of getting useful sidelights on
his own period may find that he has to wade through
pages of generalizations of doubtful value on past
ages, concerning which the author was insufficiently
informed. At the worst, he will arrive at some conception of the prevailing mentality of certain sections
of society at the moment when the work was written.
And that is something achieved ! When he has read
Simon Fish's *Supplicacyon of the Beggars*, or Martin
Marprelate's tracts, or *Histrio-Mastix*, or the *Tale
of a Tub*, or *Thoughts on the Present Discontents*, or
Tract 90, he will appreciate what moved some people
and provoked others to wrath. He can then draw his
own deductions, affected or not affected by the argu-
mentation of an earlier age. It may be dangerous for
him to say that he has caught the spirit of the times—
for has any time one sole spirit ?

V

OF HISTORICAL PERSPECTIVE IN
GENERAL

THE moment that man begins to think about something more than the passing needs and problems of daily life, and starts (consciously or unconsciously) to make generalizations about himself and his neighbours, their ends and objects, their past and future, he has begun to look at things in perspective. From what he has seen or heard of he can glance backward and forward, for cautions and warnings, hopes and aspirations, bearing on his present position. And when he extends his survey so as to draw deductions from all that he can gather as to the past records of mankind, he is trying to look at the world in *historical* perspective. It may be that his survey covers no more space of time than a few generations—tales of a grandfather may be the limit of his knowledge. Early tribal legends generally run into mythology after a comparatively short list of remembered ancestral names. Or, on the other hand, he may know—or think that he knows—the whole history of mankind since the Creation—if he ties himself down to the idea of a Creation—and may even have ideas of the evolution of the Universe before man came into being. Such was the happy conviction of Orosius in A.D. 417, and of Mr. H. G. Wells in 1938. But whether his horizon of supposed knowledge be short or long, whether it be three generations or a hundred

æons, the man who has started to generalize about
his own position in universal history is creating for
himself an historical perspective.

What are the things that determine a man's outlook on the past and the future ?   I do not mean only
the outlook that the historian (or would-be historian)
takes, but the conceptions that governed the mind
of the average man, and of the community in which he
lived, at various epochs down to our own day.   For
there have been, and are, racial outlooks on the history
of the world, quite different from the personal conclusions drawn by individuals belonging to a race,
and these communal views are sometimes not without
their importance.

It must be remembered that there are sharp
breaks in the continuity of human thought concerning
the Past and the Future, consequent on outward
happenings in some cases, on mental and spiritual
changes in others.   To take an easy example—the
conception of world-history for the Roman of the
reign of Augustus and of a Roman of the reign of
Honorius was wholly different.   But was the change
more due to the military collapse of the Empire under
barbarian invasions, or to the triumph of the Christian
over the old official Pagan ideal ?   Or were there
countless other contributory causes, economic and
constitutional, and which of them were more potent ?
Anyhow, we have to explain the difference between
Virgil's

      'Tu regere imperio populos, Romane, memento,'

and Salvian's nightmare conception of a world morally
and physically corrupt, rightly and inevitably doomed
to the oncoming fires of the Last Judgment.

Or again, the outlook of an ordinary intelligent Frenchman, Englishman, or German about A.D. 1450 was completely different from that of his great-grandson about A.D. 1600—but was that the result of the complex cultural movement which (for want of a better word) we call the Renaissance, and of the discovery of America and the Indies, and of countless advances in science ? Or was it, in the main, the result of that great spiritual phenomenon which (again for want of a better word) we call the Reformation ? Is there any fundamental truth in the idea that the revolt against ecclesiastical traditionalism was an aspect of the general revolt against traditionalism of all sorts ? Or are we to keep carefully apart the moral revolt of the spirit against corruption from the mere cultural revolt of the Renaissance against disproved fallacies ? For this latter was by no means a puritanical wave of thought.

It is well worth while to take into consideration what are the main things that have governed man's conception of the progress of world-events, and also the way in which such conception has influenced his conduct from age to age. The beginnings of unconscious historical perspective come early : we may trace them in Homer and Hesiod and the Pentateuch, even in surviving scraps of Egyptian and Mesopotamian records— and farther back than that. A hint that divine visitations of wrath are not unprovoked ; that an impious and tyrannical king ' who does not that which is right in the sight of the Lord ' means a ruined people; or that civil wars are deplorable, or that a corrupt oligarchy ends in a revolution, may be ' glimpses of the obvious '. But historical perspective is beginning when the poet, the preacher, or the annalist sets down such things as accepted facts, and applies them as warnings to the politics of his own day.

Presently we reach the stage when the intelligent observer with a literary turn works all these observed phenomena into a little constitutional essay, as does Herodotus when—under the easy fiction of a debate between seven Persian noblemen on forms of government—he discusses the advantages and disadvantages of oligarchy, democracy, and monarchy. Here historical perspective has ripened into definite promulgation of doctrine. And Herodotus is only a hundred years distant from Aristotle, who was able to set forth the doctrine of the rise, progress, and decay of states of all kinds with a soundness of judgment that none of his successors in the sphere of political philosophy has ever surpassed.

Though moderns like Montesquieu or Lord Bryce have had the advantage of the survey of two thousand more years of history than was in the purview of the Stagirite, it cannot be said that they have greatly affected his conclusions, or refuted any of the more important of his generalizations. And it astonishes us when we reflect that between his thought and ours there lie many centuries of the Roman Empire, in which the problems of democracy, on which he pondered so much, had become out of date, and still more centuries of the Dark Ages, in which constitutional history had harked back to that primitive contest between aristocracy and monarchy that had ended in Greece three hundred years before Aristotle's day.

I fancy that the Stagirite would have found himself quite competent to make the apposite reflections on the last problem that has cropped up, that of ' dictatorships ', since it bears a high resemblance to a phenomenon quite familiar to him, that of the ' tyranny ' of ancient Greece.   In this a prominent individual of exceptional ability and pushfulness gets temporary possession of the control of a state whose people are in a state of endemic discontent, caused either by civil strife, or by chafing at a constitution that is working badly, or by economic trouble after a national disaster.   In ancient Greece he did it by means of an armed body of oath-bound satellites of his own following, or by mercenary bands not infrequently.   Tyrants who arose out of a misgoverned democracy in a time of unlucky war, like Dionysius the Elder at Syracuse, were by no means unknown. They always promised freedom from faction-fighting, and enlightened administration leading to prosperity, and pandered to national (or rather to civic) pride by great public works, and were prone to annexations. The ' tyranny ' being essentially the product of the dominating energy of an individual, often came to an end at his death, and seldom survived a second generation.   A tyrant's heir, reared in the purple, always tended to forget the popular arts by which his father had come to the front, and became a victim to ὕβρις, which usually led to his being assassinated or expelled.   The tyrant having won his way to power by the death or exile of many political enemies invariably lives in an atmosphere of suspicion, closely guarded whenever he exhibits himself in public, and he occasionally seizes and makes away with persons on whom he seemed to be most relying for support. The modern Russian ' tyranny ' has shown fine examples of this—also the modern German ' tyranny ' on a somewhat smaller scale. The old story of the ' sword of Damocles ' has its twentieth-century parallels.

Of what comes after, when a ' tyranny ' has run out, Aristotle gives many examples. Not being a prognosticator, but only an observer of modern phenomena, I cannot follow him, for (as I have said before) there is no safe arguing from analogies, and ' political prophecy is the most futile of all forms of human mental activity '.

But we are at present concerned not with the future but with the past. We are contemplating the outlook on the records of mankind, not as it is to be found in Aristotle, or Dante, or Bacon, or Voltaire, or Montesquieu, or Lord Bryce, or any other ' master mind ', but as it comes to the man in the street. For the general historical perspective of a generation, the conclusions of the average intelligent person, who reflects the public opinion of his day, are as important as those of the ' master mind '. The latter is sometimes only ' a voice crying in the wilderness ' to an uncomprehending audience. Wherefore we have to study not only political specialists, but the writers who best express the common views of their contemporaries, even if they are somewhat limited in their purview.

History, as I have defined it above in its narrower meaning, when we have got past cosmogonies and theories as to the creation of the universe, begins with monuments and epics and folk-tales : afterwards written evidence comes into the sphere of the annalist

6

—often a very barren compiling of genealogies inter-
spersed with isolated notes of unusual phenomena
which caught his attention. Take as an example
the annalist in Judges xii. who writes : ' Elon, the
Zebulonite, judged Israel, for ten years, and he died,
and was buried in Aijalon in the land of Zebulun.
And after him Abdon the son of Hillel, a Pirathonite,
judged Israel : and he had forty sons and thirty
nephews that rode on three score and ten asses' colts :
and he judged Israel for eight years, and died and
was buried in Pirathon in the land of Ephraim.'
There is no comment on either personage—but we
happen to know from Egyptian as well as from
Hebrew records that Palestine was in a pretty disturbed condition all through their century. Similarly the old English annalist, whose jottings are
inserted in the early part of the Anglo-Saxon Chronicle,
gives us under the year 773 a typically unhelpful
entry : ' In this year a fiery cross appeared in the
heavens about sunset, and wondrous adders were
seen in the land of the South Saxons.' One would
have been glad to know whether this was a plague of
some sort of unwonted serpents, or whether, since
they were only *seen*, and are not said to have done any
harm, they were some sort of supernatural portent.
The early Roman *Fasti* which Livy used, were full of
casual notes of such uncanny happenings, mostly
objectless, but evidently of high interest to the Augurs.

But real historical perspective soon comes, when
among the bald annalistic record of judges' names
we find inserted the hero-stories of Gideon, Barak,
or Jephthah, deliverers who were needed because
Israel from generation to generation lapsed back

and ' went a whoring after false gods, and bowed
down before them, and turned out of the way in which
their fathers had walked '. The Lord sent champions
who delivered the people from time to time, ' but it
came to pass that when a judge was dead, they turned
back and corrupted themselves more than their
fathers, and ceased not from their doings and their
stubborn ways '. ' In those days,' says this melancholy compilation in its very last verse, ' there was no
king in Israel, and every man did that which was
right in his own eyes '. Historical perspective has
arrived and deductions are being made.

The same is the case with the Anglo-Saxon
Chronicle, when the compiler, breaking away from his
arid yearly entries, taken from some earlier annalistic
screed, bursts out in indignation against the wickedness of his own days. ' The Earth bears no corn :
you might as well have tilled the sea : the land is
all ruined by evil deeds, and it is said openly that
Christ and His saints are asleep.'

Such commentary in Palestine or England implies
the beginnings of reasoning and of judgment on cause
and effect. The chronicler is making himself the exponent of the thought of his generation, and expresses
its opinions as to the consequences of a political tendency or a moral degeneracy which has begun to
work itself out. The individual has begun to generalize
on the aspect of his own time, and presently he will
do the same on the aspect of times past, and even sometimes of times to come. For a consideration of the
problems of to-day involves, in comparison, a consideration of yesterday, and perhaps of to-morrow.
And when a man begins consciously to compare

yesterday, to-day, and to-morrow he is constructing
for himself a historical perspective. It may be only
the perspective of his own nation, or even of his own
city, or quite possibly of no more than his own class
or caste within that city or nation. Hesiod, Theognis,
Aristophanes, Juvenal had all got class and party
perspectives, not general ones. The tendencies
which they denounced were those which bore with
special hardness on men of their own standing.

But there are those who have a world-perspective,
like Orosius, or Jean Jacques Rousseau, or Karl
Marx, or Mr. H. G. Wells, but a perspective entirely
settled and circumscribed by their personal predispositions and theories, rather than by a true and
unprejudiced survey of all the historical evidence
that was available for them. Such generalizers are
often lamentably ignorant of detailed historical facts,
and tend more to *a priori* philosophical reconstruction
of the characteristics of past ages, as they imagine
them to have been. Prehistoric anthropology does
not give evidence for Rousseau's picture of the primitive virtuous man, destined to oppression at the hands
of kings and priests. The primitive man was more
like Hobbes' conception of a creature living a short,
bestial, dangerous, ' nasty ' life, before he learned
to get a little more security by arriving at a ' social
contract ' very different from that of which Jean
Jacques dreamed. And to envisage world-history
as dominated by the pestilent capitalist is as absurd
as to conceive of it as blasted by malevolent priests
or kings.

As I said before, the philosophers are the enemies
of history, trying to make out of a series of strange

and perplexing happenings which we have before us, something logical and tending to an end—evolution, progress, illumination, what you will. Each, to back up his particular conception, rummages occasionally through the records of the past, and picks up the items that suit him to point an argument. Other items that do not fall easily into his conception are left judiciously alone, or perhaps are declared to have no real importance. I must confess to a sneaking sympathy for the philosopher from practical experience in grubbing among sources : occasionally one comes upon a particularly tiresome piece of evidence, affecting one's estimate of a man or one's narrative of a battle. It cannot, in honesty, be ignored : is it to be attributed to mal-observation or malice in a witness, or to blurred memory of something seen in the past, or to second-hand information ? Anyhow it has to be faced—probably it will have to go into a footnote, with a caution to the effect that the author is not convinced as to its authenticity. What I have to complain of on the part of the philosophic generalizers on history is that they too often ignore these tiresome pieces of evidence altogether, and sweep on with an undisturbed flow of exposition, in which only the items that happen to suit them float obviously on the surface. ' Progress ' or what you will has to be proved ; why worry the audience with incidental things that have to be explained away if you mention them ? They had better be consigned to oblivion— in the hope that some tiresome critic will not rake them up from the bottom of the stream. The general public does not usually study critical reviews. Of the tens of thousands who have read the eloquent

histories of Macaulay or Froude, how many scores
know of the elaborate demonstrations of inaccuracies
that have been discovered by patient and sometimes
hypercritical researchers ?   And if this is true in
definite histories of a period, how much truer is it
in indefinite summaries of the general progress of
mankind, which sweep through the ages to prove the
plausibility of the world-perspective presented by some
philosopher with a political theory in his brain ?

For almost invariably these people have some
special hobby of their own, or some ' axe to grind ',
and are set on persuading these contemporaries that
they have the key to all knowledge.   When most
occupied in denigrating the past and all its iniquities,
they are working for their interested aspirations for
the future.   And so the record of the history of mankind has to be generalized into a logical process
leading to the desired end.   But, as a matter of fact,
history is not a tale of inevitable tendencies, but a
series of happenings, some of them so startling that
they may deserve to be called ' cataclysms '.   One
has to study them, with a cautious conviction that
things might have gone otherwise, and that no word
is so dangerous as the word ' inevitable '—except
perhaps the word ' evolution ' when used in an
unscrupulous fashion.

But leaving alone for a moment the propagandic
historical perspectives of the few, let us first examine
the less sophisticated historical perspectives of the
many—of generations and ages as they pass.   For,
as we have seen, mankind comes in a quite early stage
of cultural development to compare the surroundings
of to-day with those of the past—whatever the range

of backward knowledge may be in various races and periods. And when this pondering has begun, and explanations are sought, historical perspective has come into being.

The judgment of the man who moralizes on history, in any age, may be either Optimistic or Pessimistic. Which it may be is settled either by the atmosphere of the moment—the thinker's nation or class or religion may be faring well or faring ill— or by his personal mentality and character. For there have been Optimists in dark ages, and Pessimists in times of apparent prosperity.

VI

OF HISTORICAL PERSPECTIVE—THE
PESSIMISTS AND THE OPTIMISTS

ON the whole Pessimism is the more ancient and
universal creed of mankind—Optimism only
crops up at intervals.

Impressed by the tales told us by respected grand-
parents most men have been prone to think (with
Hesiod and Horace) that they are themselves a degenerate race. All over the world nations have been
content to believe in the ' Good Old Times ', the
' Golden Age ', which has been lost owing to the
perversity of the younger generation. Our ancestors
were divine or semi-divine. They walked the earth
thirty feet high, like the Moses of the Talmud and
several Celtic heroes, or they possessed all the mystic
knowledge of Odin. They lived three hundred,
four hundred, nay seven hundred years. They could,
like Homer's Hector, use as missiles stones ' which
scarce two of the strongest of modern men, straining
hard, could tear from the soil '. They bestrode
elephants, and used palm trees as walking-sticks.
And the earth on which they dwelt was a more genial
clime than ours, which produced three harvests a
year, and flowed with milk and honey.

But by some ancestral fault—because Adam and
Eve ate the bitter apple of knowledge, or because
Pandora opened the fatal box of plagues and diseases—
evil came upon the human race, and progressive

decay has been its lot. Hesiod formalized the conception for the Western world into the scheme of the Five Ages—each worse than that which had preceded it, till mankind had slipped through those of Silver and Bronze into the age of Iron, in which his own unhappy lot was cast. Passed on by Greece to Rome, and by Rome to the Middle Ages, the conception was as popular fifteen centuries after Christ as it had been nine centuries before his birth. And the more pessimistic spirits finished it off with the *Sexta* and *Septima* Aetas Mundi, which were to see Antichrist, the destruction of the world, and the Last Judgment— all due in a very few years. For men, it was said, have grown steadily worse, and each generation thinks that its own particular faults are so startling that divine retribution is long overdue.

This conception of mankind as a dwindling race, doomed to a merited extinction, might be considered as a fit product of the most gloomy and sin-conscious ascetics of the Middle Ages. But it is much older than Mediæval Christianity. Some of the Greeks had a glimpse of the general *débâcle* ' when Dinos (" the Whirl ") reigns, having driven out Zeus '. The Buddhist considered the world of matter as a vain, perishable thing, and would withdraw into Nirvana to escape—though this is perhaps only a different sort of annihilation. Most queer was the Norseman's conception of the end of all things—' Ragnarok ', the day of chaos, when gods, heaven and earth should go up in flames, after the powers of hell and destruction had got loose. This was a much more grim conception than that of the Christian Last Judgment— since there the just receive their reward, and only the unjust go down to eternal damnation. But if the universe bursts up on the day of Ragnarok, what has become of the eternal distinction between right and wrong ?

The conception of the history of the world as a process of consistent deterioration, from a Golden Age down to a catastrophe well earned by degenerate mankind, is not a very cheerful or inspiring one to guide the individual along the way of life. The most obvious deduction from it is ' let us eat and drink, for to-morrow we die'. The average man finds within himself no power to resist the stream of tendency in which he believes that he is being carried along toward an unhappy end. He does not even exclaim with Hamlet :

> The World is out of joint : O cursed spite
> That ever I was born to set it right !

For few minds ever conceive the idea that it is their duty to stand against the spirit of the times— hard though the task may be. Such minds, of course, there have been in all ages—even in those of chaos and decay, when there was not even a saving religion to promise a reward in another world for steadfast adherence to the fundamental laws of honour and righteousness. The Stoics of later Greece and of Roman Imperial times—who, without any faith in the discredited gods of Olympus, stood up to bear witness that right was right and wrong was wrong, and that the self-respecting man must cling to the right, come what may—were certainly examples of such a type. They lived in the midst of a most corrupt civilization, their way was certain to be difficult and dangerous, but they were ready to walk in it—on first principles and whatever the consequences. Stoics have never been numerous, and have been accused of being self-conscious and pedantic by their unsympathizing contemporaries. Nevertheless they merit our respect.

Their lot was much harder than that of other Pessimists, who like them believed in the degeneracy and wickedness of the world, but stood out against its influence, because they were supported by the inspiration of a religion which promised salvation to the individual, though it prophesied destruction for the world. Among them I can include the Buddhist— though his idea of salvation was one that seems to many of us peculiar—absorption into the Godhead without the survival of personal identity. But to the Christian or the Mohammedan pessimist the protest against the evil world took the simpler shape of the duty to save one's own soul—incidentally the souls of others if possible, but primarily one's own. Hence all the fakirs and troglodyte hermits—St. Simeon Stylites on the top of his sixty-foot pillar, or St. Antony among the lions of the desert—eschewed all touch with the wicked world, because they felt themselves unable to convert it, though they might by untold austerities macerate their own sinful bodies so far as to establish an *ad misericordiam* appeal for pardon from a just but jealous God. This form of Pessimism was as self-regarding as that of the Stoics, and less justifiable, since it ignored the immensity of God's mercy, and thought only of His omniscience and justice. No doubt the self-inflicted torture was in many cases atonement for the evil-doing of earlier years—many anchorites had sad memories of the past. But some appear to have had no such record, but to have wished simply to cut themselves off from a world of sin.

This was certainly much less amiable than the asceticism of St. Francis, who with no less profound a belief in the wickedness of the world was able to think of the souls of other men as well as of his own. Nay, he could spare a kindly thought for bird and beast, as well as for human sinners. But Francis of Assisi, though an ascetic, was an Optimist, and that makes all the difference between him and Simeon Stylites on his pillar, or St. Guthlac in his swamp, or any self-torturing Indian fakir.

Pessimism has not been peculiar to the Ancient World, or to the Middle Ages—it continues down to the present day. After all the enthusiasm bred by the Renaissance, and the self-satisfaction of the cultivated and illuminated ' superior person ' of the eighteenth century, and the progress-cult of the nineteenth century with its evolutionary ethics, the disappointed twentieth century, which has seen the Great War end not in the League of Nations but in rampant discord and practical ' might is right,' is back again in the same depression which befell Orosius or Gildas, and feeling that some sort of a Last Judgment is the deserved reward of human perversity.

The Optimist has always been a rarer creature than the Pessimist, because enthusiasm is rarer than the grumbling acquiescence in one's surroundings into which the majority of men slip so easily. Caustic remarks about the worthlessness of one's contemporaries and the rottenness of one's *milieu* are easy things to make. To take arms against the conventions of a settled society requires more energy than to satirize it. It is also in many cases a much more uncomfortable and dangerous occupation. Moreover, periods when optimism seems justifiable, even to a man of cheerful disposition, are much less frequent in the world's history than periods in which man's outlook appears gloomy or at least doubtful. It is seldom that even the poet can cry out that at this moment to be alive at all is bliss, and to be alive and young is very heaven, as Wordsworth once exclaimed. It is rare to stand upon some peak in a spiritual Darien and to see a new, beautiful, and unknown sea of possibilities spreading before one. Rarest of all, perhaps, is it to desire to call to the passing hour to stay, because it is so fair.

Yet Optimists there have been, and perhaps may be again, though their optimism is sometimes a little forced, and more often a little illogical. Was Virgil, chanting his song of the glories of the foundation of the Roman race, and the restoration of the Golden Age in the hall of Augustus, a genuine Optimist, or was he but an amiable court-poet singing for his supper ? I prefer to believe the former alternative, for I love Virgil. But Augustus was not really a very likeable person, and I fancy that Virgil knew it.

When Jean Jacques Rousseau wrote sweetly of a former age of primitive virtue and innocence, and suggested that a future age of a similar sort was possible even for the jaded and artificial folk of the eighteenth century was he a prophet or a charlatan ? Considering his life's record one is inclined to take his whole attitude for a mere pose. But, if so, it was a pose which fascinated a whole generation, and changed the historical perspective of millions of his contemporaries.

But there have been other Optimists of whose genuine inspiration no one can feel a doubt. And first and foremost among them may be reckoned those good men who have had before their eyes a religion of universal salvation, rather than one which relies on the fear of hell-fire as an efficient element in propaganda. When one is thoroughly convinced that one is doing one's best for the righteous cause, which will, and must, triumph in the end, one has the right to be an Optimist, even though incidentally one may have to be a martyr. One's personal sufferings count for little if thereby the cause is advanced, and a just God will not fail to take them into account, when one's good and evil deeds go into the divine scales. Wherefore there have been epochs of primitive faith, and later epochs of revival, when a genuine optimism prevailed, and the good cause went forth conquering and to conquer. The early apostles making their first assault on the world in obedience to their Master's last earthly words, the missionary friars of the thirteenth century, the evangelical missionaries overseas in the earlier nineteenth century were all Optimists, insomuch as they looked forward to conquering the whole world. So I suppose were the Buddhist preachers who pervaded all Eastern Asia, in the centuries shortly before the Christian era, and undoubtedly the Jesuits who worked in the same regions in the sixteenth century.

All these I reckon Optimists because they aimed at universal conversion of mankind. And therein they differed from people like Tertullian or the narrow disciples of Calvin, whose conception of heaven was that of a place reserved for a limited number of the elect, while the sinners in thousands of millions groaned below. I should call these last Pessimists, however sure they might be as to the salvation of their own little souls. And with them, I fear, must be reckoned all Predestinarians, from St. Augustine downward, who took for granted the reprobation, by divine decree, of legions of those who were never to ' have a chance ', because they were earmarked for the downward road.

But it has not been in times of religious fervour alone that men had an optimistic outlook on the world. There is such a thing as social and political optimism : and one would be loth to deny the name of Optimist to the eighteenth-century enthusiasts drafting the ' Rights of Man ' and dreaming of a second Golden Age to be reached by the simple method of ' liquidating ' kings and priests, and re-lapsing into a supposed ' State of Nature '. It was of such an outlook that Wordsworth sang :

> In which the meagre, stale, forbidding ways
> Of custom, law, and statute took at once
> The attraction of a country of romance.
> Where Reason seemed the most to assert her rights
> When most intent on making of herself
> A prime enchantress—to assist the work
> Which then was going forward in her name !
> Not favoured spots above, but the whole earth
> The beauty wore of promise—that which sets
> The budding rose above the rose full blown.

Alas for the poor Optimists, French and English, of 1792, who had before them no Golden Age but Robespierre and Bonaparte—the Luddites and the ' Six Acts '.

A generation later I should not be disposed to deny

the name of Optimist to another and a much more
sober set of political enthusiasts—or perhaps one ought
hardly to use the word ' enthusiasts ', for enthusiasm
was hardly the badge of their tribe—but at any
rate deeply convinced political dogmatists. I mean
those very superior persons the Whigs of the earlier
nineteenth century, who thought that a bicameral
constitution, with a constitutional king—or president
if necessary—was a panacea for all human ills.

There was a wave of genuine optimism passing
over Europe when serious men thought that Greece,
Naples, Portugal, or Spain, needed only the application of the Whig formula to make them happy. Nay,
with the substitution of a constitutional president for
a king, it might even work for Venezuela, Mexico,
or Honduras. From that easy solution of the difficulties of mankind we are now far away !

> How small of all that human hearts endure
> That part which laws or kings can cause or cure !

Did not Lord Bryce, in his admirable *Modern
Democracies* confess, as the last heir of the old Liberal
tradition, that constitutions are after all far less important than national character in the working of a state ?
The old Liberal Optimist of the nineteenth century
used to help himself into a comfortable beatitude by
talking of 'Progress'. The conception worked down, as
I have already observed, to Victorian schoolboys. ' We
are better than our fathers, because we have the railway, the steamer, the electric telegraph, vaccination,
improved sanitation, and a reformed parliament.
Evolution is the scientific explanation of all things,
and all evolution will be on the right side.'

This crude theory of optimism overlooks the fact that the close study of history shows that it is not merely evolutionary—it is also not infrequently cataclysmic—I mean that things happen which could not have been foreseen by the wisest, and are purely unexpected and not infrequently destructive. So far is it from being true that all history is a record of progress, there are countless examples of its having been a record of decay and disaster. The Liberal idea of Progress was a rash generalization from the single epoch of the nineteenth century, which took into no consideration the set-backs in the history of civilization. What of the end of the old Egyptian or Mesopotamian empires, on whose sites the observer of the early nineteenth century could see miserable fellahin squatting among the ruins of a magnificent culture ? What had become of the Christian Church of North Africa, the church of Cyprian and Augustine ? What of the Roman Campagna, Isauria, or Trans-jordan, where the traveller rode for long miles through uninhabited wilds studded with relics of ancient architecture ? Was progress to be detected in the breaking up of the Roman Empire, or of the Christian Church in the Middle Ages ? Rather ' decline and fall ' in many a case.

To my mind history is not so much a record of Progress, or Evolution, but a series of happenings of various tendency. And so far is it from being an impersonal, logical process, that there is more truth in the much-decried theory of Thomas Carlyle, that it has been largely affected by the working of individual men of mark on their contemporaries. Personalities like Alexander the Great, Julius Cæsar, Mohammed,

7

Bonaparte, or even Lenin were not mere typical developments of their generation, but men who turned the course of history from its normal channel, because they were abnormal. Who can dare to say that if Alexander the Great or Mohammed had not existed, some other Macedonian king or Arabian prophet would have upset the world ? One of the silliest epigrams that I have ever seen was to the effect that if Bonaparte had not been Bonaparte, Moreau would have been. Compare the character and talents of the two men ! In short let us never talk of the world-stream, or of inevitability, but reflect that the human record is illogical, often cataclysmic, anything rather than a regular progress from the worse to the better all down the ages.

VII

HISTORICAL PERSPECTIVE—CONCERNING
CATACLYSMS, POLITICAL AND MORAL

WHETHER the individual or the generation be pessimistic or optimistic in historical perspective, it is undeniable (as I have said before) that there have been certain cataclysmic events from time to time which have compelled a revision of values —a general modification of outlook. It is a misfortune that we cannot trace things back to the beginnings of conscious thought, because we require some written record to help us. No doubt there must have been such revisions of outlook when man first discovered the use of fire, or of agriculture, or of the domestication of animals. We can have a better appreciation of what happened when the people who had discovered the use of metal weapons burst in upon their neolithic predecessors. But we can only guess at the unpleasant surprise to the vanquished.

But certainly races have been forced to make a sharp change of historic perspective when national religion received a shock at the same time as national ambitions. This must have happened both in Egypt and in Mesopotamia. But the first episode of the kind of which sufficient literary evidence survives to enable us to visualize the catastrophe, is that which befell the Jews when the destruction of the house of David and the kingdom of Judah synchronized with the burning and desecration of the Temple of Jerusalem. When a religion has come to centre around a single shrine, when indeed its more enthusiastic votaries have been for generations working to destroy all minor shrines, and to concentrate all worship and ceremonial around the Great Temple, it is an awful thing to see it deliberately cast down and gutted by an overpowering alien enemy. More especially was this the case when Nebuchadnezzar's wrecking of Solomon's temple came along with the end of a hereditary kingship many centuries old, and a transplantation to foreign lands of all surviving members of the royal and priestly castes.

Many local worships and royal dynasties had perished before. ' Where are the gods of Hamath, and the gods of Arpad, and the gods of the city of Sepharvaim?' as Sennacherib had asked, a long century back. He obviously conceived, and it was the spirit of the time, that the gods and the cities perished together. The God of the Hebrews survived, unlike all the Baalim of Syria, to become ultimately the God of the Christian World. That of course could not be foreseen by any human being in the seventh century before Christ. But the religious outlook of the Hebrews was profoundly modified by the catastrophe of the destruction of the temple. They came to understand that Jehovah could be worshipped otherwhere than in the great shrine at Jerusalem, even when after the seventy years of desolation it could be restored on a modest scale. Scattered Hebrew communities would enjoy his patronage in alien lands. The great lesson was that a God invisible and omnipresent was independent of arks and altars and local ceremonies, and that a national creed could persist, like the nation itself, independent of cohabitation around the ancestral shrine.

This was a case of both religious and national perspective upset by a catastrophe. Two centuries and a half later there was a good example of political perspective being transformed for a whole nation, not by catastrophe but by sudden expansion. I allude, of course, to the Greeks, and the result on their view of the world caused by the exploits of Alexander the Great. The Macedonian conquest of the East revolutionized the relations of the active and high-cultured little states of Greece both with each other and with the outer world. Civic patriotism received a blow, but in return the establishment of the new Macedonian Empire offered many compensations to the individual. If a man consented to forget that he was a Thessalian, a Corinthian, a Cretan or an Athenian, and merely to remember that he was a Greek, what could be more inspiring than to see that the old Hellenic genius for colonization was not extinct, to behold every land from the Ægean to the Indus covered with Greek cities as large and often as splendid as those of the old Motherland. For every active-minded man—soldier, artist, architect, scribe, merchant, and seaman—there was instant honourable and lucrative employment—even for poets and philosophers a little later. Those Greeks who threw themselves into the new life of the conquered East looked back on the old times of the ' balance of power ' and the constant strife between democracy and oligarchy as something rather petty. Even Aristotle's wonderful analysis of the constitutions and tendencies of the

Greek civic states was getting a little out of date not long after its author was dead.

Shortly after Alexander the Great won his crowning victory over Persia at Arbela, news came to him of a battle in Greece. Agis, King of Sparta, had fallen, and with him five thousand brave men more. But the Macedonian turned to his generals and said, ' It seems that while *we* have been conquering the Great King there has been a battle of mice in Arcadia.' While the empire of the Eastern World was being won by the Tigris, fights at home between small armies for a strip of plainland or a border fort seemed contemptible. Yet Thucydides or Xenophon would have considered them matters of the most vital interest. For the Greeks who had thrown themselves into Alexander's great adventure the national perspective had suddenly been enlarged from a view round the Ægean to a view as far as the Oxus and the Indus. Why discuss constitutions any more, or indulge in civic faction fights, when the man with a brain and a sword had the wide world at his feet ? And so it went on for generations long after Alexander's own generals had perished or founded dynasties. Was not Euthydemus of Magnesia to reign as king over all the Bactrian realms, and the Cretan adventurer Lasthenes to rule as a nominal vizier over Antioch and the broad lands of Syria ? One might start from nothing, and end by wearing a bloodstained and probably evanescent diadem, or build temples of Zeus and Tyche somewhere east of Taurus, or grow sleek as a court poet or philosopher at Antioch or Alexandria.

The vision was elusive, the change of historical perspective demoralizing. They ended in a veneer of Greek civilization imposed on the East for a few centuries, at the cost of the exhaustion and debasement of the civilizer. There was an end of the Greece of Aristides and Pericles and Socrates, remembered only in some academic cliques at Athens or Rhodes. And in return there was produced the Levantine mongrel—the Greek had little or no trace of colour-prejudice—as the Romans knew him, and as we know him to-day—Juvenal's *Greculus esuriens*, the talented adventurer and charlatan, master of all trades save those in which honesty is indispensable—the degenerate heir of Ulysses, Themistocles, and Alcibiades, if not of Solon, Plato, and Epaminondas. What a deplorable result of what a long and magnificent endeavour ! Search for the ruins of Seleucia, and marvel at the broken columns in Transjordan.

The Greek's intoxication of empire and exploitation, ending in spiritual debasement and racial demoralization, had its pendant or parallel in the fate of the Roman. The people of the tough little republican state on the Seven Hills who fought the Etruscan, the Samnite, and the Gaul, had a mentality of their own and an outlook of their own. The Romans were limited, well-balanced, intensely pervaded with local patriotism, disciplined, and constitutional. Cato the Elder, no very amiable figure but a great citizen, was a perfect exponent of their character. To these Romans came, because of their splendid military organization, and their unbounded loyalty to the state, that same delusive boon which had ruined the Greeks—a world empire won by the sword. They lost their religion, their honesty, and their liberty in the process.

Compare the historical perspective of Cato the Elder with that of the half-cosmopolitanized but yet patriotic Cicero, and again that of Cicero—who still thought that liberty might be saved—with the melancholy outlook of Lucan and Tacitus and Juvenal, who saw that the things which made life worth living were gone, though life itself had become incomparably more splendid, luxurious, and complicated under the Emperors who had slain Liberty.

Virgil had sung, in well-remembered lines, that Art and Culture and Philosophy might be the province of the Greek, but that the Roman had discovered the greater art of ruling East and West :

> Parcere subjectis et debellare superbos.

Truly the Romans had done so, but at what cost ! ' What shall it profit a man if he win the whole world and lose his own soul ? ' and this the Roman had done.

There has not often been a century more morally dead than the culminating period of the Roman Empire, the Age of the Antonines—which Gibbon vainly praised as the time in which the greatest number of mortals in recorded history enjoyed the greatest possible amount of peace and prosperity. Outward prosperity no doubt there was, and the monuments of Hadrian arose in similar splendour in every province from Britain to the Euphrates. But it is not true that

> Whate'er is best administered is best,

and even the administration of the Antonine age has found its critics.

A period in which the old official Roman religion was defunct, and practically replaced by the absurd

institution of Cæsar worship—the test for unlucky
Christians before a magistrate—was also one when
ideals were dead, and liberty a name with which emperors sometimes played as a solemn farce. What did
Hadrian mean when he struck coins commemorating
LIBERTAS PUBLICA ? I suppose it was a jest of that
most freakish and talented person. Another emperor
who was a philosopher saw the shallowness of the whole
business, and did not shrink from setting it down.
The *Meditations* of Marcus Aurelius give some of the
most melancholy pages in literature. The world
professed to worship Cæsar, and Cæsar was a stoic
of a resigned cast, and thought that the world was
hollow, and that the good man could get no pleasure
out of it. Indeed, putting people of trivial life aside,
I doubt if there were any real optimists in the Antonine
period save the Christian propagandists, who often
came to a sad end in this Golden Age. For Marcus
Aurelius, odd though it may appear, was not merely
a depressed Stoic but a persecutor of Christians.

The soulless outward prosperity of the second
century crumpled up into the military anarchy of the
third century, during which some thirty emperors
and some fifty usurpers asserted in turn on their
coins that they were about to restore happiness to
the Roman world—FELICITAS TEMPORUM, SAECULUM
NOVUM or RENOVATIO ROMANORUM or RESTITUTIO
ORBIS TERRARUM, before they came to their untimely
ends by the swords of a mutinous soldiery. The
UBIQUE PAX of the much-harried Gallienus takes the
prize for mendacity. The time was as debased as the
currency struck by the ephemeral wearers of the purple.
And it looked at one time as if the Roman Empire

was about to break up—partly to coalesce into new local states like the Gaulish Empire of 258–274, or the Syrian Empire of Zenobia's family, partly to become the prey of the incoming barbarian, Goth or Persian.

From this particular disaster (if it would have been a disaster, which some may possibly dispute) the civilized world was saved for a time by the line of tough soldier emperors of Illyrian blood—Aurelian, Probus, Carus, Diocletian, whose military ability and organizing power gave the Empire another century of survival—with boundaries intact, if vitality hopelessly impaired. For the state as Diocletian left it was a bureaucratic reconstruction, living on an exhausted tradition, and with no inspiring ideal of religion or patriotism. Mars and Jupiter were as dead as Cincinnatus or Cato. There only remained a vague confidence in the diuturnity of the Roman Empire, as an inevitable ancient fact. To the people of this exhausted and dispirited civilization came in the fourth century two cataclysms—the one preceding the other by a couple of generations—the triumph of Christianity and the triumph of the outer barbarians—each a complete negation of the old Imperial theory of the world as a Roman Empire ruled by a divine Cæsar ' Deus et Dominus noster ' in the style of some third-century coins and inscriptions.

There had been warnings of the approach of these two cataclysms—there had been emperors who were more or less affected by Christianity in secret, and already the barbarians had been seen for a moment at Aquileia, at Delphi, at Trebizond, at Ephesus, and at Antioch in the evil days of the third century. A moral or political cataclysm put off for some decades is not thereby averted. The triumph of Christianity and the triumph of the barbarians were both inevitable, because the moribund imperial system had no inspiration or enthusiasm left in it, while both the Christian propagandist and the wild men of the North were overflowing with vitality—however unamiable the one might appear to a pagan pedant like Julian the Apostate, or the other to a cultured litterateur like Sidonius Apollinaris.

Between A.D. 320 and A.D. 420 the whole outlook of the civilized world had to change. The greatest revision of historical perspective ever known was forced upon every man. There was never such a complete alteration of moral and political values in such a short time, before or after. Imagine Horace or Tacitus faced with the problems of Justification by Faith, or the precise definition of the doctrine of the Trinity, as the most important intellectual problems of mankind—the all-engrossing topics for discussion by the philosophically-minded individual. The conception of such discussions would have appeared even more impossible than the idea of a Gothic king reigning at Ravenna, and dictating orders to a subservient Roman Senate—the astounding phenomenon which was to be seen some two generations later than A.D. 420.

It was a terrible jar to those reared under the old Empire to accept the incoming system of Christianity with its morality, which was obviously superior to that of paganism, but imposed a new category of virtues and vices, which the man in the street found it hard to work in with his sordid daily life. ' Blessed

are the meek ' and ' Blessed are the merciful ' sounded
strangely to a people accustomed to the pompous
ostentation of the imperial system, and the thousand
statues and reliefs representing the Roman trampling
down dying enemies. The man in the street had been
accustomed to gloat over the bloody sports of the
arena, where prisoners were thrown to the beasts,
or hirelings paid to kill each other in duel—with
copious betting on the events by thousands of interested spectators. It was one of the greatest triumphs
of Christianity when that devoted monk Telemachus
(A.D. 405) threw himself down into the arena between
the contending gladiators, to meet death by brutal
violence, but also to give such a shock to public
opinion that the government had to put an end to
those horrid exhibitions.

But the clash of moralities in the fourth century
synchronized with the breakdown of the external
defences of the Empire, and the irruption of the
barbarians of the North into the heart of the civilized
world. Some of the last pagan philosophers tried to
argue that the downfall of the Roman régime was the
direct consequence of the spread of Christianity—a
religion for slaves and what we should now call
pacifists. In this plausible hypothesis they erred,
for the Empire was ripe for its fall long before Constantine. The real diseases were bureaucracy, over-
taxation, the lack of local patriotism, and of any decent
nucleus of citizens in Rome itself, with perhaps most
fatal of all, the gradual supersession of the old national
army by innumerable new corps of mercenary barbarians. A pagan empire would have crumbled as
inevitably as did the Christian empire under the weak

sons of Theodosius and their successors, perhaps even
more rapidly.

The enormity of the change of historical perspective for the civilized world was felt most acutely
at the time.   Orosius wrote his immense general
history about A.D. 417 at the request of St. Augustine,
who was at the same time composing his *De Civitate
Dei*, both grappling with the great problems on more
or less the same lines, in the endeavour to explain the
cataclysm that had come upon them.   The saint
solved it with his conception of the two hostile cities,
the city of God bound to be spiritually triumphant,
while the earthly city came to the crash.   He disposed
with ease of the hypotheses of pagan philosophers
to the effect that the course of the world depended on
τύχη—blind chance, or that there was a recurring
cycle of periods, which brought mankind at intervals
back to the starting-point, or that Christianity had
been the latent cause of ruin.   The world was blind
and rebellious, what happened to it would be of little
concern, considering that the city of God triumphed
in the salvation of the individual Christian man :
not of all mankind, for there are reprobates excluded
from divine grace by the degree of Providence.
Orosius worked on parallel arguments to a similar
conclusion.   From the earliest records of Babylon
and Egypt down to the Gothic invasions of his own
day, as he demonstrated, mankind had been a sinful
race, vexed by well-deserved wars and disasters.
Empires had crumpled up, nations had been exter-
minated all down the centuries. Rome was now
following Nineveh and Carthage.   Salvation was
for the individual soul : sin was the dominating fact

in the world, and sin involved punishment by a just God. Man must look after his own soul, and by the grace of God might preserve it—but there was no official or bureaucratic guarantee of salvation for an individual as a citizen of the Roman Empire or even as a baptized Christian. Indeed Christian heretics were undoubtedly among the worst of the reprobates. Whether salvation could be gained mainly by faith or partly by works, or by the fiat of the Divinity unconditioned by mere faith or works, was another problem, and that problem was to be discussed by the Christian world down to our own day.

This fifth-century revision of all historical perspective, making the outward happenings in the world insignificant compared with the fight of the individual soul for salvation, was a complete revulsion against all old ideas. History became a sort of phantasmagoria, only worth studying for its warnings. For a thousand years on from the day of St. Augustine and Orosius, Christian Europe had as a whole a perspective in which sin and grace were the dominating factors, and the salvation of one's own soul, and if possible the souls of others, was the all-absorbing task of righteous men. In its meanest and most selfish form the idea led to the self-maceration of thousands of ascetics in cells and dens of the desert. In its more generous aspect it guided to missionary effort to give other men, heathens or heretics, their chance of salvation : it mattered not what happened to the missionary's body, if his soul was safe. The ordained instrument of salvation was the Church, and in comparison with the Church earthly kingdoms, which were usually fleeting and ephemeral, were of comparatively little importance. The old idea of the diuturnity of the Roman Empire was superseded by the new idea of the diuturnity of the Church. What were states like the Vandal kingdom in Africa, the Ostrogothic kingdom in Italy, the kingdoms of the Burgundians, Lombards, or Suevi, but things of a few years or a few centuries which vanished away? The Church might be for the moment rent by Arian and Trinitarian disputes, by schisms between East and West, by local heresies, but by divine providence it was to continue as the leaven that sanctified the world.

The conception of the universal Church as the dominating fact for mankind ran on. There was but one other conception which for long centuries was complicated with it, and occasionally became hostile to it. The Holy Roman Empire of Charlemagne was a vast but unreal archæological reconstruction, falsified of its original intent ere its founder had been dead a hundred years. And the Holy Roman Empire of Otto the Great had not even the pretence of universality which had rendered the creation of Charlemagne imposing. It turned into nothing more than the attempt of three German dynasties to maintain a precarious sovereignty over Rome and Italy. And the attempt failed—to the lasting misery of Germany and Italy alike.

Meanwhile the dominating idea of a thousand years was not the Holy Roman Empire, but the Holy Catholic Church. And the vitally important thing was not who called himself Emperor, and had got himself crowned at Rome, but the conquest of outer Europe by the Church. The conversion of the

Hungarian, Scandinavian, and Slavonic peoples
doubled the size of Christendom, and created a new
community of nations bound together by a spiritual
tie, often loose and ineffective, but still existent and
always usable for an appeal. The old conception of
the Crusades as a spiritual inspiration has, no doubt,
been attenuated by the modern demonstration of their
commercial, economic, and political aspects. But it
remains true that they are not explicable as 'the
foreign policy of the Papacy' nor as a 'grab at Mediterranean commercial monopoly by the Italian naval
powers,' nor as an 'explosion of land-hunger among
the younger sons of feudal Europe.' They were
originally inspired by a religious motive, and for
generation after generation the spiritual appeal continued to affect idealists—such as St. Louis of France—
who were free from meaner personal motives. They
were in the end ineffective in keeping back the oncoming Moslem, and some of their episodes were
repulsive—more especially the wicked 'Fourth
Crusade' which destroyed the Byzantine empire—
the old buffer-state of Europe toward the East. But
the Crusade-motive was genuine, and its debasement
into final discredit and insincerity was one of the main
causes which brought about that revision of historical
perspective in Christendom at large which led to the
pessimism of the fifteenth century.

The failure of the originally spiritual crusading
inspiration was but one of three convictions of disillusionment which pervaded that unhappy century.
The other two were the parallel extremes of debasement into which the Holy Catholic Church and the
Holy Roman Empire had fallen. Their clash was

perhaps inevitable from the first, but it was the dishonest, violent, unscrupulous methods employed on each side, which ended in that disgraceful moral anarchy, lasting for generations, which disgusted the righteous man. It was not that popes set up anti-emperors, or emperors set up anti-popes that did the mischief, but the sordid details of intrigue and chicane. When the great struggle between Church and State, Guelf and Ghibelline, verged to its end, it became clear that the Church—the victor in the strife—was rotten through and through, no less than the Empire. The flight of Clement V from Rome, ending in the 'Avignonese Captivity' and the deplorable spectacle of the Vicar of Christ no longer able to dwell by the tombs of the Apostles, and touting for support in every court of Europe by undignified and unscrupulous methods, was a sufficiently disheartening spectacle.

But how much more appalling to the Christian mind was the 'Great Schism' of 1378, when Catherine of Sienna brought back the exiled Gregory XI to Rome, only to see in the next year the whole effort wasted by the outbreak of a double election of doubtful legality. There had never before been much doubt in the minds of the orthodox as to the legitimate holder of the papal title, though anti-popes had been common enough. But Urban VI had been elected at Rome indeed, but by a minority of the Cardinals, terrorized by a Roman mob, while Clement VII, though chosen at Anagni only, had been nominated by a clear majority, almost entirely Frenchmen. The princes of Europe acknowledged Urban or Clement for purely political reasons—in about equal strength, and the Church was rent in twain.

8

The obvious end of the Schism should have been that on the death of one of the competitors, his partisans might have consented to recognize the other. Nothing of the kind happened—each party among the cardinals went on electing a successor to its first nominee, and the Schism was perpetuated for forty years. The Roman and Avignonese popes fought with all the chosen weapons of ecclesiastical wrath—declaring each other to be impostors, simoniacal blasphemers, and children of the Devil. The one could excommunicate in as sounding terms as the other. The scandal to Christendom was terrible ; no man could be quite sure in his inner heart that he had not adhered to the wrong pontiff and risked damnation.

But things got even worse when the general feeling that the scandal must at all costs be ended led to the great ' Conciliar Movement ', and the Council of Pisa in 1409 declared that both Benedict XIII at Avignon and Gregory XII at Rome were doubtfully authentic, declared then deposed, and elected Alexander V, a worthy scholar of Greek extraction who had studied at Oxford as well as at Paris. But each of his rivals was still protesting that the election was illegal, and that he alone was the true pontiff. Hence in 1409 there were three popes in existence, mutually excommunicated. Unfortunately Alexander V died only a year after his nomination, and the council made the hideous mistake of giving him as successor an ambitious and intriguing cardinal, Balthazar Cossa, who took the title of John XXIII. His enemies soon discovered that he had a lurid past and a none too reputable present, and formulated their indictment —to quote the sarcastic paragraph of Gibbon—in the

terms that ' the more scandalous charges being put
aside, the Vicar of Christ was only accused of piracy,
murder, rape, robbery, and gross sexual abnormalities.'
There is no doubt that he was a most abandoned
adventurer.

Though the Council of Constance four years later
(1415) ultimately succeeded in discrediting all the
three rival popes, yet the wounds of the Church were
not healed by the election of Martin V, who was
recognized round almost all of Europe.   Nor, we
may add, did the Council do much to promote Christian
unity by burning the unfortunate John Huss, and
provoking the long religious wars of Bohemia.   The
restored papacy did not take in hand the general
reform of ecclesiastical abuses—the programme of the
day—but started on a lively contest with General
Councils, things hateful because they had claimed and
exercised the right to deal with scandalous popes.
After forty years of strife the Papacy triumphed—a
very Pyrrhic victory, for by defeating the party of
the Councils, which stood for reform from within,
the Papacy committed itself to the policy of non-
reformation, and the internal condition of the Church
reverted to all the scandalous abuses of the fourteenth
century.   All the old grievances—pluralities and
provisions, the corruption of the Curia, the supreme
spiritual court of Christendom, the misuse of political
excommunication, the proclamation of bogus crusades,
scandalous nepotism, continued to prevail.   'Romæ
omnia Venalia '—especially indulgences.

No man could say with honesty at the end of the
fifteenth century that the supremacy of the Papacy
was exercised in the cause of justice, reason, or

morality, either in the internal management of the
Church, or the international relations of Europe—
least of all in the local quarrels of the Italian states.
The climax seemed to come when in 1492 Alexander VI, Rodrigo Borgia, was crowned with the
tiara—an even more disgraceful figurehead for the
Church than John XXIII had been. As it chanced,
the year 1492–93 is distinguished also with the lowest
water-mark of the Holy Roman Empire, the death
of the aged Frederick III, who after a reign of fifty-
three years (1440–93) died at the age of seventy-
eight, an impotent person who had been driven out
of his own dominions by the Hungarians, and had
wandered in exile among the free cities of Germany,
an unwelcome and expensive guest. The long
dynastic contest for the imperial crown between the
houses of Wittelsbach, Luxemburg, and Hapsburg
had destroyed the old prestige of the ' Holy Roman
Emperor ', and left his realm a medley of quarrelsome
feudal princes.

Hence a profound feeling of disillusionment,
political and moral, all round Europe. The Papacy
and the Empire had been tried in the balance and
found wanting—their influence was as dead as that
of the splendid old crusading-motive. I do not
think that I can give a better example of the depressed
outlook of Christendom at the end of the Middle
Ages, than that shown by that splendid folio, the
great *Nuremberg Chronicle* printed in 1493. History
is conceived in the well-known theory of the ' Seven
Ages ' of which the sixth is dismal, the seventh, or
the end of the world by the Last Judgment, very near.
After the annals of the year 1492 there is a blank of

six pages, left white for the owner of the volume, who can fill them up in manuscript with the few entries required before *Septima Aetas Mundi,* where we get the whole screed of the Book of Revelations— the rise of the Beast, the False Prophet, and Antichrist, the martyrdom of the Two Witnesses, the pouring out of the seven vials, and finally the cataclysm of the Last Judgment. All are profusely illustrated with the grim woodcuts of Michael Wohlgemuth, who excelled in the representation of devils and disasters.

The historical perspective of Christendom in 1493 is desperate. Men felt the blankness of the outlook everywhere. The ' Dance of Death ' which Dürer drew was a typical expression of the spirit of the age.

Here comes one of the cataclysms of the human mind. Turning on a few years we find this disillusionment gone, and the world full of explosive ideals, moral, philosophical, cultural, social, religious. The change is complete and astounding, we cannot explain it by looking back to the heretics and humanists of the earlier fifteenth century. A new envisagement of the world has begun, and men are no longer sighing after the imaginary Golden Age that lay in the distant past, but speculating as to the Golden Age that might possibly lie in the oncoming future.

As I said already, in another context, it would take a long book to discuss the question how far the Revival of Learning, the spiritual revolt against wickedness in high places which was one of the inspirations of the Reformation, the opening up of America and of the Cape route to the Indies, or the scientific discoveries which knocked the Geocentric theory of the Universe on the head, played their respective parts in demolishing the mediæval tradition. But the change was complete and astounding, and the foundation of modern ways of thought had been laid.

I would not ascribe too much importance in the formation of the new age to the great movement which we vaguely call the Renaissance. It was coming, nay, had already come in 1500. It was an intellectual awakening, a cultural revelation, but it was not a moral movement. The votaries of the Renaissance included many of the most immoral spirits of the age—high and low. Popes like Leo X and princes like Ludovico Sforza were its patrons—objectionable people like Aretino and Benvenuto Cellini found their pleasure and profit in it. It was an attack on mediæval traditionalism not because it was noxious and evil, but because it was absurd and often untrue. It was a free-thinking movement of a dissolvent kind, and had no profitable reconstruction of the world to offer. The way out of the disillusionment and spiritual apathy of the late fifteenth century was not by the cult of beauty, nor the study of the models of antiquity. It is conceivable that if this movement had not synchronized with the spiritual revolt against the corruption of the Church, its net result might have been morally destructive.

The other element in the general revision of spiritual outlook which marked the early sixteenth century was fundamentally an honest rebellion against the ancient spiritual abuses. The need for reform was felt even among the supporters of the old régime—the Counter-Reformation did represent some sort of a revulsion against ignorance and evil-living. The clash of controversy between Catholic and Protestant on the highest matters of faith produced an enthusiasm on both sides which shows that the moral fibre of Europe had tightened up to a surprising degree. Friars and Jesuits went to the gallows, Protestant preachers to the stake, with a good grace and a splendid confidence. Men braced themselves up to face the hard duty imposed by conscience and a sense of spiritual obligation, in a way that had been much rarer in the Middle Ages, when the easy method of recantation had been far more prevalent. So Martin Luther's ' Here stand I : I can do no otherwise : God help me ! ' and Thomas More's ' I pray God preserve me in my just opinion, even to death ' are the typical epigrams of the age. The lethargy of the fifteenth century was over.

The age of the Reformation and the Renaissance (I use the terms without prejudice) was certainly the one which saw a change in the historical perspective of mankind which had no parallel save in the chaos of the fifth century, with which we have already dealt. It took several generations to work out. The welter caused by the interplay of all the various new developments—including the doubling of the size of the known world by the great navigators, and the destruction of the Geocentric Theory of the Universe by the great astronomers, took a long time to settle down into a new outlook. The most obvious results of the spiritual struggle were the ' Wars of Religion ', which cannot be reckoned to have reached their end till the Peace of Westphalia in 1648. But the last period of the Thirty Years' War was no true continuation of

the first. The strife which had commenced with the
conflict of Protestant and Catholic interests in Germany in 1618 had become in its last stage no contest
of faiths, but a renewal of the old rivalry between the
French monarchy and the House of Hapsburg, which
had filled up so many contentious years in the first
half of the sixteenth century. The change of intent
is typical of the date.

We have already passed on into the period of wars
of territorial aggrandisement and also of economic
rivalry, with no high religious or intellectual inspiration
behind them. Two Protestant powers like England
and Holland, both republics at the time, did not find
any hindrance to a commercial war in their common
dislike for the Pope. Nor did the Emperor Leopold
disdain the help of William of Orange on account of
the Calvinism of the Dutch. Both happened to
nourish a sincere objection to the designs of the
most Christian king, Louis XIV, on provinces in the
Netherlands or on the Rhine.

No change in historical or intellectual perspective
can be discovered after an investigation of all the wars
and alliances of the days of Louis XIV. We have
got back to the simple dynastic rivalry which had
started in the age of Francis I and the Emperor
Charles V. The ' Roi Soleil ' was an accumulator
of territorial scraps, and got the chance of drawing
Spain into his solar system. The Hapsburgs, Leopold,
Joseph, and Charles VI were thinking of the restoration
of the supremacy of their House, which had existed
before the partition of 1556–7 had severed Vienna and
Madrid. In all this contest we cannot detect anything save diplomatic and dynastic contention and

many treaties and campaigns. It had no inner spiritual meaning.

But a new change in historical perspective was just about to be presented to a doubting world. The importance of the eighteenth century from the point of view which we are taking has nothing to do with the Hapsburg-Bourbon conflict, or the *Renversement des Alliances* that ended it. It comes from the new intellectual urge which supervened on a somewhat jaded and artificial society—the Liberal, Modernist, Scientific, Humanitarian, propaganda with ' Back to Nature ', the ' Rights of Man ', ' Liberty, Equality, and Fraternity ' as its slogans. In a way it was as much a revolt against authority as the Reformation had been, but the revolt was primarily against the old social authority, with the revolt against religious authority only as a secondary inspiration. Free thought was the ideal of all its votaries, but not all of them were ' Free Thinkers ' in the technical ecclesiastical sense. Indeed their views ranged over a large field so far as creeds went, from a liberal Christianity, through various shades of Deism, including the rather nebulous ' *Etre suprême* ', to blank and stony Atheism. Even Voltaire, so often stigmatized as the great breaker-up of faith, appears to have had private views of his own as to a directive providence, though he inflicted such bitter sarcasms on the dogmas and administration of the Catholic Church of his day. While all superior persons would admit that Reason should guide their path, it was not necessary to create a militant Goddess of Reason who trampled upon all altars, and whose blatancy was offensive to staid and philosophic persons. The directive idea

common to all who would call themselves ' illuminated '
was the destruction of ancient hypocrisies and social
inequalities by an intellectual appeal. Unfortunately
this conception got tangled up with all sorts of absurd
historical delusions, e.g. that primitive man was an
innocent and virtuous being, who had become the
victim of malignant priests and tyrants. The illu-
minate were not anthropologists, and did not investigate the habits and mentality of the noble savage, or
the ' horde theory '. There was a sad illusion to the
effect that it was only necessary to sweep away
admittedly bad modern social conditions, in order to
restore the imaginary Golden Age. As Pillet, whom
I have quoted elsewhere, remarked, the ideologists
fancied that by setting their propaganda to work,
they would themselves some day become philosopher
kings in an ideal state. Unfortunately when honest
indignation has created chaos, at the end of a bad
régime, it is not the philosopher only who gets his
opportunity, but demagogues, cranks, military adventurers, and *arrivistes* of all sorts. And the study of
mob-psychology does not lead to the conclusion that
it is safe to rely on the momentary impulses of a
sovereign people, either in street rioting or in plebiscites.

And so a generous impulse, under unforeseen
conditions, could lead to a sort of Jacquerie, civil
wars, the guillotine, general disillusionment, and, as
an end to corrupt administration by adventurers, to a
military despotism such as had not been seen since
the days of Julius Cæsar. The effect of the whole
French tragedy on the sympathetic observer can be
followed by comparing Wordsworth's lines on the
fascination of Liberty, which I have quoted before,

with his melancholy outbursts against the 'blind adulterous France' which had wrecked Swiss freedom and fallen into the old annexationist methods of the Bourbon kings.

Yet not even the awful example, when not a succession of Washingtons, but Robespierre, Barras, and Bonaparte descended on France, sufficed to end the revolutionary urge. Its appeal had been cosmopolitan not merely French, and the name of 'friends of humanity' had been known all over Western Europe. Enthusiasts like 'Anacharsis' Clootz and Baron Trenck had gravitated towards Paris, the central focus of the movement—and had got guillotined there, but they, of course, were only flies on the wheel. The propaganda of revolt against tradition had permeated far beyond France, and had found its admirers in every clime from South America to the Baltic, where governments of the old régime were in possession. A Venezuelan exile, Miranda, commanded a wing of the Republican army in Belgium— a Polish exile, Dombrowski, headed a legion of his countrymen in the Republican army in Italy. There were many Irish refugees in the French ranks, besides those who, like Wolfe Tone, came over the sea in the ineffective descents on their own country. In Italy, the home of some of the most benighted rulers of the age, the movement of revolt had been welcomed by the intellectual malcontents in every city. And so it came that when the blight of Napoleon's military despotism had been removed, the revolutionary cosmopolitan inspiration revived, to attack the reactionary régimes all over Europe, and after long years Metternich died disappointed.

But the nineteenth century was not destined
to see a mere continuation of the impulses of the
eighteenth ; quite a new historical perspective
emerged in men's minds when the idea of Nationalism
came cutting across the idea of Cosmopolitanism,
with its appeal to half-forgotten race-feeling, of which
the eighteenth century had made such mockery.   In
this new outlook to be a ' friend of humanity ' was
to be suspect.   At the time of the Reformation,
English, Scottish, French, Netherland, and German
Protestants had fought in line cheerfully against their
Catholic fellow-countrymen.   At the time of the
eighteenth-century intellectual revolt, the ' illuminated ' of every country considered themselves brethren,
leagued against the traditionalists of every ancient
régime.   And later, British enthusiasts sailed off by
hundreds to join Bolivar in South America, and by
scores to follow Byron to Greece.   Eight thousand
British volunteers once went in a body to aid the very
uninspiring cause of Queen Cristina in Spain—merely
because it was called liberal—and the opposing
cause of Don Carlos was certainly reactionary.

But the idea of Nationalism tended to damp down
the idea of Cosmopolitanism and the universal brotherhood of mankind.   Ancient memories of blood and
culture and historic glory were exhumed from oblivion,
ancient grudges and neighbourly enmities resuscitated
also.   It was not only in countries where a national
grievance was alive and obvious, such as Poland or
Hungary, that the spirit flared up, but in regions where
local memories seemed to be almost dead, such as
Bohemia or Croatia or Holstein.   The political devices
of alien statesmen had linked Holland and Belgium,

Sweden and Norway ; after years of trial of the experiment the nations in each case felt the union intolerable, and scission occurred. It was still more extraordinary to find that in cases where local as opposed to national pride had been the ruling sentiment, the people finally consented to merge themselves in larger national units. Italy, of course, supplies the most obvious example. The rising against Hapsburg domination in 1848 had failed, because the *risorgimento* started with old regional patriotisms—the Venetians declared their ancient republic revived— the south gave no practical help to the armies of Carlo Alberto in the north. The error was obvious—and when the chance came again, the plebiscites of 1859–61 surrendered old particularisms, and the veteran republican condottiere Garibaldi handed over his southern conquests to the half-trusted Sardinian king, reluctantly—but national patriotism prevailed.

The case of Germany was even more interesting, regional loyalties going back to the Middle Ages were very strong, and Prussia was detested not only by courts but by all men high and low in many a state and free city. I can still remember from my own experience the bitter dislike that prevailed in Hanover, Frankfort, and Bavaria to the New Reich under the House of Hohenzollern as late as 1880–90. The hegemony of Prussia had been enforced by the bayonet in the war of 1866, accepted with some reluctance after the triumphs of 1870–71 over the old French enemy. Bismarck was detested outside the old Hohenzollern dominions. But in forty years of compulsory union the elder generation died out, and the attraction of the prestige of united Germany prevailed over many old regional discontents. German Nationalism, which had once seemed likely to be liberal and even anti-monarchical—as witness 1848— became arrogant and imperialistic.

These tendencies have survived all the disasters of 1914–18, and have taken the strangest forms in the Hitlerian dictatorship, when a sort of pseudo-historic legend has been invented to the effect that the Germans are a pure Nordic race, fit to be labelled with the mistaken and old-fashioned name of Aryan. It is perfectly certain that their purity of race is a fiction, as everything east of the Elbe has a Slavonic racial base, and all the south country an ' Alpine ' admixture, from the Rhætians and other provincials of the Roman Empire who were overrun by the Bavarians and Swabians. Nationalist enthusiasts even go so far as to clamour for a German religion, some content with cancelling the Old Testament as hope-lessly Hebrew, others going further and cancelling the New Testament also, as being both meek, ' a religion for slaves ', and cosmopolitan—preaching the brotherhood and equality of all men. Hence the ludicrous framing of a ' national German ' religion, going back to traditions of Woden and his kin, and worshipping force and ' Aryan ' supremacy instead of Christian brotherhood. The enthusiasts who teach these follies are not frowned upon by the dictatorship, whose indignation is reserved for Catholic or Protestant clergy who make protests in favour of the freedom of political or religious opinions. Independent thought being prohibited, when a pabulum of official brain-nourishment is provided by the State, the expression of it is a form of civil disobedience, and leads the stiff-necked to a concentration camp.

This persecution of opinion has a fine touch of mediæval mentality—how much more so the revival of the *Jüdenhetze*, so often seen in the thirteenth and fourteenth centuries. It is true that this has not taken the form of mob-murder, but only that of a development to logical extremity of the system of restrictions, inhibitions, and insults known to earlier ages, with the ultimate end in view of the extermination (in the literal sense of the word) of the unfortunate Hebrew. The methods of repression show in some cases a curious lack of sense of humour—e.g. the exclusion of the lyrics of Heine from school-books of German poetry, and the ban on the music of Mendelssohn. Imagine the parallel effect of removing from British school-histories any account of the activities of Benjamin Disraeli.

This sort of militant Nationalism is a form of autolatry, reproducing the way in which ' Dea Roma ' was worshipped officially, until the spread of Christianity and the disasters of the fourth century destroyed the idea that the goddess Rome was not merely long lived but ever victorious and immortal.

All the more strange therefore is it to see the parallel development of racial autolatry in Italy, where the modern race is even more mixed in blood than in Germany. How many of the inhabitants of the Peninsula can have a plausible pedigree back to the three tribes who dwelt on the seven hills of the Old Republic ? Or even to their Latin, Samnite, or Umbrian neighbours ? It is far easier to trace clear signs of Lombard or of Saracen blood in the north and in the south. The Italian of to-day has many brilliant pages of history on which to look back, but there is a gap between them and the memories of the Old Roman Empire. And to remind Gauls, Britons, Spaniards, Greeks—or for the matter of that Balkan-Slavs, Turks, or Egyptians—of the universality of the dominion of Augustus Cæsar is surely tactless. I have never met any British writer who keeps harping on the fact that Boston and New York were once in the empire of George III. This is a historical fact also.

Deplorable as some of the developments both of eighteenth-century cosmopolitanism and equalitarianism and of nineteenth-century nationalism may have been, the clash of them in the twentieth century produces a crisis still more deplorable. The extremes of both of them lead to moral chaos. The conception of class-consciousness as dominating all other social ideas : or the rejection of the old-fashioned idea of ' Liberty ' as inconsistent with inquisitorial state-control : or of ' Fraternity ' because a real or alleged majority refuses to acknowledge certain sections as equals, are repulsive whether visible at Moscow or at Berlin. We who study the working of the Bolshevist ideal on one side and the extreme Nationalist ideal on the other, are sometimes tempted to relapse into the mental pose of the chronicler of 1493, who saw Antichrist and the Last Judgment looming close at hand. Twenty short years ago we had the League of Nations and universal brotherhood before us, and spent our breath in denouncing the wickedness of bloodshed. To-day we see force glorified, and a particularly vicious kind of war already in progress in West and East, while the League of Nations—much shrunken—can only ingeminate disapproval. The Pessimist is enjoying one of those periods in which he is able to snarl ' I told you so ' to a disconcerted world.

Historical perspective is gloomy—as in 417 or 1493 : the Stoic or the convinced Christian must harden his heart—he has his duty to do :

Si fractus illabitur orbis, impavidum ferient ruinæ.

and ' If hopes were fools, fears may be liars.' Right is right, and wrong is wrong. One can, at the worst, go down fighting, and mutter like Sir Ralph Percy at Hedgley Moor, ' I have saved the bird in my bosom.' St. Augustine would sympathize. And the world-mind works by action and reaction.

9

VIII

OF INDIVIDUALS AND 'PROCESSES' IN HISTORY

AGAINST vague theories of 'Progress' and 'Evolution', in which I disbelieve—holding that history is a series of happenings, with no inevitability about it—we have to set the hard fact of the appearance of occasional individuals, of the few men who have turned the stream of events into unexpected courses. Very often these courses were wholly divergent from what seemed at the moment the natural trend of the current. The theories of Thomas Carlyle do not command much approval to-day, but he was not far wrong in holding that the 'Heroes', as he called them, have in some cases left their impress not only on their own time, but on long centuries to follow. His choice of heroes was eccentric and unconvincing, but there have been certain outstanding examples of men who have left their mark on the annals of the world.

The worshipper of evolution seems to be infected with an equalitarian dislike for figures that appear too great to fit into the frame of the theory of regular progress. He tries to whittle down the abnormal personality into a mere typical development of the tendencies of his age and his race—whose greatness shall not offend the susceptibilities of smaller men, and sin against the doctrine of inevitable tendencies. If the picture can be painted so as to represent the hero

as a mere incarnation of his race or the *Zeitgeist* so
much the better.   He ceases to be a stumbling-block
and becomes a mere example.

Of course we must be careful not to insert in our
very restricted list of cataclysmic figures personages
who were of importance in their own day, and seemed
for a time, but only for a time, to have turned back
the course of events, such, for example, as Sulla or
Metternich—the great reactionaries who built dykes
that were destined to be swept away.   Nor would I
include meteoric phenomena, however brilliant, who
swept across the world-horizon for a moment, but
left no trace behind, save perhaps :

To point a moral and adorn a tale.

But there have been individuals who have not only
impressed their contemporaries, but have left age-
long results of their activities behind them.   Sometimes we do not know too much about them—Carlyle
included in his hero-list Moses as well as Zoroaster,
Buddha and Mohammed.   Moses must have been an
impressive personality—though we do not know
how much of his record is true Moses, and how much
is priestly accretion put in by the compilers of Deuter-
onomy and Leviticus.   But obviously no mean personality was required to create the Hebrew brotherhood
of tribes and faith.   Zoroaster must have had some
similar power in Iran, to persuade worshippers of
many and various local deities to accept his plausible
dualism, and crusade for Ormuzd against Ahriman.
And Buddha was certainly an astounding phenomenon,
a revolutionary against the whole complicated social
and religious system of his day, whose ascetic fervour

was to draw away millions spread over a whole continent from the worship of power and pleasure and caste-pride into the new conception of the duty of man, and his ultimate absorption into the divine unity. His effect on Asia continues to this day ; though the Buddhists of later generations have made strange additions to his simple teaching, the idea of ascetic self-denial still persists. I suppose that we can best realize him by trying to conceive what St. Francis might have become, had he not been born into the atmosphere of mediæval Catholic Christianity.

Buddha is a somewhat shadowy figure, though his right to be considered a cataclysmic personality cannot be denied. But Mohammed, whose career falls into times well known, is a perfectly clear-cut example of the abnormal individual who turns the course of history into new channels, and leaves his mark behind him to this day. I have never yet come across any historian who has made the attempt to prove that the prophet of Mecca was no more than a logical and inevitable product of the intellectual and economic conditions of Arabia in the seventh century after Christ, and of the queer assortment of creeds with which he was more or less acquainted. No one dares to say that if he had not lived some other prophet must have arisen to launch the Saracen invasion upon the Roman and the Persian empires. There have been many prophets of the fighting sort from Simon Bar-Cochba in the second century to the Soudanese Mahdi in the nineteenth. But it required a prophet of a very exceptional personality to frame a theory of militant religion which should sweep over half the civilized world from no better base than the deserts of

Arabia. It is worth while remembering that in the whole of human annals that great peninsula has never again produced a man who exercised any notable influence outside its limits. The early Kalifs were not warriors but inheritors of a tradition of war—all elderly men who sent out their fanatical generals to do the fighting. For what their troops must have been like, I suppose that we must consult the memoirs of Colonel Lawrence. Mohammed was anything but a normal product of his time and race. At the most, all that the advocates of logical evolution can plead is that he had an exceptionally lucky chance before him, at the moment when the Roman and Persian empires had just bled each other to a desperate pitch of exhaustion, after a war of twenty years. But such opportunities had occurred before—the Persians had been at Antioch and the Romans at Ctesiphon on several previous occasions—but there had been no Mohammed to take advantage of the exhaustion of the old combatants.

The founder of Islam was undoubtedly a cataclysmic personage, whose career could not have been foretold from any consideration of antecedents. But there have been others, not prophets or teachers like Buddha or Mohammed but men of action—Alexander the Great was certainly one. It would be absurd to say that the Macedonian conquest of the Near East, which added Asia Minor, Syria, and Egypt to the block of European states for nine hundred years, was in any wise a necessary development from the existing state of affairs in the Levant in 335 B.C. There had, it is true, been some indications from the march of Xenophon's Ten Thousand, and from the campaign of Agesilaus in Lydia that the fighting power of the Persian Empire was not so great as had been thought. But it was only the brain and energy of Alexander which created the enormous Hellenistic East. No one before him had thought of anything more than of nibbling at the empire of the Achæmenides—except indeed that the Athenians had once hoped to assist Egyptian rebels to cut themselves loose ; but this project had failed long ago.

Consider the circumstances of 335 B.C. Supposing that Philip II on his assassination had been followed by a son of moderate or poor ability—let us say by Alexander's actual successor, his incapable half-brother Philip Arrhidæus. Can any one doubt that the recently acquired Macedonian authority over the states of Greece would have vanished, and that the kingdom itself would have dropped back into obscurity and dynastic civil strife ? There would have been no Macedonian conquest of all Western Asia, no Hellenization of Syria and Asia Minor, no Greek kingdoms established as far east as the Oxus and the Indus. Not merely three hundred but a thousand years of history beyond the Bosphorus might have taken a completely different aspect. For no second Alexander was ever born in the Hellenic lands. Or suppose a different chance—had the ' Macedonian madman ' been killed at his first battle on the Granicus, when he exposed himself most recklessly, or mortally instead of slightly wounded in some later mischance, before his career was fully developed, it is certain that his imbecile half-brother, or his intriguing captains—his infant son was not yet born—would have been wholly incapable of conceiving the vast schemes which lay in his brain. Everything turned on the great personality of one man, and his ability not only for war but for organization. It is, of course, another question whether Alexander's dream of Eurasian Empire as a reconstruction of the civilized world was the best ideal. But such as it was, it worked for long centuries, though the net result may have been that the Greek lands had been exhausted in men and morale, and the Asiatic lands varnished with a somewhat superficial Hellenism. The Romans thought that the Eurasian human product was degenerate, and scoffed at their too numerous and shifty oriental co-citizens, when, as Juvenal complained, ' In Tiberim defluxit Orontes'. Alexander had no colour or race prejudice—many Romans had it strongly. But whether Alexander's dream was wise does not matter when we look in an objective way at its results—they were certainly cataclysmic at the time, and world-history had a new turn to be recorded.

The next figure that deserves a note as having put his mark for centuries on the world, and rationalized what looked like chaos by his cautious but hardhearted statesmanship was certainly Augustus Cæsar. I do not count his great-uncle Julius as the important personality : he was a man of genius, and smashed up the constitution (if so it may be called) of the decadent Roman republic, which Sulla had tried in vain to save. But he left no system behind him—it is impossible to say what his ' dictatorship ' would have meant, if he had been spared for a dozen years, in which to deal with the problems that lay before him. When he perished by the daggers of the Ides of March,

no man could have prophesied what was to happen.
Some dreamed that the republic might be resuscitated,
and were ready to fight for it—though what sort of a
republic Brutus and Cassius would have reconstructed
had they, by some unlikely chance, been victorious
at Philippi is difficult to conceive. But the army was
really the thing that mattered, and with Cæsar's
veterans the name of Cæsar was all-powerful. This
was the one thing on which that extraordinary young
man Caius Julius Cæsar Octavianus could count,
when he came to Rome after his great-uncle's murder,
with nothing save his name and a moderate stock of
borrowed money to help him. As an example of
long-sighted and unscrupulous intrigue the early
career of Octavian has few parallels for success. We
may add that chance bore no small part in his favour,
when the republican generals Hirtius and Pansa both
died in battle, and their army passed into his hands.
This gave him the opportunity to carry out one of the
great betrayals of history—to lead the legions levied
in the name of the republic against the republic, in
an iniquitous alliance with Mark Antony, whose
rowdy individualistic rebellion had been brought to a
check at Mutina. Transformed from the loyal officer
of the senate into the furious avenger of his great-
uncle, and the inheritor of his traditions (whatever
they really were), Octavian took his full part with
Antony in the 'proscriptions' which involved a
systematic massacre of Cicero and such other members
of the senatorial party as could be caught. He then
went in company with his swashbuckling colleague
to exterminate the surviving republicans in the East.
Considering the haphazard sort of army of which

Brutus and Cassius were in command, victory was certain. It is humorous to remember that the re-publican generals had been forced to officer their levies with any one that could be found. Horace (of all people) was a legionary tribune : no wonder that he and his men fled ' relicta non bene parmula ' before the veterans of the old army of the West.

After Philippi the career of Octavian becomes even more interesting. He had to cope with a colleague much his senior, and with an established military reputation, popular too for a time with the army for his bluff geniality. He himself was still absurdly young, reticent, somewhat of a poser, but with a keen eye for reading the minds of other men, quietly un-scrupulous and untiring in work. Nothing can better exemplify the contrast of the two men than their portraits on their coins as ' Triumvirs for the recon-stitution of the republic ' which they struck together in great quantities. Lepidus, their insignificant colleague, issued very few. Antony shows his big fleshy neck, his brutal jaw, and his somewhat staring eye : on the other side of the coin Octavian's regular classical profile suggests a very young rather enigmatic Apollo.

In the clash of two such personalities there could be no doubt which would win in the end. The effect on the world of the correct, conciliatory, business-like, untiring young man was much more attractive than that of the rather elderly Don Juan, somewhat bibulous, besotted on an intriguing Eastern queen, on whom he lavished provinces and diadems. Even the military repute of Antony suffered badly in his unlucky Parthian campaign, to which he went out in person, to return somewhat abashed. Octavian had his troubles in war, while dealing with the pirate Sextus Pompey, but his early checks were cancelled by his final victory, and he had never taken to the sea in person, but left the responsibilities to his admirals— Agrippa and the rest.

When eleven years after the murder of Julius in 44 B.C. the necessary final rupture between the two masters of the Roman world came to pass, the result was inevitable from the first. Antony ruined the morale of his army by his inexplicable waverings, and it surrendered *en masse*, in a most placid fashion, after his disappearance at the end of the naval fighting at Actium. His suicide in Egypt was the natural end of the show—whether it was caused by Cleopatra's false message, or by more rational political despair. What else could he do ?

And so Octavian, aged twenty-nine, had the Romans at his feet, to do what he chose with them ; and his policy from Actium onward constitutes the justification of the statement that he was one of the few men whose personality turned history into a new channel, and influenced the civilized world for centuries. Part of his proverbial good fortune was that he was destined to survive for no less than forty-six years, and to see all the elder generation, which remembered his not very creditable first start in politics, die out before him. When at last he passed away old memories were forgotten. ' Quotusquisque qui rempublicam vidisset ' as Tacitus astutely remarked : there was no one left who remembered the old republic, with its glories and its mishaps.

The   system   which   Octavian—now   saluted

Augustus after his Actian triumph—succeeded in evolving was a complicated one. Primarily he made the Roman dominion into a solid empire with natural boundaries, while the republic had only owned scattered provinces along the Mediterranean. He rounded it off by conquering the remoter corners of Spain, and all the lands up to the Danube and the Rhine—he would have made the Elbe his boundary but for the famous disaster of Varus. In the East it touched the Euphrates and the Armenian mountains ; the few client states left unannexed were encircled by Roman territory. In Africa the Empire reached from Egypt almost to the Straits of Gibraltar—only a trifling tributary kingdom of Mauretania being allowed to exist for another generation. These boundaries and the precept ' coercendi inter terminos imperii ' were his legacy to his successors. Practically nothing was added by them save Britain and a temporary possession of Dacia. Otherwise the limits stood firm for over four hundred years.

But the constitution and administration of the newly created empire were the particular invention of Augustus. Avoiding the provocative names of king and dictator, he yet gathered all the reins of government into his own hands by accumulating a miscellaneous group of ancient powers, offices, and titles ; the new thing being their union in one individual. The phrases were familiar, the result achieved a portentous innovation. All sorts of survivals of republican usages continued—the senate retained many formal rights, e.g. that of striking copper money —though the emperor after a time monopolized gold and silver issues, which were the important thing.

All sorts of business could be transacted by the senate
without any danger to the emperor, because the
individual senators were at his mercy. His grim
successor and son-in-law Tiberius managed much
dirty work in this way, as witness many trials for
læsa majestas when sycophantic or terrorized senators
destroyed each other.

Provincial administration was prodigiously improved—under the republic an unscrupulous governor
could do almost anything, and risk an acquittal when
prosecuted, because he could probably corrupt the
jury that tried him. Under the Empire the large
majority of the provinces, including all those of
military importance, were in the hands of the emperor's
nominees, and responsible to him. Naturally every
ruler objects to his subjects being unreasonably
exploited by any one but himself, and provincial
governors were as a rule careful and efficient. Even
when, in the days of some of Augustus' more unsatisfactory successors, tragedies were rife on the Palatine
and in the senate, misgovernment would appear to
have been exceptional far from the focus—though one
may quote the causes that provoked Boudicca's
rebellion in Britain. The Gaulish troubles a few
years later seem to have had political rather than
economic origins (A.D. 68–71).

Augustus after Actium was able to assume the
pose of the Saviour of Society, and the inaugurator
of a Golden Age of peace and prosperity—the Proscriptions and Philippi were a long way in the past
and, like Horace, most people were content to forget
them. It was better to think of the Secular Games
and the quiet times of to-day. After all, the nightmare

years were over, and the new régime seemed very
tolerable to those who could ignore the past.

So Augustus had achieved his end—Divus Julius
was in the stars—Cæsar Divi Filius radiant on the
Palatine. Possibly he himself hardly realized what
he had done—but he had turned the channel of
history into a new course. The names Cæsar and
Augustus were to run down the centuries in regular
sequence at Rome for over four hundred years—to be
remembered at Constantinople for long centuries more
—in a less genuine succession to be heard in the West
from Charlemagne to the year 1805, when Francis II
of Hapsburg acknowledged that he was no longer
IMPERATOR ROMANUS SEMPER AUGUSTUS, but only
Francis I of Austria. But the name Cæsar (Kaiser)
remained a permanent token of supreme power, just
as the name Augustus remained affixed to the mid-
summer month for ever—and no one remembered the
prosaic Sextilis, which had passed away with the poor
old Roman republic. That is not the only trace of
Octavian which still remains—I will not recapitulate
others.

There were, of course, stages and changes in the
history of the long régime that started with Augustus—
and many notable figures—but I do not reckon
Diocletian, Constantine, or Justinian among the
personalities that can be counted as 'cataclysmic'—
to use the word that I have been employing for
Alexander and Augustus. Mohammed, of whom
I have spoken already, did certainly merit that de-
nomination. But after him I fail to find any one
of whom we can say that he not only made history,
but turned the course of history in Europe into a new

channel, till we come to Charlemagne. The founder of the ' Holy Roman Empire '—that strange theoretical continuation of the pagan Roman Empire of Augustus, is rather an enigmatical figure. Wherein lay the special greatness that enabled him to do what he did ? There had been warlike kings of the Franks already— Italian invasions were not unfamiliar, nor thrusts against the Saracen and the Saxon, nor alliances with the Papacy. Apparently what Charlemagne had, and which his ancestors had lacked, was the genius for organization and the aspiration for culture and civilization. He substituted conquest and administrative schemes for the raids and infliction of homage on his neighbours with which his father and grandfather had been contented. He obviously had some notion of providing natural boundaries for the Frankish realm, even if this involved rough work spread over years, like the subjugation of Saxony or the establishment of the Spanish March beyond the Pyrenees, or the crushing of the Avars. His ambition for domination in Italy smashed up the rather promising Lombard kingdom—a mistake whose results endured for centuries, for Italy was never really incorporated in spirit with the Empire. The vast structure which he had put together split up again into three parts before he had been fifty years dead, and though the title of emperor continued, his grandchildren were really the kings of three national states, and the great imperial name became rather ridiculous when held by Charles the Fat or Guy of Spoleto.

All his annexations and his reorganization of the Frankish state might have been the work of a mere conqueror and a hater of misgovernment, something

like Theodoric the Ostrogoth on a larger scale. The
really epoch-making part of his activity was his
proclamation of himself as the successor of Augustus,
the lord of all the Western lands under the never-
forgotten Roman imperial title. It is unnecessary to
suppose that the idea was suggested to him by Pope
Leo, though he pretended a certain modesty and
surprise at his actual coronation at Rome on Christmas
Day, 800, as if the pontiff had been acting unexpectedly under divine inspiration. It is obvious that
he must have been searching for some more all-
embracing name of dignity than that of a mere king
of the Franks, which had been borne by many
insignificant Merovingian princes. And the idea
that a ' barbarian ' could not bear a Roman title—the
thing that had kept Odoacer and Theodoric from
proclaiming themselves emperors—had long been
dead. The actual holder of the name at this moment
was the disreputable Empress Irene at Constantinople,
and it was only at Constantinople that the notion
lingered—where angry formalists persisted in calling
Western emperors ' Ῥῆγες τῶν Ἀλλαμάννων ' for many
generations. Charlemagne did not think of himself as
a barbarian, but as a Christian monarch of supreme
importance, a patron of letters and art, and it was
worth while to receive his new status in the old imperial city, and to get himself crowned by the head of
the Western Church. That popes would some day
arrogate to themselves the privilege of making and
unmaking emperors cannot have entered into his
head. Leo III was his protégé, for he had saved the
papacy from the Lombards, and his father had done
the same thing a generation back.

And so the ideal of a supreme Western monarchy, all-powerful in authority and blessed by the Church, came into being, and was destined to be a mainspring in all European thought for long centuries. It may have been a mistaken ideal, since the realm was not homogeneous, and might break up not only from local particularisms, but because of the old Frankish habit of granting royal appanages in the family. Despite of this the theory of a universal Christian monarchy survived, and after all the dark times of the later ninth century was strong enough to be restated by Otto the Great with considerable if limited success. If not ruler of all Charlemagne's lands, Otto was, by the union of Germany and Italy—and a good deal more—obviously something more than a mere local king. His imperial precedence could not be disputed, any more than that of the Roman patriarchate. The tradition of the œcumenical Papacy was not broken even by all the disreputable Johns of the tenth century, any more than that of the Holy Roman Empire by Guy, Lambert, Berengar, and Ardoin. And Christendom went on after Charlemagne all through the Middle Ages, dominated by the new conception which he had given it of an organized unity with a religious sanction, however much the actual state of affairs might differ from the ideal. It was moribund, perhaps, yet not dead, by the time of the Renaissance and the Reformation. Probably the oddest testimony to the vitality of the imperial theory is that Napoleon after the collapse of Austria and the abdication of Francis II, exclaimed, ' Now I am no longer the Emperor of the French, I am Charlemagne.'

When the personality of Charlemagne is left

behind us, it is hard for a time to add another name
to the list of men who really changed the course of
history. There are, of course, many notable figures,
such as Otto the Great—who was after all only a
reflection of Charlemagne. And in England we have
King Alfred. But undoubtedly we must take some
note of two figures of the late eleventh century. The
first is Gregory VII, the indomitable pontiff who
undid so much of the work of the great emperor, by
showing that the spiritual power might strive with
success against the temporal, who brought the excommunicated Henry IV to the dreadful humiliation of
Canossa (1077). When we consider the way in which
Henry's predecessors had dominated over the papacy,
and contemplate the list of unsatisfactory popes in the
preceding century, and the scandalous state of the
clergy in general, which Hildebrand set himself to
reform with such energy, it is astonishing to find that
in the clash of wills of two such persons as Henry IV
and Hildebrand it was the latter who triumphed,
though by a chance of the moment he died in exile.

It was not all fair fighting, and undoubtedly the
perpetual disloyalty of many German feudal princes
gave an advantage to the pontiff without which he
might have fulminated in vain. He himself backed
rebellious dukes—his successor Paschal II did not
shrink from the most unscrupulous of all moves—
that of setting the ambitious son against the un-
popular father. In the end it must be acknowledged
that Gregory made the fatal breach in the predominance of the imperial idea—in all the three centuries of
strife which followed between Popes and Emperors
neither side ever forgot Canossa. And unfortunately

10

for the layman the general view of pious Christians was that the Papacy stood for reform and the imperial authority for abuses. Neither conception of the situation was wholly true.

It is perhaps from a rather British point of view that I feel inclined to add Gregory's contemporary, William the Norman, to the list of decisive individualities. My reason for doing so is that for the last few centuries Great Britain has played an all-important part in world-history, and that without William I the modern Britain could not have come into existence. England's history, so far as we can judge, would have been more like that of the Scandinavian countries, cut off from the general politics of Europe, if the Bastard had not won at Hastings in 1066. Both the Conqueror and his opportunity were unique : it seems safe to say that if he had fallen instead of Harold Godwineson on the ridge of Senlac, England would have remained an insular state, and would never have been tangled up with continental complications because of the long union with Normandy— which led to the still longer union with Aquitaine. There could never again have been such a personality as William at the head of the Norman duchy, with such ambitions and such military and organizing genius. England under a dynasty starting with the very capable Harold would have proceeded on isolated lines of its own, as it had done for the last two centuries. The optimist may hold that the development of England under continental influences was so infinitely superior to what that development would have been under purely national influences as to justify all the miseries of the Conquest. This may be so—but what is certain is that the Conquest made England an active participator in West-European politics, and that she so remained under the Plantagenets, with the net result that for all the ages to follow she was an integral factor in all the struggles of Christendom. It is impossible to believe that, if she had remained isolated, she would ever have become the great naval power of the West, and the nucleus of a world-empire. All this must be put down to William the Bastard ; hence I reckon him one of the personalities which made a landmark and a starting-point in general history.

For long centuries after 1066 there is no such singular figure—the great movements of the Middle Ages do not depend on individuals. The Crusades, the Renaissance, even the Reformation do not take their origins from a single man but from the interplay of the activities of many men—it would be absurd to link the start of the Crusades with the dominant influence of Peter the Hermit, Gregory VII, Godfrey of Bouillon or any one else. As I have demonstrated elsewhere—they were a world-movement like the barbarian invasions of the Roman Empire in the fourth century. This is equally true of the Renaissance (taking the word in its vaguest sense) : one may recapitulate lists of writers, artists, princes and prelates, but no one name is dominant : they were typical developments, as the evolutionists would say, many of them important, most of them interesting in personality, but no one figure stands out as directing the change in the European outlook on the world, which is yet obvious enough.

And so with the Reformation. There are plenty

of dominant figures, but no single personality which can be said to direct the whole movement. Erasmus, said the scoffer, ' laid the egg and Luther hatched it '. This is an absurd epigram. It would be rather true to say that the spiritual world was full of explosives, and that Luther applied a match at a leaky corner of the magazine. To find a directing mind it is no use to go back to the old heresiarchs—Wycliffe or Huss— or to search among the scholars who picked holes in the mediæval traditional conventions—from Laurentius a Valla to Erasmus. Luther's reconstruction of faith had only limited success : Calvin, a bolder if a less sympathetic personality, estranged as many as he attracted with his rigid Augustinian theology and his theories of the State and the Church. He was certainly the most trenchant personality that the Reformation threw up, and the father of many spiritual children. But Puritanism did not sweep the world as they had hoped, but merely convulsed certain sections of it. The Reformation-century left Europe divided in faith and changed in outlook on the universe. But the new perspective was not merely the result of the long religious controversy. It had also been affected by more material development which had nothing to do with the soul—such as the revelation of the outer world of America and the Indies, the destruction of the geocentric theory on which the mentality of the Middle Ages had been based, and countless discoveries in science. Yet it would be as absurd to ascribe the outlook of the new age to Columbus or Copernicus, as to attribute it solely to Luther and Calvin. Not one but many influences created modern Europe and its ways of thinking and acting. A

cataclysm had come to pass, but one cannot ascribe
it to any one cataclysmic human personality, though the
number of remarkable figures that had passed across
the stage was notable.

We are drawing near to the age when the two
movements which I described as dominating respectively the eighteenth and the nineteenth centuries
began to operate.   Perhaps we are still too near to
both to dare to pronounce conclusions on their results
or to decide whether their leading personalities deserve
record in the limited list of those who have turned
history into new channels.

To take first the earlier of the two movements which
were to shake the civilized world.   We have already
had much occasion to speak of the ‘ enlightened’ of
the Age of Reason and their propaganda for spiritual
and bodily freedom from old conventions, with the
slogan of ‘ Liberty, Equality, and Fraternity ’.   The
fundamental idea is still alive, though it has gone
through many deflections in one direction and another,
ranging from the worship of the imaginary primitive
virtuous man, to the theory that the best government
is that which makes the least interference with the
individual, and *laissez-faire* in general.   While on the
other side its humanitarian and benevolent impulses
may lead it into many such interferences, all for the
good of the individual, as Reason may dictate.   And
no less its basic idea of getting rid of superannuated
conventions, for the benefit of humanity at large,
may lead to trouble, when it comes in contact with considerable sections of humanity who think that these
conventions are not at all superannuated, but play
an important and valuable part in the conduct of life.

And what if the ' Equalitarian ' urge, which was an essential part of the original eighteenth century way of thinking—and which revelled in the idea of making an end of criminal kings and priests—gets complicated with the equally fundamental urge for the raising of the standard of life for all men—when there shall be no kings and priests but also no poor ? Equalitarian democracy may become a militant thing, jealous not only of those who enjoy ancestral privilege, but of all whose ability enables them to make a more profitable thing of life than their less gifted contemporaries.   Hence the creation of the capitalist as the most hateful bogey that can be imagined. And without doubt the capitalist has always existed, and is often in actual life a decidedly objectionable person.   If anything is more provocative of jealousy than wealth accumulated by ancestors, it is wealth newly acquired through energy, laudable or unscrupulous—it may be either—by one who has started on the same level as the man who envies him, because he himself has not been similarly gifted with capacity.   And so it may come to pass that the *carrière ouverte aux talents* which was once the ideal of the democrat, may become hateful to him because it produces inequality.   In the early days of the Russian Revolution the experiment was tried of rewarding every man with the same salary, whatever his work, because all kinds of work are equally necessary to the community, and one sort should have no preference over another.   This ingenuous theory had to be abandoned after a serious attempt had been made to put it in practice, because it was found that, except in the case of a few enthusiasts, capable men will not exert themselves to the limit of their capacity when they see that incapable neighbours are receiving the same reward for services of much less difficulty and practical value. If all work is equally remunerated, it is obviously less exhausting to take up the easier jobs, when there is neither profit nor credit to be got from carrying out the harder ones. The sincere fanatic may throw himself into obscure and perhaps repulsive labour on the inspiration of the theory, but he is in a minority. The general result of equal salaries is slack work and the discouragement of energy. Hence the revised system now prevalent in Russia, by which pay is proportioned to the value of the services rendered by the individual to the community. But when once differentiation of salaries gets established, the equalitarian theory must be thrown overboard, and gradually a bureaucracy of capable people with ambitions establishes itself over and above the proletariat. The desire to get into this ring of the well-remunerated produces all manner of competition, legitimate or unscrupulous, and finally classes are established once more, and ' class consciousness ' becomes as real a source of jealousy as in the old state of society. Only the hated governing class will be a bureaucracy, not the traditional aristocratic or capitalist amalgam. Envy is the enemy of enthusiasm.

And what names are we to attach to the inception of this world-wide movement, which started with humanitarian and intellectual aspirations, and which leads in the end to bureaucratic domination maintained by ruthless despotism over the individual ? Influential figures crop up, from Voltaire who destroyed old conventions by sarcasm, and Rousseau who held out hopes of a return to primitive virtue, through many unexpected developments ranging from extreme individualism to rigid suppression of the individual. The original impulse has been transformed, and the logical sequence of changed mentality is astounding. The explanation, I fear, is the frailty of human nature, if one may use the phrase. Equalitarianism makes no proper allowance for that most fundamental of all passions, the jealousy of the man who thinks that he is being exploited, against those whom he thinks are exploiting him. This works not only against kings, priests, aristocrats, or capitalists, but equally well against commissars and nominally democratic dictators.

Turning from the eighteenth-century intellectual movement, and its strange results, to the now competing movement which I have elsewhere called Nationalism, we find it easier to pick out dominating personalities, but the difficulty is to see whether they can be called permanent contributors to the development of human history. For the end is not yet. Peter the Great and Napoleon occur to one's mind at once— but what of Hitler and Mussolini? And would it be fair to consider that the activities of Frederic the Great and Bismarck have ceased to have any effect in 1939?

Peter the Great, I consider, must on the whole be held to have vindicated his claim to count among the permanent epoch-makers. For he turned the Russia of his day into a European power—which it had hardly been before. The 'window into Europe' which he opened has let in many things which he would have detested—such as communism. He intended to create a systematic organized monarchical despotism on the ruins of a decayed mediæval society, which was several hundred years behind its neighbours in the matter of civilization. Elizabethan travellers had envisaged the Muscovites as not so very different from the Tartars and Turks whom they much resembled in dress and habits. When Peter shaved his boyars, and put them into knee-breeches and silk stockings, he did something more than transform their outward appearance—in spite of the old adage that 'if you scratch the Russian you will find the Tartar'. The Western influences worked in devious ways and under many restrictions of despotism—in the end cosmopolitan ideas produced Russians who were enamoured of the beauty of constitutional government, and other Russians who had caught the revolutionary virus and wanted to destroy the past—the Nihilists as we used to call them. It took generations to sap the ingrained belief in the orthodox church and the divine Czar among the descendants of the moujiks of Peter's day. But for all that happened I suppose that he was responsible—he let in the Western civilization, without which the Russia of to-day would not have become what it is. No doubt in spite of all lip-service to cosmopolitan phrases, and a crazy urge towards industrialization (that most doubtful boon) there is a basic residuum of the old serf-mentality surviving—otherwise how could any one tolerate Stalin as despot ? But, for the matter of that, how can any one tolerate Hitler ?

Napoleon has a somewhat more doubtful title than Peter the Great to be considered as an epoch-maker. Of course we do not think of him, as some of his contemporaries did, as a sort of destructive meteor of momentary brilliance like Attila or Charles XII of Sweden. Nor can we define him as ' Robespierre on horseback ' as a certain statesman did at the time. Nor can we dismiss him as a negligible quantity after Waterloo, nor call him a ' Charlemagne *manqué* '—the universal monarch whose scheme did not come off. His contribution to history is twofold— he created (as he intended) the organization of modern France, but he also (what he did not intend) became one of the main originators of the urge towards nationalism which was to be the most prominent movement of the nineteenth century. These, and not the tactics of Austerlitz or the strategy of Jena are the things that must be remembered.

So far as we may draw a conclusion, when only a century plus forty years has elapsed since Napoleon took over the disorganized and bankrupt republic from the hands of the Directory, he must be credited with having made a lasting settlement of France. All the constitutional changes that have passed over the country since his day affected the surface of things rather than the foundations. The ' Restoration ' was compelled perforce to accept his settlement in the main, though the returned émigrés would have liked to upset it. The centralized bureaucratic organization and the Code Napoléon continued to exist, whatever might be the title of the ruler, or the organization of the senates or chambers of the moment. Revolutions, bloodless or not, have affected the personnel of the government rather than the administration of the country. The monarchy of 1815 or 1830, the Bona- partist revival of 1852, the Republics of 1848 and

1870 had all to use the same administrative machinery, however different their programmes and however they might work their plebiscites. Napoleon's personal additions to the programme, the establishment of a dominant empire for all Europe—he once (as we have already mentioned) called himself Charlemagne—and the endowment of a very greedy family of Corsican relations, had of course to vanish. But the organization of modern France remained, and France is a world-power.

The great Emperor's other contribution to history was his wholly unintentional assistance to the cause of nationalism. He himself, though he talked even in his last will and testament of his affection for his dear France, was really individualistic in his outlook ; he cared nothing for national boundaries or national aspirations, and made Rome, Amsterdam, Barcelona and Hamburg prefectures in his octopus-like imperial state. But unconsciously he helped on the idea of national unity. It worked in Italy, by teaching the Milanese, Venetians, Modenese and Bolognese to live together in common citizenship and to recognize their common aspirations. It worked in Germany by the imposition of a tyranny over all populations—whether annexed or handed over to subservient client princes—which was felt everywhere, and produced common hatred to the oppressor, his *Rheinbund* and his 'Continental System'. Incidentally his arbitrary rulings out of old boundaries, and enforced unions of districts which had no ancient feudal connections, broke down traditional particularism, and helped new conceptions of larger national homogeneity. Even in Poland he set going a revived enthusiasm for the creation of a national state, though after talking of ancient glories, he then disappointed the aspirations he had raised, by refusing to create a Polish kingdom, and leaving Galicia to his Hapsburg father-in-law. Even in Great Britain we may detect the tightening up of national spirit by the fixed determination not to bow down to the 'Corsican Ogre'. The great armaments of 1805 when the French lay at Boulogne, and all was deliberately risked on the hazard of the seas, are less a token of it than the obstinate determination of 1810–11; when all European allies had failed, and the outlook seemed so forlorn, with Masséna before Lisbon, Soult before Cadiz, with an American war obviously impending, and much industrial and financial distress at home. But Bonaparte must not win—the national spirit was firm : personal hatred of the enemy had braced it up— the last thing that the emperor understood.

To what precise extent Napoleon's activities may be considered one of the primary causes of the growth of nineteenth-century nationalism we need not further consider. We are at the present moment looking out not at movements in general, but at particular individuals who may be scheduled among those who may be said to have given history a new turn. Hence many famous names and some obscure ones do not come within the scope of our inquiry. We need not catalogue all the Italians of the Risorgimento, neither Mazzini nor Cavour nor Garibaldi, nor the Hungarian Kossuth, nor the German liberal idealists of 1848, nor the forgotten nationalists who tore Belgium away from Holland in 1830, or Norway away from Sweden in 1905, nor the Pan-Slavs, Russian or Balkanic,

nor the first preachers of Czech, or Yugo-Slav, or
Rumanian independence. But perhaps a word should
be said about the individuals who produced modern
Germany, since two of them are outstanding figures—
shall we have to add a third—or are we watching a
temporary phenomenon at present ? The first was
anything but a nationalist, but we have to include him
as we have already included Napoleon in our list.

Frederic the Great was not a German patriot,
but a Prussian dynastic individualist : he despised the
German language, used it as little as he could, and
aspired to become a minor French poet among other
things. It is odd to find this admirer of Voltaire
among the makers of modern Germany—but he
certainly must so be reckoned, since he is responsible
for ' Prussianism ', the worship of military force and
rigid administration, a certain ruthlessness and a
certain narrowness. He built up the armed state
which was destined to dominate all the minor powers.

And with him certainly we must reckon Bismarck,
Prussian at heart but a German nationalist in practical
working, who made the Hohenzollern kingship into
a Deutsches Reich, and had ambitions beyond the
Rhine, in all the ends of the earth. I can just remember
the old Germany of the petty states and the local
patriotism, in which I saw the survival of anti-Prussian
feeling which refused for a generation to merge into
general German national consciousness. That it
did so merge was Bismarck's work—helped above all
things by the chance which blessed him with a venerable and convenient head of the state, who survived
long enough to allow the new régime to take root and
acquire the prestige of time and of success. If

William I had died at threescore years and ten, instead of living to be ninety-one, Bismarck would have found himself confronted quite early in his Chancellorship with a Liberal-minded monarch who disliked him and all his ways, and was deservedly popular. There must have been a clash—it will be remembered that William I was born in 1797, and was three years over the Psalmist's reasonable limit of age before Sedan ! Imagine the results if Frederic had succeeded to the Prussian throne in 1867— Bismarck would not have had his long term of power, in which to create the Reich and give it many years of practical working. He got the chance—and became the second maker of modern Germany. His final removal by William II came too late to affect his life's work, and the third and last Prussian Kaiser took over the conditions that the great Chancellor had created— and used them in his own eccentric fashion, with the results that we all know. It was a great experiment !

Post-war developments all round the world I leave untouched. It is still uncertain whether we are dealing with epoch-makers or with striking temporary phenomena. I am a historian and not a prophet. As a British prime minister remarked very recently, governments do not last for ever ; but they may leave very short or very long consequences behind them.

IX

A PLEA FOR MILITARY HISTORY

'EVERY battle of the warrior,' wrote the prophet Isaiah, 'is with confused noise and garments rolled in blood.' It is most unfortunate that many historians have never got much further in their appreciation of war than did the ancient prophet. The few who had some real military knowledge have usually confined themselves, like Julius Cæsar, Maurice de Saxe, and William Napier, to writing on military subjects, not on general history. Gibbon, it is true, had once been a captain of militia, and though he never heard a shot fired, yet observed that his limited experience with the Hampshire Militia had not been wholly useless to him. Machiavelli, a civilian steeped in ancient history, presumed to philosophize on the art of war, but got hopelessly wrong : he 'backed the wrong horse' in almost every one of his recommendations. He thought that firearms were going to continue negligible, that the day of cavalry in battle was quite over, and that infantry was going to continue in very large units, using neither pike nor arquebus, but short weapons for close combat like the sword of the ancient Roman legionary. His forecasts were hopelessly erroneous.

But the civilian-historian dabbling in tactics was an exceptional phenomenon. Both the mediæval monastic chroniclers and the modern Liberal historio-graphers had often no closer notion of the meaning of war than that it involves various horrors, and is attended by a lamentable loss of human life. Both classes sometimes strove to disguise their personal ignorance or dislike of military matters by depreciating their importance and significance in history. One may dislike war just as one dislikes disease : but to decry the necessity for studying it, and estimating its meaning and effect, is no less absurd than it would be to minimize the necessity for medical investigation because one disliked cancer or tuberculosis. `

After all, war has been throughout the ages one of the most prominent phenomena in man's dealing with man. One may hold that it is fundamentally immoral, but that does not obviate the necessity of endeavouring to discover its characteristics. Even the most convinced pacifist cannot deny its existence, however much he may deplore it, and he is but deluding himself if he tries to maintain that it is a negligible factor in the annals of mankind. Yet there was a generation of historians who were blind enough to hold this view. To show their mentality I may quote a paragraph drawn from the *History of the English People*, by J. R. Green—a typical product of the old Liberal optimism, which still to-day has thousands of readers because of its attractive style, and still goes through new editions.

Green wrote : ' It is the reproach of historians that they have too often turned history into a mere record of the butchery of men by their fellow-men. But war plays a small part in the real history of European nations, and in that of England its part is smaller than in any. The only war that has profoundly affected English society and English government is the Hundred Years' War with France (1336–1451), and of that war the results were simply evil.'

This is an astonishing paragraph, and the perversity of the mental attitude implied in it grows more obvious as we ponder on each of its sentences. Did Green, who was after all a historian, conceive in truth that the campaign of Hastings did not profoundly affect English society and English government? Did he regard Plassey and Quebec as negligible happenings in the history of the development of the British Empire? Still more perhaps might we wonder at the implied judgment that the campaigns of the War of American Independence, which forced Great Britain to give up her old theory of colonial administration, had no effect on the future government and growth of her empire. We cannot now in fairness ask the historian, long since dead, whether he would have persisted in his idea that the miserable Hundred Years' War was the only one that had permanent and marked effects on national life. I should have thought that this vain and immoral venture had less lasting results than several other wars that could be mentioned. It merely put an end to the ambitions of the Plantagenets to build up a continental empire, and wrecked the very shaky ' Lancastrian constitutional experiment.' That it did not impoverish English society is sufficiently shown by the growing wealth of the fifteenth century, demonstrated by a thousand magnificent Perpendicular churches and an ever-growing commerce. And the marked decline of the power of the feudal baronage, and the development of the ' new monarchy ' was surely a result of the Wars of the Roses not of the unfruitful attempt to conquer France.

II

If two wars had to be selected as having had the most important consequences for English society and English government, surely the first must be the ' Great Rebellion ' struggle of 1642–48. It was Marston Moor and Naseby that settled the problem whether Britain should or should not become a despotic monarchy dispensing with the old constitutional checks. The net result was that Charles II, when restored, was determined ' never to go on his travels again ', and that his brother James, not so wise, did have to go on his travels in 1688.

And if a second war must be named, of whose existence Green knew, it would be that of 1756–63 which created the British Empire, establishing the hold on India and on America which was not to be broken even by the successful revolt of the Thirteen United Colonies, or by all the complicated Indian wars of the later eighteenth century. This war not only created the British Empire, but also created the British naval predominance which was to make the maintenance of the empire possible, and to persist in 1793–1814 and again in 1914–18.

The comfortable theory that wars do not much matter, prevalent among many old Liberals and humanitarians in Green's day, who had been reared in the Optimism of mid-Victorian thought, received a severe shock in 1914–18. Hypnotized by the nineteenth-century conception of ' Progress ' and fortified by the happy invention of the term Evolution they had ignored the obvious facts of history, and had decided that war was brutal and its study useless. The revulsion was sharp.

One may trace several separate strands of prejudice in the minds of those who decried military history. One very comprehensible one is reaction against what was called the 'drum and trumpet' history of many of their predecessors. It is quite true that social and economic annals were somewhat neglected by many who spread themselves on the narration of wars and treaties, and called economics 'the dull science'. But it was possible to go to the opposite extreme of unbalanced thought, and to preach that 'history is the history of peoples, as opposed to the personal adventures of kings, statesmen, and generals' as if the personalities of kings, statesmen, and generals made little difference in the history of the peoples. I have tried already to show that, so far is this from being the case, that the abnormal individual has not infrequently changed the whole course of the world's movements, and sometimes by the sword.

The second fundamental prejudice against the study of military history was the purely sentimental and humanitarian dislike of the horrors of war— things that had better be cursorily dismissed with a frown at the errors of our ancestors. This feeling cropped up again very fiercely in 1919, after 'the war that was to end all wars', when we fondly supposed that the League of Nations was to guide us to eternal Peace. No doubt general disarmament was to follow, and the world would be able to devote itself to universal brotherliness, social services, and economic and scientific progress. This being so, the study of the details of wars ought to become a mere archæological inquiry, infinitely less important than many other lines of antiquarian study. This idea was founded on

a misconception of human frailty, and took no heed
of the unfortunate fact that some nations, like some
individuals, are selfish and greedy and have a profound contempt for other nations. It has even been
found that the hateful word ' glory ', which we supposed to have become completely out of date, had still
an unholy fascination in some quarters, in spite of all
its associations with self-advertisement and lying
bulletins. Quite recently a prominent continental
statesman has announced that war alone calls out the
highest aspirations of the human soul in the way of
self-sacrifice and lofty patriotism, ignoring the fact
that these virtues are to be practised to the detriment
of some one else, and cannot be entirely self-regarding.
In fact we find a revulsion to the American admiral's
famous ' My country, right or wrong ', with a complete forgetfulness of universal brotherhood and the
moral law, which were to be enunciated from Geneva.

An obvious deduction follows from the unhappy
certainty that wars are not out of date, as we had
hoped, and that the conflict of clashing ideologies—
as in Spain to-day—or of national grudges, still leads
to armed conflict, and this conflict is made all the more
dreadful because mankind has recently become
possessed of several new ways of molesting an enemy.
Clearly if war is still with us, there is every reason to
study military history, because it gives the explanations of many of the great cataclysms which break
up the annals of the world, and (what is more important) suggests deductions which will be necessary
for the future. For, as I have said before, history
cannot make prophecies, but it can offer cautions and
warnings.

There have been a limited number of epoch-making events in history which were purely the result of military happenings, which could not have been foretold from any mere study of constitutional tendencies, economic conditions, or social institutions. Occasionally the fighting man has put the clock forward or backward in the most unexpected fashion. Sometimes this has been from the appearance of an abnormal personage—but not always, for there have been cases in which all-important wars have been brought to momentous conclusions without the appearance of any transcendent genius upon the winning side. Sometimes indeed the genius has been on the losing side—as when Hannibal fought the Romans, or Napoleon was crushed by Schwarzenberg and Blücher in 1814. In each of these cases the genius had everything against him, made a wonderful fight, but succumbed inevitably.

We may take a few examples of the cases in which an event of supreme importance was settled by the individual leader of an army. I have already dealt with the smashing up of the old Persian Empire by Alexander the Great, and of the republican system at Rome by Julius Cæsar—men who both created and trained the armies by which they turned world-history. But in some ways a clearer example may be drawn from our own English annals. William the Conqueror, as I have already observed, was a dominant personality, but the result of the campaign of Hastings in 1066 was by no means a foregone conclusion, and if the result had fallen otherwise the subsequent history of England—perhaps of Europe and the world—might have borne a different aspect. In fact this was one of the great ' Ifs ' that we must always bear in mind. It is easy to be wise after the event, and to say that Harold's defeat was made possible by Anglo-Saxon localism, want of a strong executive, and employment of antiquated tactics. But granted all this, it was still quite possible that the Duke's enterprise might have had a disastrous end. If the English fleet had continued to hold the sea, as it had been doing till a few days before the Normans set sail, the overloaded ships of the invaders might have been beaten before they ever saw the shore of Sussex. Had the Duke been a less skilful general, had he been an ordinary feudal chief, and trusted for victory to the furious rush of his cavalry alone, his expedition might have miscarried, and Domesday Book might never have been written. Had Harold Godwineson used better tactics and succeeded in keeping his levies in better discipline, above all had been furnished with a few hundred mounted men, he might have founded a dynasty and died peaceably in his bed. And suppose that the axe-blow which, as we know, brained William's horse had fallen instead on the rider's head and slain him, it is certain that the battle would have been lost, and the Norman Conquest never carried out ; for there was no other military figure beyond the Channel in that or the succeeding age who had the genius and the initiative required for such an enterprise. Both the Conqueror himself and his opportunity were unique.

There are other military events which might well have gone otherwise, and whose results, if different from what they actually were, would have turned European history into strange channels. Such are the great sieges of Constantinople by the Saracens in 672–76 and again in 717–18, when the waves of the original Moslem flood washed up through Asia Minor and threatened to make an end of Eastern Christendom. This was in the worst time of the Dark Ages, when at the other end of the fighting-line the same invaders conquered Spain (711–13). There was in Christendom no other state which could have made the slightest effective resistance if the great Byzantine barrier had broken down. It is quite certain that all the barbarous and still pagan tribes who occupied eastern and central Europe would have become the subjects of the Kalif and the votaries of Islam. The Franks were still in the time of the *Rois Fainéants*: it was only in 719 that Charles Martel, after much fighting in East and West, became Mayor of the Palace in both the Neustrian and the Austrasian Frankish realms, having crushed the last Merovingian king who tried to have a policy of his own at the battles of Vincy and Soissons. Meanwhile the Saracens from Spain were at Narbonne and Nismes. Wherefore the purely military exploit of Leo the Isaurian in saving Constantinople from the army and fleet of Moslemah in 718 was a far more important historical landmark than Charles Martel's turning back of the last Saracen invasion of Gaul at Poitiers in 732. The eastern push of the Kalif's armies on the Bosphorus was so decisively checked that Constantinople was not in danger for three centuries. If it had fallen in 718 there would have been such a cataclysm as the European world had never seen, even when Alaric sacked Rome, or Theodoric reigned at Ravenna. For the unaided West could not have stood the tempest.

Sir Edward Creasy, whom J. R. Green much disliked as the exponent of 'Drum and Trumpet History', once compiled a book on the *Fifteen Decisive Battles of the World.* I should be inclined to endorse several of them—e.g. Arbela, Pultowa, Saratoga, and Hastings, certainly not the Athenian disaster at Syracuse, or Joan of Arc's relief of Orleans, or Blenheim, while for Valmy, Fleurus ought to be substituted, and for Waterloo Leipzig, and for Marathon Salamis. But there are other military crises which had world-wide effects, and do not come into the selected fifteen. There would be fair reasons for including either the successful defence of Vienna in 1529, or the vast naval battle at Lepanto in 1571, one or both of which may be said to have brought to an end the second great Mohammedan assault on Europe, by land and by sea, which looked so dangerous while Christendom was torn asunder by the rivalry of Hapsburg and Valois, and by the simultaneous outbreak of the troubles of the Reformation.

Military crises have repeatedly been ended by the sudden removal of the dominating figure, sometimes by a chance accident of battle. One may speculate on the logical effects of the death of Attila or of Gustavus Adolphus of Sweden. But the 'Ifs' are as interesting on the other side—what would have happened in Asia if Alexander the Great had perished in the first battle on the Granicus, where he gave the enemy every chance of killing him? It is equally impossible to see what might have occurred if Bonaparte had been hit by some chance bullet at Montenotte or Arcola. The French Directory might, no doubt, have been cast down by some other successful general

—but no ordinary dictator who had executed a *coup d'état* would have been of the calibre sufficient to enact the after-career of the Corsican, to wear the crown of Charlemagne, to carry his victorious eagles to Vienna, Berlin, Madrid, and Moscow, to make modern France what it is, and to leave behind him influences that have not even yet ceased to work. An anonymous musket-ball or canister shot might in 1796 have made all that impossible. He himself once remarked that if General Bonaparte had fallen in his first campaign as commander-in-chief, a good many paragraphs in historiesof Europe would not have beenwritten.

The heroic individual figure counts for much in military history, as in all history, but it cannot be denied that occasionally the fortunes of war have been settled, and the world's annals deflected not by a single commanding genius, but by a school or succession of leaders not rising to any surprising personal eminence, but applying a system of tactics and organization developed as a national or professional heritage. The best example of this phenomenon on record is the subjection of the inner Mediterranean world by the consuls and proconsuls of the Roman Republic, before Julius Cæsar arose. The men of outstanding ability among them—such as the Elder Scipio and Marius—were few, and we do not even know to whom we should ascribe the first organization of the legion, the great military machine with its peculiar and effective infantry tactics, which proved able, when properly handled, to deal with any enemy—with the formidable Macedonian phalanx, the mailed horse of the East, the agile Numidian light cavalry, the furious onset of a Gaulish or German tribal levy, or the guerrilla tactics of the Ligurian or Iberian mountaineer. We must study not only the campaigns of the greater generals—Scipio, Marius, Sulla, Pompey, Cæsar, but the not always successful operations of many minor commanders reared in the same national school of legionary tactics, if we would understand the rise of Rome to empire.

So, similarly, with more modern instances, we are bound, in order to understand the history of Europe, to study the rise, domination, and fall of other schools of war, such as those of the Mongol or Tartar horse-bowmen, the terror of Western Asia and Eastern Europe for more than a century, and of the English archery of the fourteenth and fifteenth centuries, the men who won Halidon Hill, Crécy and Agincourt. Not least must we note the history of the Swiss pikemen, who not only created their own small and heterogeneous cantonal confederacy, but were the arbiters of battle—much to Machiavelli's disgust—on a hundred stricken fields in Italy. The Ottoman Empire—essentially a military creation—is inexplicable without a knowledge of the tactics of the janissaries and their comrades of the Turkish feudal light horse, who beat both East and West—as witness Kossovo, Nicopolis, Varna, and Mohacs, no less than Tchaldiran and Ridanieh. They built up an unnatural imperial state which reached from Budapest to Bagdad, and from Kufa to Algiers. Many of their leaders of the House of Othman were men of capacity, but it was the machine and its tactics which created the empire, though the machine was in the end destined to run down when it fell into the hands of a succession of degenerates and imbeciles.

Wherever a military discovery or innovation in organization, armament, or tactics has affected the general course of history, it is obvious that it should be investigated and explained with the same care with which modern historians treat economic and social changes. Otherwise we get a lopsided history of the world. There are apparently at present many who study the development of the woollen industry or of steam navigation for one who tries to make out the exact method of the introduction of gunpowder into war, or of the rise of the modern standing armies. The invention of the breech-loading rifle was (as witness Sadowa) no less an important factor in the history of Europe than any mechanical invention of civil life. And the military use of the aeroplane is, as we know too well, a more momentous thing than its much vaunted civil convenience.

More especially is the need for the study of things military necessary, now that at the end of the Great War of 1914–18 we have to recognize that universal peace has not been secured, that treaties can be repudiated, and that strife is with us once more, despite of all paper guarantees. The history of the world in 1914–18 turned on purely military problems. Would a great strategic conception—von Schlieffen's ' New Cannae ' for enveloping the forces of France by a vast westward wheel in August–September 1914— succeed or not in the hands of the younger von Moltke ? Was the submarine, ruthlessly used, capable of bringing a sea-girt state like Great Britain over the edge of starvation to surrender ? Would air-raids by Zeppelins or smaller craft, or the employment of poison gas, or the invention of the tank have any decisive effect, or any effect at all, on the settlement of a campaign ? Is it possible to break through a deep system of fortified positions, adequately manned by defenders who have line after line behind them on which they can fall back ? It is obvious that the fate of the world turned on these practical military problems, not on any ethical or metaphysical considerations. ' Militarism ' was at least twice on the edge of winning the war. Do not let us deceive ourselves by pretending that its failure was from the first inevitable, or that it can never try the experiment again.

We must grant then that history should teach on the military side. The directing classes in any nation should have a certain general knowledge of the history of the Art of War, just as they ought also to be instructed in economic or constitutional history. ' What touches all is the business of all ', and it is no more right to hand over the study of military history to professional soldiers alone, than it would be to permit no one but lawyers to touch constitutional history, or no one but business men and manufacturers and trade union leaders to study economic history. Till some such general knowledge exists, it is open to any person, military man or civilian, to ' pontificate ' upon the most crucial national problems without being recognized at once as a crank or an ' interested ' person by those whom he is addressing. In Victorian days it was not uncommon to hear members of parliament proposing the solution of some difficulty by sending the British fleet to places which happened to be quite inaccessible by water. I have been reminded of this old folly quite recently by vehement orators who have been urging British intervention in quarters where our power to intervene would be impracticable, if not ruinously dangerous. As long as we live under the present form of constitutional government, our ministries must be influenced neither by blind popular agitations, nor solely by the precepts of their official military and naval advisers.

I am quite aware of the perils of 'amateur strategy', having some knowledge of the insane adventures on which the British Governments of 1793–1809 not infrequently sent out expeditions to perish in the West Indies, South America, or Holland. One need only think, to come a little later, of the tribulations which M'Clellan and other Federal generals endured at the hands of the Washington Government in the great American Civil War. But to 'trust everything to the soldier' is equally dangerous.

Military supreme authorities, like other human beings, are fallible. Take an obvious example—the Austrian Government in 1805 handed over the control of operations against Napoleon to General Mack, a professional soldier whose plausible personality and power of self-assertion had gained him an undeserved reputation in military as well as in political circles. He happened to be an incompetent theorist, and in six weeks after the outbreak of war had surrendered the main body of the Austrian army, and let Napoleon into Vienna. To come nearer to our own day, every one knows that the French Government in 1914 trusted its professional advisers at the outbreak of the Great War, and those advisers (who had been pondering for years over the proper strategy for a Franco-German War) adopted their famous 'Plan No. 17'. This was a deplorable document, which argued from erroneous premises to false conclusions, and based itself on the theory of the old Napoleonic *offensive à l'outrance*. Within a month the German armies were within thirty miles of Paris—only to be foiled by the misguidance both of their General Headquarters and of the two army commanders at the front. Hence the so-called ' Miracle of the Marne '. On both sides the soldiers were wrong.

I do not see any infallible receipt for dealing with the two opposite dangers that arise from ' amateur strategy ' on the one side and military authoritarianism on the other. It is clear that the civil heads of the State must retain some power to criticize, even to remove, a general who has proved himself incompetent. On the other hand, light-hearted interference with details by the civil power, or sudden orders to the commander-in-chief to change his objective are obviously unpardonable. The better acquainted with the rules of war that the minister is, the less will he be tempted to interfere without necessity. But all through history there have been examples of commanders who proved themselves, on trial, incompetent to carry out the task allotted to them. This was particularly evident in the old days when commands were given to royal princes, court favourites, or political protégés of a ministry. That danger, at least, is not likely to recur ; but there always remains the chance that an officer with a brilliant record in minor duties may prove disappointing when larger ones are imposed upon him. The supreme responsibility of removing him after well-defined failure must rest with the Government ; all the more, therefore, is it necessary that ministers must have some knowledge of military possibilities and impossibilities. And so I am driven to the conclusion that a reasonable knowledge of military history at large, no less than of military details of the moment, should be required of those with whom rests the supreme decision. I see no fatal objection to a supreme war council to advise the minister, though here lurks the old danger of differences of opinion in such a body. The story of the old Austrian ' Aulic Council ' dealing with the generals of the Revolutionary War is not reassuring. The one outstanding conclusion is that the more that knowledge of the Art of War, historical as well as practical, is diffused among responsible persons, the less will be the peril of disaster.

X

ON HISTORY AS A HINDRANCE, AND POISONOUS HISTORY

I SAW in a recent monthly magazine an article entitled 'Poisonous History', and though I found myself not at all able to agree with the classification of historical books which the author made, I am bound to hold that such books do exist. There is a preliminary remark to be made—history in the wider sense (the record of things that have happened) is sometimes a most deplorable hindrance to the world-settlement which we should all desire. But this is not all: matters being difficult enough as they stand, there are certain tendencious books which aim at exacerbating them. To these I should restrict the title 'poisonous history'. These books are sometimes consciously, sometimes unconsciously, malicious; they are intended to twist the record of history in some period—short or long—to the profit of some cause—national, religious, political, personal, or what you please, by the methods common to all tendencious historians, *suppressio veri, suggestio falsi*, even sometimes more than *suggestio*, by the deliberate assertion of untruths. Many writers of 'poisonous history' have been conscientious men according to their lights, but so set on proving their thesis that they deliberately ignore all counter-evidence, even when it must be known to them. But more, as I believe, have been arrogant and ill-informed persons, who, destitute of any sound general knowledge of a period, choose to 'pontificate' upon it, after the manner of propagandic party journalists, and rush into print when they have discovered some facts that seem to tell in their favour ; they do not wish to know of any others. There is another class of meddlers with history who simply accept all rumours and legends, however obviously worthless, because they have no critical sense, and never take the trouble to verify a story. Much mischief can be done by all these sorts of 'historians' ; some of their perversions that I shall be mentioning go back to very remote ages, yet have their surviving effect to this day ; others are deliberate modern forgeries, yet have caught on to the popular ear—like the celebrated 'Protocols of the Elders of Zion' in which Hitlerians believe.

The very earliest samples of 'poisonous history' are generally justificatory legends, invented to cover offensive wars or old antipathies ; they often remind us of Æsop's fable of the wolf and the lamb. It is comparatively rare for a king or a nation to fall upon a rival without any plausible pretext given, on the simple line of arrogant brute force, demanding submission to the larger army or the stronger will. Such action may, of course, be found in early 'Dark Ages' invasions by barbarous hordes : Attila and Genghiz Khan did not take the trouble to formulate *casus belli*, though Edward III, Frederic the Great or Napoleon or Adolf Hitler thought it worth while to do so, in more sophisticated ages. The idea of 'retaliatory action' as a justificatory cause for war goes very far back, and was familiar to the minds of our earliest historians, as witness the curious pages in Herodotus'

12

first book, as to the ancestral feud between Europe and Asia having originated in the rapes of Europa and Medea, revenged by those of Io and Helen. He himself grants that the explanation seems to him hardly adequate, and fathers it upon his informants. But old-established racial feuds have generally some such legendary grievance or insult at their start, as for example those of Corinth and Corcyra, the Lombards and the Gepidæ, the Amidei and the Buondelmonti, or the MacLeods and Macdonalds. The tale of the provocative insult which brings about revenge is so familiar throughout the dimmer ages, that I always feel inclined to be sceptical about it when we have got into comparatively modern times. The stories of the ' Brides of Venice ' and the Sicilian Vespers have a certain suggestion of the old justificatory myth about them, and no less the tale about the Dauphin's present of tennis balls to Henry V, which Shakespeare allowed himself to utilize in order to create a scene of fine indignation.

The state of mind of deeply rooted racial dislike, prevalent through all ages, is undoubtedly one of the main sources of what may be called ' poisonous history ', i.e. tendencious and biased statements intended to put the blame on an enemy. And the historian of to-day has to be most careful to guard against it, whether he is investigating a chronicle from the Dark Ages, or a declaration of war by an eighteenth-century or nineteenth-century monarch. Sometimes the researcher of to-day gets so obsessed by the obvious overstatements of the document before him, that when he tried to write justly, and to make a fair judgment between causes, he may be driven by sheer repulsion to put the blame on the more blatant stater of grievances. This is by no means a safe criterion of right and wrong. One may be driven to an error which I have stigmatized ere now, that of attenuating misdeeds or whitewashing offenders merely because the case against them is set forth with too great venom. Of course one has to allow for the chronicler recording a provocation, or the statesman drawing up a declaration of war, being naturally ' propagandic ', and making no allowance for ' extenuating circumstances ' in the rival, and naturally he will be silent about contributory provocation by his own side. A Hebrew's views on Canaanites or Philistines and their habits, a Roman's on Carthaginians, a Welshman's on Anglo-Saxons, a Greek's on Turks, a German's on Poles (or a Pole's on Germans) cannot be expected to be stated with impartiality.

But there are limits : the historian obviously must not swallow without testing them, all the indictments brought by nations, or by individuals, against each other. And one of his most difficult tasks is to arrive at some general conclusion, as fair as he can make it, after a careful consideration of all the evidence. It is quite conceivable that it may have to be rather a negative one, and that, like Alice in Wonderland pondering over the respective turpitudes of the Walrus and the Carpenter, the historian may have to decide that ' they were both very unpleasant persons '. I have often felt in such a way myself, when trying to sum up the balance of moral guilt between two ancient opponents, such as the Romans and the Carthaginians, or some mediæval pope and emperor. One can but set down what happened, to the best of one's ability, remembering that unlike Plutarch or the Venerable Bede, our end is not ' to persuade the attentive hearer to imitate that which is good, and to shun that which is hurtful and perverse ', but rather to arrive at facts, not to make moral judgments.

Nevertheless one may perhaps pardon the reader of history if he chance to be somewhat of a humanitarian, or infected with the general idea of ' Progress ', or swayed in all his judgments by religious predispositions, when he finds himself sliding into the comfortable conclusion that the victory of one tribe or personage over another was on the whole the best thing for the human race at large, or for some vague thing called culture or civilization or moral advance. This sort of conclusion, however pardonable, may lead to the composition of what I should call ' poisonous history ' in the proper sense of the word, and may conduce to several dangerous deductions. One is the idea that might must have been right—since it has triumphed—a delusion common among ancient Roman historians who arrived at the conclusion that Greeks, Gauls, or Carthaginians ought to be crushed, because their crushing was necessary for the great end of Roman domination in the world.

Tu regere imperio populos Romane memento.

By this I mean the pandering to autolatrous lust for universal empire, more or less disguised under fine phrases. The Romans are not the only race liable to such accusations in a more or less degree. There is a dangerous tendency to believe that one's own race are a ' chosen people ' for whom no destiny is too great. The ancient Hebrews had certainly such

conceptions ; modern foreign writers ingeniously
discover similar aspirations in British mentality, and
have read very sinister meanings into ' Rule Britannia ',
never quoting the rest of the verse, which merely
makes the declaration that ' Britons never never never
shall be slaves '—which is hardly an incitement to
universal domination. Modern British writers discover similar latent propaganda in ' Deutschland über
alles '—which is also susceptible of a less general
and blatantly ambitious interpretation. I fear that
I cannot say the same for Adolf Hitler's *Mein Kampf*—
which does seem to be pervaded by a very dangerous
underlying idea that the nation of which he claims
to be the guide is a ' peculiar people ' superior to all
others. This is a very quaint notion, for every one
knows that the modern German nation is no ancient
homogeneous unit, but has absorbed immense pro-
portions of Wends, Sorbs, Gallo-Romans, Rhætians,
Prussians, Silesian Poles, etc. etc., and is, in short, as
mixed in blood as the English or the French. In
A.D. 900 there were no Germans east of the Elbe.
Some one called the East Germans of to-day ' camou-
flaged Obotrits '. Hence one can only say that
theories of ' racial purity ' are a poisonous delusion,
especially when turned into justification for the persecution of some minority which the exponent of the
theory considers particularly objectionable. I can
understand a policy of exclusion to keep out a race
intruding into a region where it has not already existed,
e.g. the Americans desire to keep Chinese out of
California, or the Australians to prevent Japanese or
Kanakas settling down in large quantities in Queens-
land. But to evict by slow and elaborate legislation a

minority which has been permitted to dwell for long centuries in a state, and to cover that legislation with propagandic tales whether exhumed from the Middle Ages, or forged the day before yesterday, is a very different thing.   I can imagine nothing more disgraceful than the leave given by the Nazi Government to malignant journalists to re-publish unhindered both the stories of ' ritual murder ' which go back to the thirteenth century, and the ' Protocols of the Elders of Zion ' forged in the early twentieth century by the abettors of Russian ' pogroms '.   This is one of the phenomena which make the rational observer doubt of the future of the world—there are others, alas ! in plenty.

But I must not wander too far from the point on which I am now insisting, viz., that the distortion of history for propagandic purposes is and always has been poisonous.   Few nations can plead ' not guilty ' after a survey of their past.   The intention may have been fanatically religious—a glance through a collection of English pamphlets of the period of the Popish Plot is not a pleasant survey.   Or it may be simply national-political—I can recall one or two books which show perfect examples of distortion.

Look through Pillet's *L'Angleterre*, written in 1813 by a Napoleonic officer, to denounce Great Britain not only as the curse of the world, but as the home of the most odious, hypocritical, and cruel race that has ever existed.   ' They live and prosper for more than a century on the ignorance, the follies, and the mistakes of all the other peoples.'   Even the errors of the French Revolution should be laid at the account of Great Britain—' Our men of letters, our philo-

sophers, our travellers, were ensnared by an adulation
for a country which seemed to be the soil of freedom
and of equal laws.   The larger part of our best
writers, caught by the sentiment of personal vanity,
aspired only to a Revolution which should place
France on the same base of constitutional liberty which
seemed to distinguish England from the other states
of Europe.   That revolution was to make them the
rulers of the State—some day they thought that their
ashes would lie in honour beside those of our kings,
as the ashes of Newton and Shakespeare (!) lie in
Westminster Abbey near the old Plantagenets.'   Sad
illusions of Montesquieu and Helvetius !   But Anglo-
mania goes further back—the Regent Orleans and his
vile minister Cardinal Dubois, the pensioner of
Walpole, were the first propagators of this pestilent
delusion.

How can any reasonable man, asks Pillet, see
anything but the basest selfishness in the English
policy which starves the Hindoo, exploits the Portuguese, and prompts the Russians to murder their
Czars ?   The governing classes go on their wicked
way with a perfect knowledge of their own turpitude.
The Prince Regent may be corrupt, prime-minister
Perceval a humbug, the Whig leaders of the Opposition, Wilberforce, Lord Holland, Whitbread, all
humbugs too—only set on getting into office ; they
all, Whig and Tory, will hang together, when it is
a question of profit for Great Britain.   ' I know England too well to believe in any real virtue in the isle.'
Machiavellian ingenuity can go no further than that
of Perceval, who when there was grave discontent
among the working classes, organized the Luddite

Riots by means of *agents provocateurs*, in order that he might have an excuse for letting the dragoons and the yeomanry cavalry loose on the masses, so as to bring about terror and submission.

England is the home of snobbery and humbug. Its numerous charities have their roots in self-advertisement, its public services are corrupt, its religion a mask, its army and navy assemblies of ruffians ; public decency does not exist, atrocious crimes are more common than in any other country of Europe— parricide, incest, unnatural offences, infanticide, cruelty to children and animals. Pillet alleges that he had actually seen one of those sales where a husband takes his wife to market with a cord round her neck and disposes of her to the highest bidder—he allows that the buyer had always been the paramour of the woman, so that the auction was a farce. He adds, that the children of such unions were legitimate in the eye of the law, an astounding invention of his own.

And how, Pillet asks, does this community of gangsters continue to exist, nay, to prosper ? He concludes that it is due to an astounding racial pride, which links all classes together in stupid self-complacency. They are really without any justification for their arrogance—but national contempt for all foreigners is universal : the mob despises ' froggy ' as much as do the aristocracy. And they never despair in hard times: ' the last guinea and the last man ' was the cry in 1811–12, when all looked so desperate before the Moscow disaster. When you find a people recklessly resolute to sacrifice everything for an end— be it right, be it wrong—it is a people hard to beat. But what a hateful people !

This stuff of Pillet's is the venom of a prisoner of war, who had broken his parole, and had consequently been shut up in very uncomfortable quarters on a pontoon-ship. He spent his time in collecting excerpts from the police news, hence his sometimes detailed narratives of murders and divorce cases. Probably Pillet is one of Dr Goebbels' ' bedside-books.'

A work certainly much more poisonous in actual effect than Pillet's *Angleterre* was the renegade Houston Chamberlain's volume on the British Empire, published in Germany shortly before the Great War of 1914–18. It had certainly a part in producing that general impression of British carelessness, unpreparedness, and moral decadence which pervaded Germany just before the crisis came. It had also the characteristic of being blatantly anti-Jewish.

We cannot acquit some English writers of having given unnecessary offence abroad by contemptuous descriptions of foreign countries. Attempts to be amusing at the expense of neighbours sometimes bite deep—e.g. Charles Dickens' description of the life and manners of the United States in *Martin Chuzzlewit* was not forgotten for many years in America. But we were no worse than other nations in this game, as witness Dumouriez's description of eighteenth-century Portugal, and several French and German pictures of Italian society in the same period. Of course the traveller who wishes to secure a good sale for his book always emphasizes scandals, which are sometimes more or less true, and undoubtedly make more interesting reading than statistics or descriptions of scenery.

It is comparatively rare to find formal histories,

as opposed to travellers' notes or propaganda of the moment, which are pervaded by a fixed purpose of denigrating some other race or state. We may sometimes detect it in rather unexpected places—e.g. Mommsen's great *History of the Roman Republic* had no good word for the turbulent, arrogant, and self-centred Gaul—by whom he really means the modern Frenchman. Treitschke, more obviously, wrote a history of modern Europe in which England is always the sinister and selfish intervening power—generally guilty of running counter to Prussian aspirations of the moment. One expects Spanish narratives to be hard on Queen Elizabeth and William of Orange, and French republican narratives to be full of the ' gold of Pitt and Coburg ', but it is a more serious matter to sit down after long years to write a tendencious screed on a one-sided appreciation of history. I still find foreign history books of anti-Protestant inspiration, which ascribe the Reformation in England entirely to the matrimonial misfortunes of King Henry VIII, and his obstinate autolatry. This is about as fair as the verses of the parodied English poet who was made to find Bonaparte's malignity at the bottom of all evil :

> Who makes the quartern loaf and Luddites rise,
> Who fills the butchers' shops with big blue flies,
> Who with a whirlwind devastates Caraccas
> To raise the price of brandy and molasses ?

Or, to take a French parallel, to believe that all modern unhappiness when it is not ' la faute de Voltaire ' is the ' faute de Rousseau '—a parody of Victor Hugo on onesidedness like the verses on Bonaparte stated above, but no doubt true as an exposition of the views of many sincere French reactionaries.

There is, alas ! no doubt that history—I mean the record of actual past events and not historiography, the art of dealing on paper with those past events—is occasionally a very sad hindrance to that general ideal of reasonable brotherliness for all mankind which sought its 'realization in the ' League of Nations '. There always have been, and still continue to be, clashes between states and races which leave behind them rational prejudices. These are sometimes wholly comprehensible. Welsh nationalism, voiced in the early ages by the Merlin-prophecies, full of aspiration for the removal of the intrusive Saxon, and not wholly extinct to-day ; the more lively nationalism of the Irish Celt, based on unhappy memories of what happened in the twelfth and seventeenth centuries, are fine examples of history standing in the way of peace. So are Polish memories of Catherine II and Frederic the Great, or Italian memories of the long German domination of Italy. I may say the same about the obvious dislike of the Portuguese for the Spaniard, which I have often had occasion to test. Races have undoubtedly inflicted grievous wrongs in the past on other races.

Is it possible not to forget them—that is hardly conceivable—but to regard them as atoned for or pardoned, and to write them off the slate as practical motives for malevolence at the present day ? Sometimes this seems to have happened—Anglo-French relations in 1939 do not seem to be much affected by memories of William the Conqueror, or the burning of Joan of Arc. And the bitter civil wars of the old

Swiss cantons with each other do not appear to have much effect on Swiss national consciousness to-day. My Orkney ancestors were abominably maltreated by the Stuart earls after their annexation to the Scottish crown in 1469, but except a few bookish men nobody remembers the fact.

But all too often the ancestral grievance has left behind it surviving practical evidence—generally lost lands and lost boundaries, which mark the result of some ancient clash of nationalities. Can old wrongs be righted, or had they better be ignored when the present relations of the parties concerned are taken into consideration—and an ideal of world-peace is the dominating conception of the time ? Unhappily the dream of the League of Nations, which was to wipe out old scores, and to inaugurate a brotherly toleration of the *status quo* under conditions of impartial administration, does not seem to have commended itself in the quarters where its acceptance is most necessary. And as long as the unsatisfied groups are strong enough to terrify the satisfied groups, it is difficult to see how any stable equilibrium of universal security and content is to be reached. The difficulty is that international problems are not based on simple matters of rights and wrongs, but that there is usually much reasonable argument to be produced on either side. Two ' rights ' in collision are much more dangerous to world-peace than a right and a wrong.

The historian is to-day often called upon to deliver verdicts between rival propaganda—not merely between diametrically opposed ideologies, such as the theories of Totalitarianism and Communism — I apologize for using two much abused terms—but between more ancient and more particular grudges and ambitions. The more they are contemplated, the more does it seem hard to arrive at a decision. The most plausible and the most impossible is to lay down the rule that every race should be given its own ancient territories. I remember a vehement speaker in the House of Commons urging that what was needed for the creation of an earthly paradise was that every people should be given what it rightfully claimed as its own. There seems to be a practical difficulty here—the thesis would appear to imply that North America should be restored to the Red Indians, and Australia to the Blackfellows. If once we concede that such a proposal is impracticable, the simple solution by restitution is given away ; we are merely thrown on the problem of determining what layer of population in any region of the world can be considered to have a dominant right to control it. For unfortunately the world is covered with regions where races are superimposed on races, and the two or even three are bitterly at variance. There are cases where a dominant minority is imposing its will on a recalcitrant majority, and on the other hand where a dominant majority is rightly or wrongly accused of maltreating one or more discontented minorities. For in states like Czechoslovakia or Jugoslavia or Poland or Roumania, we found several very vocal minorities, all declaring themselves oppressed by the existing government but entirely without any sympathy with each other.

An idealist set on ' self-differentiation ' suggests that the difficulty might be met by partition on the ethnological basis—then comes in the statistical

geographer, who shows that the races are most tire-
somely located, parishes where one of the rival strains
is predominant being scattered about in enclaves among
the main blocks of the others, so that a redistribution
on racial lines would produce something like the map
of the counties of Ross and Cromarty, in an area
that could not be rationally administered save as a
single unit.   Any one acquainted with the details of
the map of Central Europe is perfectly well aware
of this fact, sufficiently evident of late in Czechoslovakia.   It remains clear that the inhabitants of
enclaves isolated among tracts when there is a majority
of the other race will have their grievance, unless they
are treated with extraordinary consideration—perhaps
even then.   For there are people who resemble that
Scottish nobleman who, when offered reparation for
an injury by King James VI and I, replied that
he ' preferred his grievance '.   A standing grievance
produces a not unpleasant feeling of self-righteousness
and importance, particularly if it is well advertised
in print.

   We are bound to admit that there do exist in some
regions these isolated minorities which have reason to
complain of their treatment, not only the Sudeten
of whom we have heard so much—but the German
minority in South Tyrol, and the Ruthenian or
Ukrainian minority in Poland, or the Hungarian
minority in Roumania.   But these are comparatively
simple ethnological or geographical puzzles.   Let us
ask the historian what should be done with Palestine.
He must reply that when first discernible it was held
by a number of small tribes, apparently by no means
all of the same blood, who may be called in a general

way Canaanites—Amorites, Perizzites, Hivites and so forth. On them descended somewhere about the thirteenth century before Christ, the Hebrews, who themselves were probably not of such homogeneous origin as their tribal traditions asserted—all claiming descent from Abraham as their patriarch. Much about the same time the Edomites, whom the Hebrews allowed to be of near kin to themselves, the descendants of Jacob's brother Esau, came in on the south, and the Philistines, who were an alien sea-folk from the Mediterranean, seized the shore. The original Canaanites were mostly destroyed or absorbed—not so either the Edomites or the Philistines, both of whom persisted, but were intermittently subject to the Jewish monarchy into which all the Hebrew tribes were united by about the year 1050 b.c., the age of Saul, David and Solomon. This monarchy made itself suzerain over considerable portions of Syria, but when it broke up into the rival kingdoms of Israel and Judah after the death of Solomon, it lost its dependencies. Finally the northern kingdom of Israel was destroyed by the Assyrian king Sargon about 722 b.c., and its area was resettled by immigrants from Mesopotamia and elsewhere. The kingdom of Judah survived for one hundred and thirty years more, but was destroyed by Nebuchadnezzar about 586 b.c. The ' Return from the Captivity ' of the Jews, under Persian patronage after the Babylonian exile, never led to a complete resettlement of Palestine, in which large bodies of aliens continued to exist—Samaritans, Phœnicians, Philistine remnants—to which after the time of Alexander the Great were added casual Hellenized Oriental city-dwellers in many regions, especially in Transjordan. The restored Hebrew monarchy of the Maccabees only lasted somewhat over a century (143–4 B.C.), even when we add to its years the reign of their successor Herod the Great who was an Edomite and not a Jew. Something like a half of the population in the first century B.C. was non-Hebrew. But after the two great revolts of the Jews against the Roman Empire (A.D. 66–70 and A.D. 133–5), the Romans expelled the whole people : Jerusalem was rebuilt as a Roman colony, and the population of Palestine became practically of the same mixed sort as that of the other Syrian provinces of the Empire. This condition of affairs lasted down to the unhappy seventh century A.D., when Palestine, now the centre of the Christian cult, and occupied by Christian provincials, rather prone to heresies, was devastated first by the Persians of Chosroes (A.D. 607–27) who carried off the 'True Cross' and left the country very desolate, and then, after a short interval by the Arabs (635–38). These last came to stop, unlike the Persians. They settled down among the surviving provincials, and turned Jerusalem into a Moslem sanctuary. Though a Christian minority lived on, not to speak of other minorities of the 'Samaritans', and a small proportion of returning Jews, Palestine became a Mohammedan country.

It never took shape as a local Moslem state, but was swept over by various conquerors, Fatimites from Egypt, and Seljuk Turks, and then for a century fell into the hands of the Frankish Crusaders like the greater part of the other Syrian lands. But the Franks were only a dominant aristocracy, no great proportion of the inhabitants, and they vanished, expelled from

Jerusalem by Saladin (1187) and from the coast-lands
by the Mameluke sultans (1270–81). Two centuries
of Mameluke rule ended in the swamping of this
Egyptian dominance by the Ottoman Turks (1516).
Three and a half centuries of grinding Turkish rule
left the country in the state of destitution in which
Napoleon found it in 1799 or Lord Allenby in 1917—
its towns in ruins, save one or two and the cosmopolitan
holy city of Jerusalem, its hillsides and plains untilled,
lands which had been fertile and populous in old
Jewish or Roman days relapsed into mere desert.
What should be done with this derelict and thinly
peopled region ? The general rule clear to idealists
of ' giving the land to its rightful owners ' hardly
works—one could scarcely dream of handing over the
Holy City, and all that it meant to Jew, Christian, and
Mohammedan, to the thinly spread and very mixed
race, calling themselves Arabs, who were left when the
Turkish iron hand was removed. Hence the British
mandate, complicated by the idea that occurred to
Mr. Balfour of turning in the exiled Jews into the half
inhabited and ruined land that had once been their
own. The scheme was founded on historical memories
and long-nourished aspirations : a capable and pushing
influx of Jews has poured into the land, and is undoubtedly making the desert bloom again.

But what of the fellahin styled Arabs, who are
really an amalgam of many races, from the original
Canaanite down to the Turk ? They do not appreciate a revived Hebrew Palestine if it means their own
reduction to the tradition of the Gibeonites of old.
Chaos ensues ! What can the historian recommend,
looking backward at the tangled history of this land,

13

which has been under a series of foreign dominations for some eighteen hundred years ? The last programme—partition between ' Arab ' and Jew—seems as little likely to produce general content as any other device that could be contrived.

World-history, we must say, has produced a problem that looks insoluble—and who is to blame ? Nebuchadnezzar, or the Emperor Hadrian, or the Caliph Omar, or the Crusaders, or the Ottoman Turks? Or is it a case for the ' white man's burden ', as Kipling would have put it, i.e. forcible solution from outside ?

Palestine looks about the most hopeless problem in the whole wide world, though there are plenty more, as has already been shown. There has been one worked out to what looks like a moderate success, but only by a drastic method, hateful to the humanitarian mind—I mean the systematic deportation of the Greeks of Ionia and the Trebizond coast to Europe, and of the Moslems of Macedonia and the Thracian seaboard to Asia. Well over a million of the Greeks have been forcibly moved to Macedonia and to the less peopled parts of the older continental Greece, something like half a million of the ' Turks ', if so they may be called, to Ionia and Mysia and other parts from which the Asiatic Greeks have been removed. The misery and privation caused by this wholesale and involuntary transplantation, and the actual loss of life occasioned by the moving of the very old and the very young to an unfamiliar climate and surroundings is terrible to contemplate. It is not even certain that the question is settled for ever—it can never be supposed that the Greeks will forget that they were in possession of the Ionian coast-land from the earliest times recorded in history—or at any rate since a thousand years before Christ. Yet the surviving emigrants of each nationality seem to have settled down, and a constant source of trouble has been removed—or appears to have been removed. At the present moment the Turkish and the Greek governments seem to have arrived at a *modus vivendi*, inspired by their common dread and dislike for the obvious East-Mediterranean ambitions of a great power which has its outlying military and naval bases in close touch with both Greek and Turkish homelands (Rhodes).

Transplantation looks to our modern minds as recalling far too well the methods of Sargon and Nebuchadnezzar. Folk-wanderings when undertaken on the initiative of the wanderers, as in the cases of the Celts in ages B.C. or the Goths and Lombards in ages A.D. are very different from folk-transplantations dictated from outside by alien wills. On a large scale, when millions are concerned, they look repulsive. Even on a small scale it is easy to drop a sympathetic tear over them—as witness Longfellow's ' Evangeline '. To revert to Palestine—I have actually seen a suggestion that all the Mohammedan fellahin might be moved into Transjordania, or Irak, where there is certainly plenty of room for them. But consider the repercussions in all the Moslem countries of the East, not to speak of the storm that would beat upon a British government from our own domestic internationalists and humanitarians, if it ever proposed deportation on a large scale.

There remains the idea of the Mandate, fascinating enough in 1919, when it was supposed that peoples recently freed from an unprogressive and heavy-handed alien domination, would feel nothing but gratitude and relief when placed under a sympathetic and highly civilized administration, which would play the part of a benevolent schoolmaster.   Unfortunately school children after a few years tend to believe that they are fully grown up, and well able to direct their own activities, long before this is actually the case.   I need hardly mention the case of India, where the conception of a pan-Indian nationality took long decades to develop, because the peninsula contains not one but scores of languages, and not two religions only but very many more. Something by way of a constitution for the British provinces has been vamped up, but is working badly, and the idea of federation, which was supposed to be about to complete the scheme of a united India, hangs fire, because the princes who were to be thrust into it, mostly against their will, are finding effective methods of preventing its consummation. How this will work out in the end remains problematical at present : we are contemplating what seemed to many observers inevitable—the resolute determination of Hindus and Mohammedans not to work together, or to trust each other. As long as this mentality prevails—and there is no reason why it should ever change, the idea of an artificial unification of the incompatible remains a dream. It is not the harangues of Congress deputies that much matter, but the bloody racial religious riots which still continue to crop up with distressing frequency.

Faced with these old antipathies and grudges all round the world, the historian is forced rather to issue cautions than to formulate universal remedies. Internationalism is a well-sounding word, but broad phrases do not solve definite local grievances, going back for long centuries. It is sad to confess it, but human nature stands in the way of easy solutions. One thing however is obvious : propagandic national histories, setting forth old claims and old wrongs can only do harm. To dig up records of ancient atrocities for the purpose of rekindling modern dislikes is as malicious as it is effective. For the end in view is always not the arrival at truth, but the exhibition of alleged rights—or wrongs. It is a long time since any English writer treated seriously the old Plantagenet claims to Aquitaine, or thought of the inhabitants of the United States as ' rebels '.

I often come upon traces of equally antiquated memories in propagandic stuff from abroad—e.g. the Italian claim to all Dalmatia, much ventilated at the Versailles Congress, or the aspiration to count the Flemish lands as essentially German and due for annexation, which cropped up during the Great War— an absurd reminiscence from the old ' Holy Roman Empire '. I remember coming upon, in 1917, a Bulgarian book with illustrative maps, which laid out a modern Bulgarian kingdom including all that had once been held by Czar Simeon or Czar Samuel in the tenth century. To come nearer home, when boundaries were shifting about in 1919, I found French writers who claimed the Rhine-boundary for France, not on ground of strategic necessity—which is comprehensible—but on reminiscences of the years between 1797 and 1814 when Cologne and Mainz were French *chefs-lieux de Préfecture*. Nor was it forgotten that in the time of Diocletian they were in the ' Diocese ' of Gaul. Perhaps the most pernicious if the most obscure, of propagandic travesties of history are to be found in school books—I have seen fine examples in Irish manuals and occasionally in American ones. There is apparently a systematic attempt to rewrite all European history in some of the recent issues of the Nazi educationalists. I note that in one there is a thoroughgoing depreciation of Charlemagne—who was not Teutonic enough, and behaved with reprehensible cruelty to Wittekind and his Saxons, who were much more representative of the real national spirit. This is odd—considering that one might have expected to find the great Charles glorified as the unifier of all German races. But he sinned by permitting himself to be crowned by the Pope in 800, and dabbling with the non-national claim to be a Roman emperor ! His son Louis the Pious deserves an even worse mark, for permitting a kingdom of France to be created for his youngest son, Charles the Bald—this West-Frankish unit should never have been permitted to get loose from the great Teutonic domination, and was destined to be a curse all through the ages.

All this is ' poisonous history ' in the highest degree—it continues to be written, and in its underground way saps at the roots of all scientific consideration of the problems of modern Europe. There is a well-known epigram, ' I care not who makes the laws of a country, if I have the making of its songs '. Not less equally true would it be to say, ' If I have the making of its primary school historical manuals '.

XI

CONCERNING RESEARCHERS AND RE-SEARCH, AND THEIR VARIOUS DIFFICULTIES

IN the course of the last fifty years I have had to busy myself with almost every form of historical research, ranging from the dry compilation of lists and figures to the widest generalizations on long periods of annals. I have found none of these tasks unattractive—though, of course, there are gradations of interest. It might perhaps be supposed that the mere copying out of lists, whether of persons or of sums of money, at the Record Office or in a foreign public library, might be depressing. This is not often the case—one is generally employed in comparison—let us say in the placing side by side of two tax-rolls of 1377 and 1381, or in the juxtaposition of the official 'morning states' of the French army of Spain on January 1, 1812 and January 1, 1813. The labour of taking down the individual figures is considerable, but is quite compensated by the result to be obtained from discovering the differences between the two sets of statistics. Deduction by this comparison is often most illuminating. Why have certain items disappeared? Why, when there has been no actual disappearance, do great differences show in the amounts accounted for under each separate heading of a certain unit? In this way one verifies or disproves vague general statements, whether made in official reports or in printed histories. For example one gets a general statement in every history of the Peninsular War, French or English, that Napoleon was withdrawing troops from Spain in 1812 for his Russian campaign. No one ever gives the items or the exact numbers, which are made to vary according to the tendency of the writer. It is a real pleasure to detect from the comparison of two monthly 'morning states' at Paris what exactly were the troops moved, and when they marched off from one theatre of war to another. One sees that some commentators have exaggerated and some minimized the changes made, and gets to the actual fact. Similarly I got a distinct pleasure from comparing the statistics of the parishes and rural deaneries of mediæval England from the *Taxatio Ecclesiastica* of 1291, and the *Valor Ecclesiasticus* of 1537. Every change in name or figures has a meaning, which has to be thought out and explained.

There are often maddening mishaps to be endured. In the middle of what ought to be a continuous roll of statistics there will be found gaps, lost or abstracted leaves, which make the general deduction to be made not quite so certain as could be wished, though reasonably sure. I was particularly worried by this when dealing with the tax-figures of towns and districts before Wat Tyler's Insurrection of 1381. Many very important items were missing among the collected scraps—I got the impression that this was not casual, but intentional, that some official, in 1382 perhaps, had taken out items for his own purpose, either to investigate the names and figures honestly, or else to suppress some of them which might be compromising to some one—perhaps himself.

Of mere careless separation of documents which should never have got apart, I find many cases everywhere. Even in our own Record Office the statistics for Wellington's army of 1813 had got separated from the bound-up Wellington dispatches. Years after my original work on that year had begun, the missing statistics turned up, roughly tied together in a brown paper jacket, in quite another section of the library. Things were much worse at Paris and Madrid. It was quite a matter of chance whether a document would be at the Paris Ministry of War or at the *Archives Nationales*. And when one did get upon the right year, there was no arrangement of the documents, which were tied up in *cartons* or portfolios by the month or the series of months, with no distribution of them into those dealing with one army or another—' Midi ', ' Portugal ', ' Centre ', ' Nord ' all mixed up. Searching for what Soult intended in a given month, one had to go through masses of what Jourdan, Marmont, or Dorsenne and all their subordinates were writing at the same time, before one came upon the dispatch that one required. At Madrid things were even worse—one had to discover whether the documents existed at all, for it seemed to be a matter of chance whether dispatches that *must* have existed had been lost : what survived was interesting but fragmentary. It was, for example, quite impossible to discover exactly what troops, in what regimental organization, took part in the disastrous battle of Ocaña. My own experience as a grubber among unpublished documents can, I am sure, be paralleled by those of my contemporaries who have done any similar work.

It is depressing when, comment and compilation being finished, some benevolent stranger shoots in upon one a number of important documents which have been for a century or more in private hands, and which give definite information as to subjects on which surmise alone had been possible hitherto. Despite of all the labours of the Historical Manuscripts Commission there are still masses of unsuspected material lurking in family desks and bureaux. Any one who has had to deal with the eighteenth century will appreciate what I mean—new letters often compel one to make some revision of one's conception of the character or intentions of some prominent man. An example which occurred quite recently to my own detriment may be worth giving. All the papers and reports of Sir George Murray, who practically served Wellington as a Chief of the Staff during the Peninsular War, were presented by his heirs to the Scottish National Library just after I had printed my last volume on that long struggle. Their existence was unknown—if I had been able to get access to them, I should have been able to solve many problems of detail on which it was only possible to frame hypotheses. And there probably exists somewhere a vast file of Lord Beresford's papers, which would be very illuminating if they could be discovered.

While this book was being written there has come out an immense series of the letters of George IV, hitherto kept unpublished, in which some astounding revelations appear. Future historians will have to take them into serious consideration, and rewrite the versions accepted till now of certain happenings.

Sometimes statistics and dry official reports contain neglected data which destroy the official and received conclusions on events of some importance. They exist, often in print, but the difficulty is to discover their lurking places and then to extract their meaning. The time that has to be spent in looking for information which may or may not exist is often wasted. The required file may not be discoverable, or, when it is discovered, may be found to be quite unprofitable to the researcher, who had expected to find something useful in it, but fails to do so.

When working at the history of the ancient world, or the Dark Ages, the danger of finding conclusions affected by the appearance of new written documents of primary importance is not, of course, so great. The main sources on Greek and Roman history are for the most part accessible and in print. It is very seldom that a lost primary authority like Aristotle's Πολιτεία τῶν 'Αθηναίων turns up from an Egyptian dust-heap, to confound all those who have been writing about Cleisthenes or Solon. The real foe to final conclusions on ancient history is the spade, not the parchment. The archæologist in his excavations turns up countless fragments of ancient civilizations, and sometimes more or less intelligible inscriptions. Our conceptions of Hellenic origins or Oriental dynasties have to be revised. Any book on Greece written before the discoveries in Troy, Mycenæ, and Crete is now worthless as regards its early chapters. Egyptian and Mesopotamian excavations reveal forgotten episodes like the early kingdom at Ur, or the heretical adventures of Akhenaton. The dimly appreciated Hittites are perpetually throwing up architectural fragments and unintelligible inscriptions which raise more problems than they resolve. Till a long, bilingual document in stone gives a key to their annals, hypotheses will continue to be made and controverted as to the extent of their empire and the character of their civilization. Even a bilingual inscription, unless very long, may not suffice to put things right. The classical scholar remembers only too well the problem of the Etruscans, known for centuries, but still unsolved, in spite of many short inscriptions with Latin parallel renderings. But the great ' Agram Book ' still remains uninterpreted, though dozens of scholars have racked their brains over it.

But these are troubles from the early ages. As to Greek and Roman history from the sixth century before Christ onward, there is no prospect before the historian of the breaking-up of accepted fundamental annals, but he has to keep in touch with the record of inscriptions, which give interesting sidelights and add minor details which we should search for in vain in Herodotus or Livy. Sometimes they prove that one of our old written authorities had gone wrong— generally on a point of minor importance. But there is no prospect of the turning up of some of the long historical narratives, which we know to have existed, from the way in which other historians quote them. It is maddening to look at some of the worthless scraps which have floated down from the classical world, and to sigh that we have not got instead of them the histories of Isidore of Charax or Apollodorus of Artamita, or the Roman annalists of the third century after Christ, to whom fourth-century authors make

allusion. Instead we have to be satisfied with countless inscriptions—often valuable. For we certainly
know more of the Roman Empire of the second and
third centuries from inscriptions than can be gathered
from the indifferent historical scraps available.

I have never, to my deep regret, been among the
diggers, and have only peered at their traces on such
home-lying trails as those of the British walls of Hadrian
and Antoninus. But their reports I have read in
great profusion and with much interest, and envy the
energy which opens up remote and often insalubrious
sites, with results which are sometimes epoch-making
and sometimes only the cause of much learned controversy. Teaching in Oxford for forty years, I have
never been able to make long stays far afield—though
I have visited many an interesting site in Italy, Spain,
and Greece. But to me research has been at the desk
rather than at the trench, and national libraries have
been more in my way than excavations. In them
I have had to spend many hours, and to take my share
in what I must call ' record-grubbing ', under the
roofs, not in the open air. It is a fascinating pursuit,
not altogether destitute of excitement, and one whose
attraction grows upon one more and more, as one
discovers new fragments of things interesting if not
always important. Often the distraction is that, while
pursuing one line of inquiry, one haps upon threads
of another, which would lead one far afield into mazes
of information on some subject quite alien from that
with which one is dealing at the moment. They must
be snapped off ruthlessly, if with regret, if work is to
be finished.

There is, of course, one danger in record-grubbing

of which I have had occasion to make mention already.
Some researchers get so profoundly fascinated with the
mere hunting for unpublished stuff, that they fall into
what a French author called the *fureur de l'inédit*.   I
mean that any new piece of information which they
chance upon assumes in their eyes a supreme importance over all sources that exist for the period in which
they are interested, and they not only insist upon its
value, but wish to discredit any other piece of evidence
which does not exactly tally with it.   Yet it may be,
and sometimes is, a record by a biased or ill-informed
person.   To turn down one's own discovery requires
a very honest and well-balanced frame of mind.

I have known even more unhappy results from pure
' research ' work :   some people get so engrossed with
the accumulation of material that they cannot stop
hunting for more corroborative evidence, and continue hunting for ever, never making a halt to co-
ordinate and arrange what they have gathered.   There
is always some desideratum not yet discovered, without
which the complete arrangement of the finished work
cannot be undertaken.   And for this desideratum
they go on searching for ever, and finally die, leaving
behind them a pile of disconnected scraps, and of
notebooks of half-arranged material.   This is ' research ' in the most literal sense of the word—for
research does not necessarily mean successful research
—as with the scientists of the Renaissance who spent
lifetimes on seeking for perpetual motion, or the
philosopher's stone.   If there is any work in the world
thoroughly wasted, it is that of the man who collects
a quantity of useful information, and then passes
away without leaving any proper record of it.   His

knowledge perishes with him, and might as well not have been acquired. Less futile, if not very interesting or informative, are other researchers who at least print in learned journals or brochures pages of statistics, or of charters, or of letters, without any proper commentary or intelligible explanation of their inner meaning. In such cases the material is at least accessible to other people interested in the same topics. These are the researchers, I think, to whom Lord Bolingbroke was alluding in a passage which I have already quoted, when he spoke of those who ' get no wiser or better for the study themselves, but enable others to study with greater ease—our obligation to them would be great indeed if they were able to do anything better.' This urge is particularly common among local antiquaries, who spend untold energy in collecting mere lists of names connected with the district in which they are interested, and arrive at almost complete catalogues of—let us say— the rectors of Aston Turville, or the Mayors of Fordwych. Or they extract from parish or manorial records lists of comparative prices of staple commodities extending over many generations. Sometimes they compile local bibliographies in which books good, bad, or indifferent go in together. A writer of larger scope may arrive at useful general conclusions by putting side by side a number of such isolated pieces of information, but when taken by themselves they are rather tokens of wasted effort.

Obviously research is not an end in itself, but only a means of getting to conclusions. And this is the reason why we, at Oxford, when creating research fellowships, put in provisos that at the end of seven years the endowed person must produce a definite piece of work on the topic which he has selected for his studies. I have known cases where the fellowship was allowed to lapse at the end of the period, because no such work could be exhibited, but only vague—if sometimes interesting—accounts of investigations which have never resulted in the compilation of anything that could be printed or published. Often this comes from a sort of ' inferiority-complex ' in the researcher, who dreads that if he does put anything on paper it might be considered inadequate to justify his endowment. But sometimes it is due to the fatal disease of ' pottering', the easy tendency to go on for years from one detail to another in a topic, from a congenital dislike to formulate general conclusions from a series of premises which is not yet quite complete.

Even the best and most capable of men may not be wholly exempt from this failing. I knew one of them well—I speak of him with all respect for he was a great researcher and almost became a great historian. I mean, of course, Lord Acton. He started to read history early, he was granted a long life ; he had ample leisure and he collected a private library of dimensions which surprised me when I went through it. And he died leaving behind him one good book, some lectures, and an infinite number of reviews and essays scattered about in the back numbers of more or less unattainable periodicals, together with a scheme for a modern history on a great scale, to be written by others, which though excellent in its plan was not carried out precisely on the lines which he had laid down.

This sad paucity of results from a man qualified to accomplish great things proceeded from Lord Acton's resolve to embrace too much, and to master everything before he completed anything. He had a great book hovering before his mind ; what exactly it was I have never quite made out. Lord Morley, his literary executor, once told me that he fancied that its subject might have been the growth of the modern idea of Liberty, but I have heard other titles suggested. Whatever it was, its compilation necessitated the accumulation of such a mass of detailed material that no single brain could have formulated it all. I went down into Shropshire to look at that famous library before it was removed to Cambridge. There were shelves on shelves of books on every conceivable subject—Renaissance Sorcery, the Fueros of Aragon, Scholastic Philosophy, the Growth of the French Navy, American Exploration, Church Councils. The owner had read them all, and many of them were full in their margins with cross-references in pencil. There were pigeon-holed desks and cabinets with literally thousands of compartments, into each of which were sorted little white slips with references to some particular topic, so drawn up (so far as I could see) that no one but the compiler could easily make out the drift of the section. I turned over one or two from curiosity—one was on early instances of a sympathetic feeling for animals, from Ulysses' old dog in Homer downward. Another seemed to be devoted to a collection of hard words about stepmothers in all national literatures, a third seemed to be about tribal totems.

Arranged in the middle of the long two-storied

14

room was a sort of block or altar composed entirely
of unopened parcels of new books from continental
publishers. All had arrived since Lord Acton's
health began to break up. These volumes were
apparently coming in at the rate of ten or so per week,
and the purchaser had evidently intended to keep
pace with the accumulation, to read them all, and to
work their results into his vast thesis—whatever
it was. For years, apparently, he had been endeavouring to keep up with everything that was being written
—a sisyphean task. Over all there were brown
holland sheets, a thin coating of dust, the moths
dancing in the pale September sun. There was a
faint aroma of mustiness, proceeding from thousands
of seventeenth and eighteenth-century books in a
room that had been locked up since the owner's
death.

I never saw a sight that more impressed on me the
vanity of human life and learning. A quarter of the
time that had been spent on making those marginal
annotations, and filling those pigeon-holes might
have produced a dozen volumes of sound and valuable
history—perhaps an epoch-making book that might
have lived for centuries. But all the accumulated
knowledge had vanished, save so far as that the dead
books, without the link of live thought, were to go
as a gift to Cambridge. And I said to myself—
intensive research, even by the most competent researcher, is wasted, unless the results are put together
and printed. It would have been better to have
written two or three solid monographs on one of the
many scores of topics on which the accumulator had
been pondering, than to have collected in one's brain

countless lights on all manner of historical subjects, whose correlation perishes when the brain is gone. Perhaps some later researcher may have to put it all together again.

In short the ideal complete and perfect book that is never written may be the enemy of the good book that might have been written. *Ars longa, vita brevis*— one must remember the fleeting years, or one's *magnum opus* may never take shape, if one is too meticulous in polishing it up to supreme excellence.

For this reason I always deprecate vast and ill-defined aims in one who wishes to do something valuable for the cause of history. It is much better to start on some definite piece of work, even though it may only be a biography, or a narrative of a short period of national annals, rather than to embark on universal histories, or dissertations on some tendency extending over many ages. The broader the sphere of research which the author undertakes to investigate, the more certain is it that in some sections of it he will be less well informed than in others. This warning is perhaps not so necessary to-day as it was in the nineteenth century, when authors sat down cheerfully in the style of Grote or Lingard to write twelve- or twenty-volume histories of Greece or England, even like Buckle to write a history of European civilization. No one would now believe himself to be equally competent to discuss Mycenæan civilization, Platonic philosophy, and the social condition of the Hellenistic kingdoms in the second century before Christ. Nor is it likely that the writer who would be best equipped to discuss the Anglo-Saxon settlement in England would believe himself the ideal person to discuss the antecedents of the Tudor Reformation, or the growth of the British colonial Empire. Manuals, no doubt, there must be, for the use of the beginner—I have myself been guilty of the preparation of two or three—but they are dangerous things—especially if some political, religious, or social bias can be detected : or if there is no such bias they may turn out to be deadly dull. We have all smiled at endeavours to prove that all possible events have been ' perhaps for the best ', as non-committal writers love to say, unconsciously set on justifying Providence or evolution, or the ' world-mind '. Such hedging can lead to no great instructional benefit. Probably every one should select his own manual, and retain his own essential views on what is good or bad, wrong or right. This necessity comes a little hard on the schoolmaster or the conscientious paterfamilias, if they are aware of their responsibilities !

It is, as I suppose, from being an author of manuals that I am from time to time beset by one of the historian's normal worries — letters from ingenuous persons outside the teaching world, who write requesting a short definite answer as to some event in history. The man in the street has a vague impression that there exists somewhere a general repertory of historical information, from which his question can be answered in a moment. His point of view is that history is a bundle of facts, which can be packed into an encyclopædia, and that every one should be able to discover what he wants to know by turning to the right page in some universal dictionary of information. Perhaps he has tried the *Encyclopædia Britannica* in vain, but still believes that the answer to his query can be found somewhere. This optimistic attitude of mind assumes that all facts are ascertainable, and have only to be caught and bottled by competent historical experts for the benefit of the general public. It comes as a shock to this simple inquirer to find that some facts are unascertainable, and that on certain others there is no universally accepted view, but only hypotheses. What became of Benjamin Bathurst? Did Alexander VI poison cardinals? Where was Brunanburh, or 'Vinland the Good'? Who wrote under the name of Junius? There *ought* to be an answer in three lines. But the perplexed historian will have to reply to this correspondent that he had better read some half a dozen controversial volumes, after which he will have some notion of the meaning of the question which he has asked. History, in short, is not what the 'practical man' would like to find, a solid record of names, dates and happenings. The few historians who have tried to write from such a point of view are unreadable—people with the mental attitude of Haydn's *Dictionary of Dates*. It is the bias of interpretation which makes what we may really call 'history', which is a way of looking at facts rather than a mere recapitulation of them.

The necessity of replying to the ingenuous demands of the 'man in the street' is only one of the troubles of those who have involved themselves in the task of dealing with history. A far more vexatious one is the almost inevitable fact that they will, from time to time, find themselves drawn into controversies with others of their own trade. Such controversies are sometimes rather pleasant and stimulating, at others very unpleasant. A good many historians are reasonable men, who will acknowledge that another author may differ from them on points of importance without any necessary moral turpitude. I am myself of that way of thinking, being not infallible. But there are a few who consider that the non-acceptance of their views implies mental perversity, and that an attempt to disprove them is impudent if not insulting. Hence bitter adjectives, and perhaps allegations of literary dishonesty. Some people like to see their attempts to refute other people in print—being well aware that many who will see the accusation will never see the reply. And a strongly worded charge is at least good self-advertisement for the prosecutor. Lord Macaulay was a great sufferer from the controversialists—his Whig history provoked Tories and churchmen, and the accusations against him of prejudice and inaccuracy were many. Sometimes they were justified—like all historians who paint on a broad canvas he was sure to be weak in some corner details. It is one of the testimonies to the fundamental merit of his five volumes of the *History of England* that controversies raised by him continue to this day. Professor Firth thought it well worth while to publish an annotated edition of the book seventy years after it had been written, with judicious comment. The general impression left on the mind is that the inaccuracies impair but do not cancel the credit of the eloquent volumes. The names of the critics have been forgotten.

Froude's picturesque history of Tudor England provoked quite as bitter and even better justified attacks. There can be no doubt that in his determination to set forth his own view of the Tudor period he not only omitted adverse evidence, but sometimes garbled the documents that he was professing to quote. His admirable power of dramatic narrative— more effective because less lurid than Carlyle's— carries the reader over many doubtful crises before suspicion arises. The desired impression is produced, which is all that a confessedly biased historian can hope for.

Both Macaulay and Froude were dealing with political and religious questions which are still alive, and provoke controversy quite apart from textual criticism of particular books. Old party and church feeling was roused by both. Hence a natural touch of bitterness. But there was no such excuse for Round's attacks on Freeman's *Norman Conquest*, where a malicious wish to advertise slips in a valuable book was much more evident than a desire to establish fundamental truths. The critic's determination to attract attention to his own discoveries by sarcastic comment on an accepted authority was very obvious. But Freeman was not the only sufferer from that ingenious pen. The craving for smart writing led Round to hunt much smaller game, even to be a terror to the compilers of family origins in Burke's *Peerage*. Much learning was devoted to short studies and monographs which might have been turned to better effect in writing a continuous history of Norman England. This Round never attempted to do—a glance at his *Geoffrey de Mandeville*—the nearest approach to a self-contained section of narrative history that he ever produced— raises the suspicion that it might not have been very readable. Apparently the hindering cause, so I was informed by one of his friends, was not ill-health—the plea was insufficient from one who lived to be over seventy, had ample leisure, and published thousands of pages dealing with very technical subjects—but a determination not to risk a reputation for infallibility by committing himself on points of detail where some of the many authors whom he had scarified in controversy might find a crack in his harness. ' I have written too many slashing reviews.'

This confidence, if it was correctly reported to me, was a typical example of the mentality of certain specialists, the writers who have made some period of history so much their own, that they come to think that they have acquired ' patent rights ' in it. No one else must meddle with this particular crisis or institution. I met such men more than once ; they are convinced that the whole course of world-history turns around their own special preserve. All the later Roman history may be a story which mainly hinges on the *tribunicia potestas*, or all English history may be built up round the ' folk ', or all German history may be explained by the provisions of the Golden Bull of Charles IV. I once knew a learned ecclesiatical historian who made the obscure tribe of Jerahmeel, mentioned twice in the Old Testament, the originators of all Jewish nationality. He did not make many converts, but he conducted much controversy, and thought very poorly of those who could not see the convincing character of his theory.

The extreme type of historical specialist is often too like the man in the adage who cannot see the wood because his attention is fixed on his own particular trees. If you trust him with a section of a general history, you will find that all other phenomena assume an ancillary position around the institution or the theory in which he himself is interested—be it constitutional, or economic, or religious. As to histories written by other people, he will assure the world in perfect honesty that they are wrong in perspective, because they do not show that this institution or theory is the central point round which all else revolves. Very often it is economic or administrative, very seldom military. Sometimes there is a bogey who has set everything wrong—very likely the capitalist, that eternal enemy of all discontented historians. When Adolf Hitler goes into historical surveys, it is of course the Jew.

The specialist may sometimes be narrow minded, but he is not so repulsive to the true historian as another class of people, who ' rush in where angels fear to tread,' and try to generalize on history without having any sufficient detailed knowledge of it. We have all met the man who, after reading a dozen popular manuals, is prepared to lay down the whole scheme of the universe, ignoring all difficulties because he is not aware of their existence. This is the type which the French call the *vulgarisateur*, the man who proposes to make history, religion, science, or art easily comprehensible to the multitude, by leaving out all their problems and uncertainties, and setting forth his own conclusions with the backing of a few carefully chosen examples. To attack world-history with no wide knowledge of languages, no power or leisure to read original authorities, no foundation of detailed studies, can only result in producing ' the second-rate at second hand '. Nevertheless the impression made on the untaught multitude by the *vulgarisateur*

may sometimes be decidedly dangerous, if he has a
trenchant style and a fluent pen, and perhaps some sort
of a political reputation.   The task is particularly
easy if the writer can pose as a democrat, a friend of
humanity, and an enemy of all shams and old
conventions.

The sad thing about the co-existence in our own
century of the extreme specialist and the *vulgarisateur*
is that between them the stabilization of true history
may be delayed.   The greater the mass of undigested
and chaotic facts that is being thrown up by the
excavators in the field of historical research, the
greater is the need for the patient men who will be
content to spend long years in sifting out the heap of
material of all shapes and values, sorts and sizes, in
order to piece together all the more important fragments into a coherent pattern.   Each new discovery
has to be fitted into the mosaic.   The specialist will
persist in spending his energies in putting together one
very small corner of the problematic heap of facts,
without any regard for the main bulk of them.   The
vulgarisateur will pretend to throw the entire mass into
some simple shape, by plastering over the whole of it
with some worthless superficial mud-wash of his own
invention, which hides all ragged corners and tiresome
edges.   And then he will say that he has produced a
certain and convincing rendering of universal history,
which leaves no problem unsolved.

The true practical ambition of the honest historian
is to collaborate in collating the sum of knowledge that
exists in his own day.   Discoveries of the future will
be for the next generation to work upon.   All that the
writer of to-day can hope to do is to keep history up to

date, so far as in him lies, by the laborious piecing together of the trustworthy ancient material and the new stuff that keeps coming in.   It will not be an easy task ; some of the new matter that he will have to study will have to be rejected, after consideration, as worthless, hypothetical, or unimportant.   All of it will have to be subjected to ruthless criticism.   But there will be a large residuum of new certainties, which must be worked into the general fabric of history.   It will be no dishonour to the great historians of older days if their works have often, with all due reverence, to be laid aside as authorities, or only consulted as interesting examples of literary style or of the mentality of their age.   Many of them will have to go up to the more inaccessible shelves of our library, along with Rollin, Lingard and Voltaire. It would be absurd to accept in 1939, as our guiding summary of history, books which were admirable in 1850 or even in 1900.   This is as true in History as in Medicine or Chemistry.   We are dealing with a progressive science, not with an infallible Bible.   Even Dr. Stubbs' *Constitutional History of England* begins to show signs of wear.

It is no doubt a disheartening thought to remember that thirty or forty years hence—perhaps at an even earlier date—our own books on history must go to the same limbo of forgotten things as the books of our revered predecessors.   There is no more finality in History than there is in Natural Science.   A new recension of knowledge is required for the new generation ; and the works of which we have been so proud will ascend to the top shelf of the Public Library—if not descend to the cellar.   We must think ourselves happy if they appear to our grandchildren rather as glimpses of the obvious than as homes of exploded fallacies.

Nevertheless we may claim that we have not been without our uses. Every generation must codify its own stock of knowledge. And the successive codifiers, if their work has been honest, have served well the men of their own time. To the younger age they can only, perhaps, say, *Morituri te salutamus*, our work must perish ; but it had to be done.

XII

HISTORY AT OXFORD

DOWN to the nineteenth century it may be said that there was no great consideration paid to history here, and no school of Oxford historians, though some very distinguished graduates of the University produced from time to time famous books —such were Walter Raleigh, Lord Clarendon and Edward Gibbon, to mention only the greatest names. None of their works were written in Oxford, nor did their urge to write proceed from any training that they received in their years of residence ; indeed, if we credit Gibbon, he got no training of any kind in Magdalen. The university curriculum had no place for history, and though the great antiquary Camden left in his will provision for the establishment of a ' prælector ' in ancient history as early as 1622, we have no proof that his benefaction had any great result in encouraging studies in the realms that he loved. Official recognition really starts—rather unexpectedly—in the reign of George I (1724). That prosaic monarch, whom one does not normally regard as a patron of culture of any sort, did send to Jacobite Oxford (as the contemporary squib remarks) rather a troop of horse than the books which he sent to the loyal University of Cambridge. But it is also true that he established a Regius Professor of Modern History, the first of a long roll. From his modest annual stipend of £400 the professor was to maintain two lecturers in modern languages—French, German and Italian—to train for the public service and diplomacy, scholars who were to be nominated by the Crown. The University received the gift with unpardonable discourtesy, sending back a short acknowledgment by the hands of a bedell ! No doubt it felt no interest in the notion of training young Whig diplomatists in modern languages, and incidentally in modern history. It was a case of *timeo Danaos, et dona ferentes* —any Hanoverian endowment must be sinister.

I should imagine that the lectures of the early professors were boycotted—their uninspiring names show no reason for believing that they took any useful part in the University. I almost doubt whether Gibbon knew of their existence. In the miserable state of University examinations in the eighteenth century, there was certainly no opening for any one who would have felt the inclination to study modern history. If many young men read Clarendon and Bishop Burnet, or glanced through Swift's, Bolingbroke's and Defoe's contributions to polemical party annals, it must have been because they were interested in the topics, not because they were of any use in the academic curriculum. Of course there was a general newspaper knowledge of current events, and those who were going to be travellers, diplomatists, or merchants had to acquire some notion of the countries which they intended to visit, just as those with parliamentary ambitions had to acquire the outlines of recent party history, perhaps even some smattering of constitutional law. When Blackstone was in his early prime he collected an audience by circularizing likely hearers in an impassioned leaflet declaring that some knowledge of English law ' was the proper accompaniment of a gentleman and a scholar '. Professors, it is to be feared, did not often go out into the highways and hedges to sweep in audiences for lectures on subjects quite outside the University curriculum. Adam Smith made the broad statement that the greater part of the professors of Oxford had for many years given up all pretence of teaching. The vindicator of professorial virtue, one Hurdis of Magdalen, could only reply that out of twenty professors then existing, four were lecturing once a week—on law, science, and (oddly enough) Hebrew—eleven others ' lecture once a term, or employ a deputy, or have ceased to lecture because they could never secure an audience '. The Professor of Modern History of 1790 did not lecture, but employed a deputy ' who would wait on gentlemen in their own rooms ' if an arrangement could be made with him. Evidently there was no audience for modern history—but possibly a private coach might be wanted for an exceptional undergraduate.

This conception of the normal duties of the holder of a chair was not confined to professors of History, but was apparently general. If the professors had employed their leisure—enforced in some cases by the absence of an audience—in writing valuable works on their own subjects they might have been held absolved. Unfortunately they did not.

In the whole century I cannot find one important book written by an Oxford professor of Modern History. Warton, a Camden Professor of *Ancient* History, did produce an excellent work, his *History of English Poetry*—he held the position of Poet-

Laureate along with his professorship. But a history of English poetry was hardly in the proper sphere of a professor of *Ancient* History : it might conceivably have passed as appropriate production for the Regius Professor of *Modern* History. Not so— it was people like Hearne, sublibrarian at the Bodleian, who edited unpublished mediæval chronicles, and Gibbon, a scoffer at Oxford teaching, who wrote the greatest of books. Of our Regius Professors, David Gregory and William Holmes, Henry Beeke and the rest, who retains any memory ?

It was not till the nineteenth century had begun that there seems to have been any stirring among the dry bones of history at Oxford. The long period of desolation had already come to an end in other subjects before historical interest began to revive. The honour schools, which superseded for all the better men the old curriculum, started in 1802, and took more definite form in 1807, when Literæ Humaniores was separated from Mathematics and Physics, so that an ambitious student might take two schools. The famous old ' double first ' became possible in 1809, when the three classes were established in each of the two now separate schools. Sir Robert Peel was the first Oxford ' double first ', it may be remarked, a fine figure to start a new form of distinction. The ' fourth class ', *not* a form of distinction, but a refuge for the mentally destitute or the idle, was added in 1830. But history was not yet considered a fit subject for final examinations.

Part of its somnolence may perhaps be attributed to the long reign of the last professor of the old do-nothing school, Thomas Nowell, Principal of

St. Mary Hall, who drowsed for more than thirty years, in the time of the growth of wider interests. The first of the new series was Edward Nares, appointed by Lord Liverpool in 1813, a man who at any rate tried to justify his existence by producing a big book—the *Life of Lord Burleigh*, on which Lord Macaulay wrote such a scarifying review. Nares was not by nature a technical historian, but a lively and many-sided person ; he was interested in theology and geology and the plurality of worlds ; he also wrote serio-comic short stories, and incidentally ran away with the daughter of a duke. Farington in his diary comes across him, and speaks of him as a most amusing conversationalist. But a book he did produce, ' swelled to vast dimensions by endless repetitions, by episodes which have nothing to do with the main story, by long quotations from volumes which are in every circulating library, and by reflections so obvious that they must necessarily occur to the mind of every reader.' ' Compared with the labour of getting through these pages, all other labour, that of convicts on the treadmill, of children in factories, of negroes in sugar plantations may be considered agreeable recreation.' Macaulay was, no doubt, rather vicious in dealing with an old Tory. The book is long but not devoid of merit : it bore witness to a newly awakened acceptance of the fact that a professor should either teach or write, and should not look upon his post as a sinecure, to be comfortably held along with a country living in Kent or Somerset, or two or three other university offices. Two of the do-nothing professors had also been heads of colleges, for example. Several were pluralists who held other

15

professorships along with that of Regius History. Nares resided, but ' thought residence an expensive and meaningless formality '—since audiences could seldom be obtained.

At the end of Nares' long tenure of office (1813–1841) the place of history in the world of learning had been generally recognized all over the kingdom. A taste for mediæval history had been one of the by-products of the Romantic Movement of the late eighteenth and early nineteenth century. Every one read Scott's Waverley Novels, and a good many people other historical tales of less merit ; they naturally craved for the recognition of modern history as a primary element of culture. The university pressed for the choice of a known master of history, whose name and works should be familiar to every one. Sir Robert Peel, who had just become Prime Minister, was an Oxford double first himself, and quite conscious of university opinion. He nominated a very famous man, Thomas Arnold, the great head-master who made Rugby the best-known school in England. He was just resigning his post there, after much good work done and much controversy on outside matters, but was remembered in Oxford as the greatest of ancient history tutors in his young days, and the author of several books, an edition of Thucydides and a three-volume history of the Roman Republic, which was in its time the best work of the kind. His nomination made a mark in the annals of historical study in Oxford, and his first set of lectures was thronged by multitudes of hearers—an unprecedented thing. Nares had complained in 1835 that he had *two* listeners to his last course.

Thomas Arnold, most unfortunately, died before he had been a year in office, and the problem arose as to what sort of man the Crown would nominate as his successor, and as to whether the influx to the lectures of Arnold had been the result of his personality, or of the growing interest in the study which he represented. Arnold's numerous admirers subscribed a sum in his honour sufficient to start the Prize Essay which goes by his name. The successor appointed by the Crown, for some inscrutable reason, was John Anthony Cramer, Principal of New Inn Hall. He was a pure classical scholar, with no modern interests, who revived the bad old habits of the eighteenth century by holding the Deanery of Carlisle in plurality, and resided very little. The audiences disappeared.

It must be remembered that there was in 1842–48 no Modern History School, and that supposing a professor was unattractive, there was no reason why any one should attend his classroom, save that in those days a certificate that a student had attended so many professorial lectures—in one subject or another—was necessary to enable him to supplicate for his Baccalaureate. As Montagu Burrows, an undergraduate in 1853–6 at Magdalen Hall, remarks :

' The fame of a professor might attract an audience : the system of compulsory attendance, in order to secure the certificates necessary for a degree, might swell its numbers. But woe to the study which was not included among those for which examinations were provided, for which the prize of honours gained by competition did not exist. Modern History was in fact dying, books were not studied, gaping hearers, pressed men, surrounded the professor, and progress was barely perceptible. The change effected in Oxford studies by the University Commission arrived in time to save what might probably have perished. The new subject at last received admission within the favoured circle, and speedily justified the wisdom of the boon. At least, if the numbers attracted to the study, when it was made one of the recognized subjects for examination, is taken as a test, the evidence is not wanting.'

This means that among the many results of the first University Commission was the establishment of a new Honours School of ' Law and Modern History ', oddly linked together just as Philosophy and Ancient History had been in the great original Honours School of *Literæ Humaniores*. The first examination in it was held in 1853 and had eight entrants ; by 1860 there were twenty-seven. The union of Law and Modern History was not appreciated by all, either among lawyers or among historians. The former thought that the ' general periods ' going back into the Dark Ages and the political economy were unnecessary to them ; the latter objected to being burdened with the outlines of Roman law and the details of English case law. The amusing comment of Burrows, whom I have quoted above, is that at least ' history supplied interest and breadth to the somewhat repulsive science of Law '. Similar acid comment as to the vagueness of history was made on the other side. In the end the two studies were severed, and the scission proved not fatal but profitable to each of the two Siamese twins whom the Commission had joined together by a link of common examination papers. The final separation took place, with general approval, in the year 1873, when there were 31 candidates for Law and 59 for Modern History.

Practically speaking, the reputation of Oxford, as a home of historical study and the breeder of a large family of historians, small and great, starts from the work of the Commission of 1852–4 and the various ordinances which were imposed on the Colleges and the University in consequence of its legislation. But oddly enough the class-lists of the early years of the new school of Modern History and Law show among the prominent names many more of persons who were destined to become Parliamentarians, Cabinet Ministers, and Ambassadors than of professional historians. Apparently the original intention of George I in founding the Regius Professorship of Modern History for the benefit of public servants and diplomatists was not without its justification. The first writer of really important books who appeared in the Modern History class-list was Lord Bryce (1861), and he was a politician even more than an author. The History Professors of the next generation had nearly all taken the *Literæ Humaniores* curriculum, obviously because their residence happened to fall before the new school came into existence. This was the case with Freeman (1845), Goldwin Smith (1845), Froude (1840), Samuel Rawson Gardiner (1851), and Stubbs (1848). Only Montagu Burrows (1857) and York Powell (1872) were products of the first twenty years of the ' Law and History ' combination.

The fact that the early records of the new school show the names of men politically minded more than of professional historians brings up before our view the great controversy which arose as early as 1854, and which goes on till to-day. What is the object of the History School at Oxford ; is it intended to provide useful citizens for the State, or furtherers of historical research—or both ? This problem got tangled up almost from the first with a long dispute between professors and tutors, and incidentally between the University and the Colleges. There was an evil tradition of slackness, dating back to the eighteenth century, hanging about the Professoriate. To this the University Commissioners had intended to put an end, not only by imposing definite duties of frequent lecturing on the professors, but by increasing their numbers and authority. The Commissioners even suggested that the conduct of the examinations in each school should be placed in the hands of the professors attached to it. They stated that ' college activities had stifled the demand for professorial teaching ' ; the narrow range of ' coaching for the schools ' had discouraged both research and the power to draw broad and useful generalizations. It was a mistake to restrict instruction to that which would lead to a good class in the schools, and to dis- courage enthusiasm for subjects which might not ' pay '.

This move by the Commissioners provoked violent opposition from the tutors, mainly those teaching in the old *Literæ Humaniores* course, for tutors in Modern History had only just begun to appear. It is interesting to read the Memorandum prepared by the ' Tutors' Association ', and signed by some names that were of weight in those days. The Commissioners are accused of depreciating tutorial teaching, and leaning to an impolitic subversion of it. As a matter of mental discipline the signatories held that college tuition was superior to the delivery of public lectures. And they were tactless enough to speak of the professors as ' a body of men raised from a comparatively unimportant position ' who were to be trusted with much power and control of university studies—obviously regarding the tutorial body as much more important. The tutors had a strange ally in Dr. Pusey, who issued a pamphlet urging that professors were a race to be distrusted on first principles. Not only did he hold that professorial teaching does not communicate knowledge well, nor give a good discipline to the faculties, but he was of opinion that where professors ruled they were propagandists of scepticism and rationalism, and indirectly responsible for a general relaxation of the moral code. Copious allegations to support this idea were given from Germany. He summed up his views in a weighty paragraph :

' The problem and special work of a University is not to advance Science, nor to make discoveries, nor to form new schools of mental philosophy, nor to produce works on Medicine, Jurisprudence, or even Theology, but to form men's minds religiously, morally, and intellectually to discharge whatever duties God in his providence shall appoint to them.'

Another odd ally of the tutors was Mark Pattison, then in his early days, who held that ' the Professorial System as the main method of education is fundamentally wrong in principle ' and that ' he could not perceive that a professor's lectures could ever have a stimulating power on undergraduates '. ' When not understood he was wasted on the auditor ; when half-understood he begot a state of the conceit of knowledge where knowledge was not '. When he wrote this Pattison was a tutorial fellow of Lincoln and a frequent examiner in the schools ; in later life, as his memoirs show, he became a convert to the necessity and usefulness of professorial teaching.

The Commissioners, little affected by their critics, produced the system under which the University was to work for many years, with a body of professors much augmented, a set of new Honours Schools, and a drastic abolition of old academic scandals—pluralisms, monopolies, and evasions of duty. The changes were generally for the good—they certainly transformed my own old college from a home of Wykehamical founders-kin drones into one of the most flourishing units in the University.

But as to the Modern History School, the hope that the professors would take a distinguished share in organizing it seems to have failed from the first. The school grew, and many good candidates passed through it, but I cannot find that the professors had any influence on it—the tutors kept a grip upon its teaching, and did not share their power with the rivals whom the Commissioners had ' wished upon ' them. This was very largely the fault of the Crown : when Henry Halford Vaughan, the Regius Professor of the Commission time, was gone—he had been a great pamphleteer against the tutors—the Prime Minister replaced the advocate of whips for chastisement of tutors with an advocate of scorpions. Goldwin Smith, a law fellow of University College, was given the Chair in 1858 and proceeded to make himself generally odious, not only to tutors but to most other

people. The *Dictionary of Natural Biography*, defining
his personality, calls him 'the Controversialist.'
He was an extreme militant radical, not only inspired
by the Manchester School, but plunging into all
extremes of anti-imperialism and bitter criticism of
every existing institution. He was a profuse pamphleteer and political propagandist. Disraeli called him
' an itinerant spouter of stale sedition ', and ' a wild
man of the cloister, who goes about the country
maligning men and things '. His career was extraordinary : denouncing every English institution as
effete, he went to the United States, and exchanged
his Oxford professorship for one at Cornell. Later
he transferred himself to Canada, where he started an
agitation for the scission of that great dominion from
the British Empire—which fortunately had no success.
He survived to a patriarchal age, and died at Toronto
as late as 1910—aged eighty-seven.

Any chance that the Regius Professor would have
a useful influence in the formation of the recently
formed Modern History School was of course defeated
by such an appointment, and his colleague in the
second new historical professorship established by the
Commissions unfortunately failed to win the collaboration of the tutors from precisely the opposite reasons.
Montagu Burrows was a distinguished naval officer,
who came up to the University very late, as a married
man. He was the first professor who took the Modern
History School, and got first class honours in it in
1857, when aged thirty-eight. He never obtained a
fellowship, but worked as a private coach in history
with enormous success, and at the same time became
a prominent figure in religious circles—as an early

member of the English Church Union, a speaker at Church congresses, and the secretary of the Universities' Mission to Central Africa. He was a devout and rather pugnacious churchman, and a militant Conservative, who took an active part in city no less than in academic politics. His election to the Chichele professorship of Modern History in 1862 caused universal surprise, as there were running against him three men all destined in later years to be Regius Professors, Stubbs, Freeman and Froude, each one of whom had already produced well-known historical work, while Burrows had as yet none to show.

Burrows was a bluff, honest sailor, with a real love of historical research ; he produced several works, small and great, of which his Life of Lord Hawke remains a standard authority. I knew and liked him well. But unfortunately his pronounced conservatism and active churchmanship prejudiced many of the tutors in the Modern History School against him, just as much as Goldwin Smith's virulent radicalism prejudiced others. The conjunction of two such opposed personalities in the professorial chairs, just at the moment when the Modern History School was growing to maturity, was most unhappy, and practically led the majority of the college teachers to drop into Dr. Pusey's old idea that professors were dangerous wild fowl. The practical boycott on professorial lectures started in the 'sixties. It was rendered complete by a university change made in 1861. Down to that time attendance at professorial lectures was one of the requirements for a certificate for the B.A. degree ; the obligation was then abolished. This came very hardly on Goldwin Smith's three successors—Stubbs (1866–84), Freeman (1884–92) and Froude (1892–94), whom I knew well, and I sympathized with their grievances. Stubbs was the most unpretending and genial of men, fetched from a country vicarage, where he had been editing mediæval chronicles, to preach the thesis that history must be studied for its own sake. The thing that vexed him when he came back to Oxford was that it was undervalued in its true character of mental training ; it was learned to qualify men to make effective speeches in politics, or to indite brilliant articles in magazines and periodicals. ' It is made the embellishment of wordy eloquence, or the source for pictures by painters who evolve groupings of personages, costumes and incidents from their own inner consciousness '. He also pleaded that instead of being made the handmaid of political or religious controversy, it should be studied for itself, with no ulterior motive. He allowed that much nonsense had been written under the name of Philosophy of History, and that it is too common to knock together ingenious theories from well-picked and insufficient data. But he maintained that history as a record of fact had its lessons—and that they can be discovered and taught. He himself was interested as an Englishman in everything that had ever happened in England.

Surely there was no danger in these views—but Stubbs' lecture-room was never full. Undergraduates were not told by their tutors to frequent his courses on the Constitutional History of England, which finally took shape in a book which served as a sort of bible for the student for two generations. He spoke to an audience of a dozen or so, while popular college tutors could command one of sixty or a hundred. It is true that his meagre band of pupils included several students who were to take prominent places among the history teachers of the future—but they had found him out for themselves—certainly had not been encouraged to do so by their tutors. This was my own case—greatly venturing (as I considered) for I was an undergraduate with no special introduction to him, I called at his charming little Jacobean house in Broad Street to ask him about a sixteenth-century source. I was so kindly received that I became his devoted admirer for ever, and one of my proudest memories is that of membership of the little Society of the younger generation over which he presided in the last two or three years of his professorship. I still cherish my photograph of him sitting benevolent in the midst of a little circle consisting of Lang (our present primate), Henson, J. A. R. Marriott, Raymond Beazley, Cooper, Ellis, Adkins (both destined to be M.P.'s), the omnivorous American Brearley, Carlyle and two or three more. We read each other essays, and enjoyed our president's humorous commentaries on them.

Stubbs, the most easy tempered of men, took the neglect shown to him by the tutorial body with equanimity, wrote away at his books, and finally left Oxford to take up the bishopric of Chester. His successor Edward Augustus Freeman was of a very different character, intensely combative as his previous career had shown. His inaugural address, which I heard, was an indictment of the Modern History School for not being sufficiently inclusive. His thesis was that it was useless to draw a line at the

year A.D. 476 and to call what went before it ' Ancient '
and what came after ' modern '. Every one ought
to look at history as continuous, from the Call of
Abraham or the Dorian Migration down to the recent
Russo-Turkish War. The thesis was inspiring, and
the protest against the custom of shutting up history
into water-tight compartments convincing. But the
application of it to the practical needs of the Modern
History School presented difficulties. Freeman tried
to illustrate his theory by giving a series of lectures on
Sicily, starting from the Greek settlement and going
down to Garibaldi and the ' Thousand '. But he
never got farther than Frederic of Hohenstaufen,
because no continuous audience could be found.
Freeman did not deliver a short general sketch, but
lingered lovingly over details of the Athenian expedition of 414 B.C. or the exploits of Roger the Norman.
In the fourth or fifth term the audience had dwindled
to four—one of whom was a middle-aged clergyman
from North Oxford, with a taste for general information. This cleric was compelled to break off his
attendance in the middle of the term, but rose to
explain to the professor that ' to keep up the quorum '
he must send his daughter, a very intelligent girl of
fourteen. Freeman, who was growing more and more
indignant as the terms went on, and the hearers went
off, broke off the series with an inarticulate groan.

Nor can I too much blame the University for
not being able to provide hearers who wanted to
hear all about Sicily throughout the ages ; the main
interest of the practical inquirer is confined within
some narrower period, and few if any dare to aim,
as Freeman did, at being encyclopædic. He himself

attributed the want of interest in many annals which were to him most attractive to the bane of the examination schools. They destroyed the conception of the continuity of history, and concentrated the attention of the student on certain periods, on which there was 'intensive' teaching by the tutors. I once heard Freeman make the rather astonishing statement that 'in the art of preparing—I will not use the ugly word *cramming*—an undergraduate for his class, the last bachelor of Arts who has just won his own class is necessarily more skilful than I am'.

One of his more rational protests was against the statute which compelled professors to deliver precisely fourteen, or twelve, lectures each term on a definite subject. This he called having to 'dance in fetters'— the fetters being the exact number of lectures to be given. For it is quite true that some subjects can be disposed of in four addresses of an hour each, while others may require forty. This necessity to issue an exact terminal scheme, measuring twelve or fourteen hours, was like 'the bed of Procrustes'. Topics had to be chopped short, or stretched to unnecessary length. Here, I think, Freeman was in the right ; for the burden of having to produce forty-two or thirty-six original lectures every year is a very heavy one, and historical topics do not naturally cut up into equal sections suited to the exigencies of the academical terms.

In a general way Freeman was in arms, all through his eight years of office, against the 'crammers', and criticized every alteration in the direction of definition which they made in the regulations for the honour school. He was a believer in the continuity of universal history, and would have liked every one

to feel the same general interest, instead of being
pegged down to Period III or Period V, or 'the Indian
special subject'. Often he would complain that
though theoretically the most responsible and important
individual in Oxford for the History School, he had
not the slightest influence on teaching or examinations.
The only point on which I remember that he showed
any reluctance to make history all-embracing, was
that he had no desire for emphasizing the literary side
of it. He was a strong opponent of the formation
of the School of English Literature, for he said that
literature was a subject upon which no one could be
properly tested, tastes being different, and no standard
of rightness or wrongness being possible. It did not
very much matter to him if the Anglo-Saxon Chronicle
was written in one style and Clarendon's *Great
Rebellion* in another. One only wanted to get at the
facts behind their verbiage.

Unfortunately Freeman could not lure an audience
to his lectures on Gregory of Tours or Geoffrey
Malaterra, and he remained a voice preaching in the
wilderness against the examination bogey, and the
general want of interest in ' things of real importance '.

He died suddenly at Alicante, while travelling in
Spain, and the Crown chose as his successor the man
of whom he most disapproved, James Anthony
Froude, with whom he had been engaged in many a
controversy. It is doubtful whether Freeman disliked
him more for being an unregenerate imperialist, for
having divested himself of his clerical orders, or for
writing in a very picturesque and dramatic literary
style. Froude's appointment came somewhat as a
surprise ; he was now an elderly man—over seventy

years of age—and had long been out of touch with Oxford. I well remember his inaugural lecture—it contrasted curiously enough with Freeman's, which had been denunciatory and propagandic. Froude's lecture was, on the other hand, not at all serious. It was paradoxical, witty, full of persiflage and half-ironical apologetics. 'How do I come to be here, Regius Professor in the University of Oxford?' he asked: and then answered with a smile, 'I was tempted, and I fell.' But putting aside his very clever and rather touching personal explanations of his attitude to Oxford, and Oxford's former attitude to him, his main thesis was a defence of the personal and dramatic treatment of history. He fully appreciated all that had been said or written against his methods and his manner, and set himself cheerfully to defend them.

He asserted that history was all the better for being written as literature, that it is the historician's duty to present it in a form that will attract as many intelligent readers as possible, and that arid narrative and technical verbiage scare away many who might have profited greatly by historical study. He pleaded that the influence of the personality of the historian cannot possibly be eliminated : he must state the case as it appears to him, not as it might appear to some ideal person destitute of all bias, convictions or prejudices.

I found myself at first in some doubt as to accepting this view of the historian's duty, but felt that for practical purposes it is the only one that produces good work. Logically, no doubt, one ought to agree with Lord Acton and Professor Bury, and to conceive of the historian as a passionless creature. But nevertheless I am driven after reflection to concede to Froude that history must be somewhat subjective. No great book ever has been, or ever will be, written by a historian who suppressed self as he wrote every word. What such a book might gain in accurate statement, it loses in spontaneity and conviction. The passionless chronicler, detailing the movements of figures for whom he must show no moral approval or disapproval, does not produce a readable book. As to those who hold that history has nothing to do with literary form, that vivid descriptive narrative is unnecessary, or even meretricious, we must of course draw the line somewhere. A good style can do no harm, but a historical ' thriller ' is to be deprecated. How far more useful would Carlyle's *French Revolution* have been if he had had pruned his verbiage, and refrained from painting lurid and chaotic scenes, in which the vehemence of the narrative sometimes prevents the reader from forming a definite and accurate picture of what did actually happen. And, above all, let us have no ' debunking ' or ' whitewashing ' of central figures, in order to produce an effective picture of a period or an incident, and to gain some notoriety for the ingenious writer.

Froude's time in Oxford was short—less than two years (1892–94) in it he gave three most interesting and attractive sets of lectures, which drew vast audiences not only of North Oxford ladies but of undergraduates and even tutors. The subjects were the Great Elizabethan Seamen, Erasmus and the Council of Trent. Advancing years had not affected the charm of his style, and every word was worth hearing. If he had survived to deliver many such courses the

16

latent prejudice against professorial lectures would have died out. But it may be doubted whether any man is physically capable of continuing such a mental and literary output for many years. As Halford Vaughan wrote, far back in the time of the first Oxford University Commission, the burden which is placed on professors by the Statutes is a very heavy one. Gibbon took twenty years to write the *Decline and Fall*. If it were measured into lecture-lengths he would have had to write the equivalent of two octavo volumes every year, and to have finished the job in six. This would have been impossible, even for a man of his calibre. Fortunately he was never a professor, nor set to write against time. Froude's short term in Oxford was a sort of Golden Age for great lectures— but I do not see how it could have continued.

The Crown—on this occasion Lord Rosebery was Prime Minister—took effective measures for breaking the cycle, and filled the Regius Chair with a successor as unlike Froude as could be imagined. Lord Rosebery had been an undergraduate at Christ Church, before his unlucky collision with the College authorities on the subject of race-horses, which led to his departure without taking the final schools. In his student days he had known and admired the then law-tutor of the House, Frederick York Powell, a many-sided and very attractive personage, but not one distinguished for order, or steady attention to routine. Having the gift of the Regius Chair in his hands, Lord Rosebery wrote to offer it to Powell. No answer came, for the curious reason that Powell, who hated correspondence, was in the habit of leaving all letters with O.H.M.S. on the envelope unopened

for weeks—they probably contained tax-demands.
Personal inquiry had to be made, and the official
letter was discovered under a pile of others. The
offer was accepted, with some doubts as to whether
acceptance was wise, for Powell knew that he disliked
formal lectures and regular time-schedules.

Every one knew and liked York Powell, but
the conception of him as even theoretical head of
the History School was difficult. A burly, bearded,
athletic man, always in a blue serge jacket, a low
collar with a wisp of black tie, and with a briar pipe,
he looked rather like the captain of a coasting steamer,
no one would have taken him for a don. His tastes
lay in the direction of boating, boxing and fencing,
in all of which he excelled. He had a wonderful
flair for picking up general information and languages,
and an interview with him usually ended far away from
the subject with which it had commenced. Continuous work was not his strong point. The one
considerable production of his life was an edition of
the *Corpus Poeticum Boreale*, the Icelandic sagas,
which he carried out in collaboration with the Icelandic
scholar Vigfusson. It was always said that when
something had to be finished Vigfusson found it
necessary to come and sit permanently in Powell's
rooms, or the particular section in hand would never
be completed. Powell would have slipped off when
not watched, for he was hopeless in keeping engage-
ments of any kind. If any particular job happened to
be required from him at any moment, he would
always find that job repulsive and half a dozen others
more attractive. He had a wonderful talent for
browsing among books—not only historical ones,

and the book that he had picked up at the moment always seemed of superior interest to the one on which a problem was put before him. The only serious piece of writing outside the *Corpus Boreale* which he ever succeeded in finishing was a short history of mediæval England, very original, and containing many odd anecdotes from chronicles which no one had used before. But he often wrote short reviews and notes.

There is an ancient Roman story of a talented young patrician whose habits were so desultory that his relatives succeeded in getting him elected into the College of the Pontifices, who had to discharge many and various matters of routine, in the hope that obligatory work of detail would make him systematic. The experiment is said to have been successful. I can almost fancy that Lord Rosebery may have had some such an idea with regard to York Powell, whose talents and knowledge he knew, and probably also his dislike of fixed duties. Some of us in Oxford certainly thought that the result of the nomination might be to cause the new professor to buckle down to regular work, and perhaps turn his obligatory lectures into valuable books. The hope, it was hardly an expectation, was destined to be quite fruitless. No change appeared in Powell's habits or his outlook on academic life.

His inaugural lecture, at which I was present, gave us a sad impression, and showed what we might expect. The whole of the senior members of the University were waiting for him, when he came in rather late and looking hurried. He had a few scraps of notes in his hand ; after paying short tributes of respect to his predecessors Stubbs and Freeman, he passed over Froude, merely saying that he knew practically nothing of him, and then developed in a few paragraphs what seemed the main thesis of his address—a complaint that historical study in England was handicapped by the lack of machinery for the facilitation of research—places where the student could be taught palæography and diplomatics, where he could have his range among manuscripts under skilled supervision, and find collections of bibliographies on all ancillary subjects. After twenty minutes, when we were expecting him to warm himself up to some general observation on the teaching of history, he suddenly put down the last of his notes or scraps and remarked, ' I have done '. The whole business had taken less than half an hour, and was but rambling talk— evidently no care had been taken over the preparation.

This start on the professorial round was a warning for what was to follow. Powell announced terminal lectures on the sources of English history, or still more vaguely promised 'informal instruction'. I understand that those who went to him heard many disjointed but interesting suggestions, and conversation on all sorts of matters, but had nothing to put in a notebook. The only persons to whom he may have been of some use were those who had aspiration toward research, but no knowledge of how to set about it. York Powell, with all his vast and miscellaneous knowledge and his many-sided brain, was always more effective in what he suggested than in what he accomplished. He produced no more books, though considering the perfunctory way in which he dealt with his statutory lectures, he must have had ample leisure to write. But, as always, he preferred to browse at large, being a perfect type of the 'researcher' who does nothing but research, and has too many irons in the fire to produce a single welded bar.

After eight years of tenure of the professorship, Powell died in 1902, leaving nothing behind him that could be published, and only a vague memory of various learning. He put in his will a request that there might be no service at his funeral, neither religious nor a secular *éloge* in the continental style. A long procession of those who had admired him in many ways, filed past the deep pit in Summertown Cemetery in blank silence, and that was all. It was a very hot day, and the effect was depressing.

So far as the development of practical instruction in the Modern History School went, York Powell might never have existed. But there was much useful work being done by the college teachers ; the 'crammers' whom Freeman had denounced. The history tutors of the period 1890–1910 in many cases did not deserve the criticism poured upon them by that apostle of universal history. They were by now men who had been trained in the Honours School themselves, and knew all about its limitations, but they also had begun to write meritorious books on the special subjects in which each of them happened to be concerned. Several of them obtained professorships in other Universities, and acquitted themselves well there. It is true that the task of preparing individual pupils with the precise information needed to obtain a good class in examination absorbed much of their interest. But this, which Freeman had called 'cramming', was not their only inspiration, and they did their best in their Faculty Boards to knock together what they considered a practical curriculum for the better sort of under-graduate. 'Periods' and 'special subjects' were being continually varied, with the best intentions, and new subjects introduced—not always profitable or popular ones.

There was, of course, one terrible handicap for the conscientious tutors, with a real wish to advance the study of history. Their colleges kept thrusting upon them many pupils of inferior intellectual calibre, who did not wish to be stigmatized as passmen ; and the tutor had to spend countless dismal hours in screwing stupid men up to the minimum standard for obtaining a third or fourth class, or (that refuge for the destitute) a certificate for Group A or Group C. In an ideal University these 'honour men by compulsion' would not have been allowed to take the History School at all—they were merely in it because they thought it rather less rebarbative than Law or Mathematics, Theology or Physical Science. Their perfunctory weekly essays were heartbreaking boredom to the tutor, who had to impress upon them that screeds produced from text-books or glimpses of the obvious would not do for the Schools.

But there were some pupils in all colleges, and many in some colleges, who had a real enthusiasm for history ; a certain proportion of them were in-tending to teach history themselves some day, but many more felt that a knowledge of it would be useful to them in after-life, not only in political spheres, but in almost every other line of life whether professional, commercial, or administrative. A minister, lawyer, banker, manager of a factory, or Justice of the Peace, or master in a secondary school, or journalist, would draw inestimable advantage from having passed through the curriculum at Oxford, in spite of all its limitations. Many of those who had to deal with the organization of the Modern History School were convinced that it was serving its purpose sufficiently well, by training the average good citizen from the governing classes in the past annals and present problems of the British Empire.

There remained, however, another question. Ought the History School to be so framed that it would produce historians ? York Powell had hinted at this, when in his truncated inaugural speech he had complained that the technical machinery required by the student who intended to devote his life to writing or teaching history was insufficiently provided by the University. This was the problem definitely raised by York Powell's successor in the Regius Chair, Sir Charles Firth (1902–25), who fell foul of the existing system because ' it did extremely little for the exceptional man who wishes to study history for its own sake '.

This was a most interesting topic, and discussion upon it occupied great part of Firth's intellectual efforts, as may be seen from his pamphlet on *History at Oxford*. His thesis was that the History School was being worked on the wrong lines, partly because it was conceived of as being good training for the intelligent citizen, and partly because the tutorial body had come to think that their main duty was to obtain good classes for their better pupils. In a way, Firth's complaints repeated Freeman's old denunciation of the ' crammers ', but he had a much better conception of the real state of affairs, because he (unlike Freeman) had passed through the History School himself (1878), had been for a short time a tutor at Pembroke College, and had frequently acted as examiner. His thesis was that the History School ought to be a training ground for historians, and he was of the opinion that its organization should be modified so as to give opportunity for the proper instruction of those who intended to take up research or the composition of books. As one who had gone through the whole system himself, and who ended in writing a long series of valuable volumes on the English history of the seventeenth century, he had special claims to be heard.

His very combative inaugural lecture of 9 November 1904 set forth his proposals. He had, he said, gone through the class-lists of the last twenty years, and found in them very few names of men who had published historical works of any kind. His explanation of the fact was that the school was not so organized as to encourage candidates to proceed to any serious study of history. It might give the ordinary citizen a training that would be of some value to him in his later career, but it did not equip the scholar with the special knowledge needed for the purpose of independent research. Examinations as managed at present were 'an excellent training for journalists', and gave the examiner an easy means of comparing the relative intellectual qualities of individual candidates. But the papers written in the schools were all derived from second-hand information, whether got from tutors or from books. There was no demand for the exhibition of the power to deal with first-hand material. He thought that the training of professional historians ought to be part of the University curriculum, and to secure this end proposed various changes in the examination system. A start might be made by allowing candidates to escape part of the normal papers by presenting theses showing original work— which should exempt them from, e.g. the details of early constitutional history, or from political economy. Early constitutional history, meticulously studied with the aid of Stubbs' Charters, was his special bugbear, ' of very little value to the persons seeking a liberal education through history, who form the bulk of our candidates '. Stress ought to be put on some mastery of other languages than English—the undergraduate comes up with little or no knowledge of any tongue but his own, save a sketchy acquaintance with Latin and Greek, sufficient to pass him for matriculation. (Even this modicum of touch with the classical languages has vanished since Firth's day). But literature bearing on history is practically ignored—questions were sometimes set on literary subjects in the schools, but, speaking as an examiner, Firth declared that no one ever tried to answer them. Another necessity was the moving forward of the date down to which the history of the constitution and the empire should be studied ; this was at the moment 1837, a ridiculous limit, when foreign history was allowed to be investigated down to 1878. This change was duly made a short time after Firth's protest had been entered.

But the Professor's main remedy for the deficiencies of history teaching at Oxford was the development of post-graduate study under the charge of the professors of history, by the aid of the then newly established baccalaureate of Letters, which gave an opportunity for a real training in the methods of research and of historiography. There ought to be courses of special study, in which, under skilled guidance, men should be adequately trained for research in medieval or modern history, so as to be competent to work independently when their baccalaureate of Letters had been obtained. Two attempts had been made to form a class of apprentice-historians of this kind, one by Freeman, another by York Powell. Though both experiments had failed, Firth was determined to make another, the prospect, as he thought, being a little brighter because of the greater number of post-graduates in residence.

Alas ! Firth's attempt failed like the others, and for a fundamental reason. No two of those who want to start on research after the schools, or who come up to try for the baccalaureate of Letters, are interested in the same particular topic ; and to be offered a training in historiography by means of the study of some period or theory in which one has no interest is unattractive. As an example of the hopeless discrepancy of aims which prevails, I may mention that the three first candidates who came under my own notice were interested respectively in the English administration of Aquitaine, the seigneurial tenures in Canada, and the Fifth Crusade. Who could form a class useful to all three ? Not even Firth's broad knowledge of England in the seventeenth century could secure a band of followers with identical interests. The only class of people who might conceivably be kept together, if enough of them could be found, would be serious students of the Middle Ages, to all of whom palæography would be necessary for detailed research. We have a reader in Palæography —what sort of audience he can command, I do not

know. Of the three candidates whom I mentioned
above, two got leave to proceed with their studies
abroad—when they were completed, how could their
baccalaureate be said to have come from training or
research in Oxford ?

If, as Firth proposed, the instruction of post-
graduate students had to be entrusted to the professors
and readers of the University, since every individual
student would be working at a different theme, the
result would be that the professors and readers would
be requested to act as private coaches to an infinite
number of isolated persons. This would effectually
prevent them from doing any fresh work of their own,
or from writing books—their position would be even
worse than that of the College tutor, whose pupils
are at least confined to a definite, if a large, list of
prescribed topics. But post-graduate students wander
at their own sweet will.

For this reason, so far as history teaching given
by professors could serve, I have had little belief in the
baccalaureate of letters, or the Doctorate of Philosophy
afterwards established. Good theses may be produced,
but they are not in any way the result of the Oxford
training, save indeed in the cases of those who have
already taken the Modern History School, and the
limited scope of that school is precisely what the advocates of post-graduate studies are wont to denounce.

Twenty-three college tutors wrote a formal protest
to Firth concerning his inaugural lecture and its indictment of their school. They acknowledged that some
of the criticism of its details were well founded, and
indeed most of the anomalies were gradually removed.
But they held that the school was made to train the

good citizen, not the professional researcher. ' The University would be false to a paramount national duty if it substituted for a liberal education through history a system and a curriculum beneficial only to a very small minority '. They also repudiated the statement that the History School bred no historians, by giving a long list of men who had passed through it and written valuable books—thirty-five names were cited. Many more could be added now. I am in complete agreement with their conclusions—though I am a professor.

Firth failed to organize post-graduate education on a professorial basis, but many of the younger generation studied his works and followed his precepts. His great achievement was the series of solid books on the history of the Commonwealth, with such valuable by-products as *Cromwell's Army* and scores of original monographs in learned magazines and periodicals.

The successor of Firth, H. W. Davis, whose tenure of the Regius Chair was all too short (1925–28), believed in the utility of the History School for the good citizen, and warned the researcher that ' the process of inquiry is not an end in itself, and is only useful if controlled by some definite scheme '—an axiom which I had laid down myself in my own inaugural address twenty years before. He was a strong advocate of Modern Studies : there was still much to be done in the nineteenth century—an immense amount of material which had been printed in public records, biographies, collections of letters and speeches, still required sifting—spadework, perhaps, but most necessary before the definitive histories can be written by some historian yet unborn. He repudiated the idea that history was an exact science, and that topics were to be studied from a detached impersonal point of view, and not presented to the world showing any trace of personal bias or scale of moral values appertaining to the historian. And he had a word of disapproval for ' Social Historians ' who ' tell us that all we must need to know about the civilizations of the past is what the poorer and more illiterate classes thought and did. I can find no justification for the belief that what the masses think to-day, Society as a whole will infallibly believe to-morrow '. On the contrary, new ideas percolate downwards—not upwards : Carlyle was not so wrong in his hero-worship.

After reading my present colleague, Powicke's, summary of his views on history, I do not think that he differs very much from Davis's or my own general conclusions. I note that he has seen the same division between the two ways of interpreting history which I have called Pessimism and Optimism—though with a slight change of nomenclature he calls them the cynical and the mystical outlooks. An eminent German historian, von Below, was thinking of much the same difference of perspective when he wrote of the dangers of ' positivism ' and the opposite dangers of ' romanticism '. Powicke writes that ' the old constructive impulses of mankind, such as the sense of race, of nationalism, of class, of the organization of the state on the basis of force, have become so incompatible with each other that we cannot take them as our guides without reducing ourselves to the scepticism from which these same impulses, when they were fresh and young, rescued our forefathers. In a wider outlook the dominant conception will be the need of mutual understanding and equitable behaviour between man and man, race and race. How the material of history will respond, and adapt itself to dictate our historical judgment will be known only to history itself. . . . At present only the widest and most tentative generalization are possible '. This conclusion, it may seem, leaves the official guide, the teacher of history, in a somewhat groping posture, watching the movement of the world with no certainty as to whither the movement is tending. But it certainly does not absolve him from setting forth his own conclusions as an honest student, with ethical and moral fundamentals of his own, as to what seems dangerous and what profitable to mankind.

As to my own personal outlook, after serving the University for twenty years as a college tutor, and for thirty as Chichele Professor, I may perhaps be allowed to state my own experiences. The first conclusion is that the Modern History School still remains a firm training-ground for the good citizen, in spite of all the changes of the last post-war years. I do not like all these changes, but think that the essential core of the school still remains healthy. I deplore the present trend away from the preliminary centuries towards the very last periods that are permissible. The proportion of examinees in the schools who offer anything before the eighteenth century seems to be decreasing, so that some one lately called the curriculum ' the School of *Very* Modern History '. Nor have I ever approved the shortening of prescribed terms of years, thinking it better to know a good deal about three centuries rather than to know a very great deal about one century, and very little about the two others. I detect a certain tendency to neglect some necessary aspects of history—for example, it used to be prescribed that every candidate should answer a question or two dealing with historical geography, and if possible should elucidate it with sketch-maps. These old ' starred questions ' are no longer differentiated from the rest, and geography *can* be eluded and I judge, from the Examiners' Report of 1938, *is* eluded. But the thing which strikes me most of all as deplorable is that knowledge of languages, however theoretically advocated, seems no longer a necessary equipment for a first-class man. This deduction I make from personal experience; every year many of the best candidates from the schools compete for the All Souls fellowship in History. They used to try, on the average, four languages in the unseen translation paper—Greek, Latin, French, German ; some had a certain knowledge of Italian. But now very frequently a candidate with the highest possible class in the History School or ' P.P.E.' only translates in two—Greek (I suppose) has been killed by the abolition of compulsory Greek in the entrance examinations, years back. But now many prominent candidates only offer Latin and French, and are not too ready with their renderings in either. German and Italian passages are not too often attempted or too well done. It looks to me as if a first-class in the present school is sometimes obtained by undergraduates who have no full and accurate knowledge of any tongue but English—a deplorable phenomenon.

However, I may say of the History School that

' with all its faults I love it still ', and that I deprecate
and shall continue to deprecate, the tendency of some
students, who might well have taken it for their mental
education, to slide away into that vague thing which
public opinion has christened ' Modern Greats ',
where a modicum of very modern history hardly
suffices to leaven a mass of less definite and more
controversial studies. For, to put it crudely, I hold
that History is an astringent and Philosophy a dissolvent for the mind of the ordinary student. As
a training for good citizens I prefer immensely the
old curriculum—and of course it cannot fail to be so
for those who intend to become historians. One
must not generalize on controversial subjects before
one has learned how to particularize on definite ones.
' That way madness lies '—i.e. theories about the
' philosophy of History ', and ideologies of all sorts.

If I may be permitted to add a few paragraphs
about my own work as a professor for the last thirty
years, I may say that taught by the experience of what
happened to Stubbs, Freeman, and Firth under my
own observation, I have long ceased to hope for large
audiences at professorial lectures. As a late Master
of University College—still with us in venerable old
age—observed long years back, ' Professors are called
on to teach in the grand style, but there are no students
in the grand style to attend their lectures '. A late
president of Corpus, who had long been a college
tutor, observed that Oxford and Cambridge are the
only Universities in the world which do not encourage
attendance at professorial lectures. It is possible,
as Stubbs found fifty years ago, to write books which
go through countless editions, but which when they

17

were in lecture-form were rehearsed to classes of nine or ten hearers. I can support his evidence by my own—one of my books which is now in its eighth edition was delivered to a very meagre attendance, another of which 14,000 copies have been sold, first and last, got a slightly better audience because it attracted many non-academical hearers of both sexes from North Oxford. The plausible advice, which I have already mentioned, that professors should devote themselves to post-graduate education is, to those who know the facts, quite farcical. The post-graduate students all wish to study different topics, and no class can possibly be formed from them. No professor, however broad his interests, could act as private tutor individually to isolated students of dozens of topics, most of which would not come within the scope of his special knowledge.

The only thing left for the conscientious professor to do is to deliver his statutory lectures, but to make them subordinate to the duty of increasing historical knowledge by writing books in which he can express the results of the particular lines of research in which he believes himself to have a competent knowledge. Since it is impossible to produce three new books of solid bulk every year, to correspond to the three academical terms, I have—while writing hard at the subjects to which I am devoted—taken to the system of giving two sets of professorial lectures each year on topics which are seldom or never touched by the tutorial teachers for the examination schools, but which come inside the curriculum, and to devote the third term to a section of one of the large-scale books on which I am at the moment engaged, which may be

called a piece of detailed research. The sets of statutory lectures may not attract any large audiences, because
they are on subjects which college tutors very rationally
declare to be of ' no use for the schools '. This comes
to some extent from the fact that students have moved
on from mediæval studies to nineteenth-century ones,
and the number of undergraduates who offer the earlier
periods is now never large. Hence scant audiences for
the Ottoman Turks, for mediæval Scandinavia and
Russia, for political geography in remote epochs, or the
later Crusades. But certain series, e.g. on the Art of
War, on the Renaissance, on the history of English
castles, or of the English coinage and currency, might
be considered courses which students might attend
without waste of time. Nevertheless they do not attend
in any great numbers, for the practical reason that few
questions on such topics are set at examination-time.
A small audience is secured for such subjects, because
there are a few undergraduates of the better sort,
who like to hear about those aspects of their periods
which are not dealt with in the tutorial curriculum.

What I can more rationally deplore is that when
I am dealing with the larger topics, concerning which
any student might reasonably be expected to have
some natural curiosity, the number of my hearers is
not much larger than if I were speaking about the
Balkan Peninsula in the Middle Ages. This is where
the ' boycott ' on professorial lectures is really felt—
there are many colleges from which I have not had an
auditor for long years, though there are others from
which the tutor sends me some of his better men.
That such lectures are not worthless is sufficiently
shown by the fact that when published they go into

all bibliographies, and some of them into many editions. That they are not inaudible (an accusation made sometimes against professorial lectures) is evident to all hearers. That they are the results of original research, and bring out information not hitherto accessible, is equally obvious. But they are professorial lectures—and not directed to some definite prescribed subject in the Modern History School !

My own aspiration would be that one of two changes might be made in the University organization for lecturing by professors. Either (but this I fear is improbable) there should be some encouragement to students to attend the lectures of professors, as there used to be before the second University Commission legislated. Once upon a time, up to 1861, it was necessary for the candidate for the Baccalaureate to produce certificates of a modicum of such attendances. This obligation prevails, I believe, in all the Universities of the world except Oxford and Cambridge. Or else, which I think is also inconceivable, professors should be relieved of the duty of lecturing, on condition that they show at reasonable intervals books which prove that they have been devoting themselves to research, and have placed the results of it in printed form before the University and the world. I have myself issued twelve such books in the last thirty years, making twenty octavo volumes, besides dozens of monographs contributed to learned periodicals, and scores of reviews of important modern works. These ' parerga ' could hardly be expected to count, since they were not primarily academical contributions. But they at any rate prove that I have not been, like some researchers, a ' potterer '.

XIII

SOME HUMOURS OF HISTORY

THE errors of our friends may provoke no more than an indulgent smile. Those of our enemies may cause distinct exhilaration—*schadenfreude* as the Germans call it. When Homer nods, as the Roman poet knew that he occasionally did, we say no more than that the most inspired bard may have his less happy moments. But when our would-be instructor, much given to pontification, produces a ' howler ', the world grows lighter for us, and we say, with some self-complacency, that no one is infallible, least of all superior persons. This is, perhaps, not a very high-minded feeling, but we are all liable to experience its not unpleasant glow. I have myself derived some satisfaction from finding that the most scientifically trained continental historians may occasionally drop into statements of the same type as those to which our own native antiquaries are prone. Did not the almost omniscient Mommsen, trespassing for once on ground with which he was not over familiar, state in one of the chapters of his *Roman Empire* that Welsh is spoken in Cumberland ? And did not Seignobos, whose *Europe Contemporaine* was in its day one of the books most read in our Modern History School, display the normal Gallic ignorance of Holy Scripture, when he stated that the Adullamites in the British Parliament of 1866 were stigmatized as murderers by John Bright? 'Adullamites,' he wrote,

' i.e. assassins, allusion biblique, parce qu'Adullam a voulu tuer David.' The cave was unknown to him. And did not I note recently, in an authoritative work, patronized by an eminent Cardinal, a statement that an Edwardian Protestant bishop was displaced by Queen Mary STUART ?

But when we are dealing with the Middle Ages, with which I have a profound sympathy, and collecting the more eccentric statements of their chronicles, I feel that I must smile at the slips of old friends, rather than exult over the lapses of old enemies. The statements are often so preposterous that one lingers over them, and endeavours to trace their origins. To understand the spirit of any age one must have some conception of its outlook on the past, for our actions of to-day are often conditioned by our views of the meanings of yesterday—though the yesterday may be a thousand years off. I have therefore collected a number of impressions of what ancient history meant to the educated inquirers of various ages. Most chroniclers, it is true, were not so much political philosophers as anecdotal annalists ; but some were possessed with that same wild ambition for writing Universal History which inspired Orosius, Sir Walter Raleigh in his prison, or in our own day Mr. Wells. It is worth while to discover what the researcher thought about that long series of centuries which to the Christian writer started from the creation of Adam, so convincingly fixed in 4375 B.C., and went down to the birth of Christ. A conservative heathen would call it the time between Deucalion, I suppose, and Augustus Cæsar.

Professional historians were numerous in the later

centuries of the old classical world, some of them framers of general histories going back to the earliest conceivable periods of human existence—though they might not take Prometheus or Deucalion too seriously, and might perhaps take the First Olympiad or the year of the foundation of Rome as a convenient starting-point. But far beyond these fixed points were mythological conceptions or primæval tribal legends, of which the historian of a sophisticated age had to take at least some account—as witness the introductory chapters of Livy's first book, and countless incidental allusions in Herodotus. Different races had different versions of the primæval world, and thought very poorly of the versions of other races. The Roman was inclined to laugh at early Greek annals *quidquid Græcia mendax audet in historia.* The Greek invented rather derogatory stories about the origins of the Romans. It was not, indeed, unusual to ascribe degrading ancestry to neighbouring and unfriendly tribes—the Hebrews alleged that the Moabites and Ammonites were the children of incest, owing to Lot's involuntary lapse—which is perhaps more insulting than the allegation of the other Thessalians that the Myrmidons were descended from transmogrified ants. But could not the Myrmidons have replied that all their neighbours had much less intelligent progenitors than ants, since they must have come from the pebbles which Deucalion and Pyrrha threw over their shoulders in their celebrated promenade after the deluge ?

As the old Hellenic world grew less credulous, and came to doubt not only of the somewhat immoral Pantheon of Olympian gods, but of all subsidiary tribal legends that depended on divine ancestors, when in short the rationalizing spirit spread abroad, we come to one of the most amusing attempts to reconstruct early history. The tendency began before the man from whom it is usually called turned it into a regular system, but it is always associated with the name of Euhemerus. He was a philosopher of the Cyrenaic School, who in his Ἱερὰ Ἀναγραφή, written in the third century before Christ, reduced all the national gods into historic characters, whose doings had been distorted and magnified by popular tradition.

He even pretended to have found in the isle of Panchæa a memorial dedicated by Zeus himself, while he was still a mortal, to his ancestors Cronos and Uranus. But no one has rediscovered the mysterious isle of Panchæa. The early Christian authors were well acquainted with Euhemerus, whose theories were utilized by Tertullian, Clement of Alexandria, Cyprian, and Lactantius, when they were set on demolishing pagan myths. From the Early Fathers the method of Euhemerus passed on to the mediæval chroniclers, who were naturally ready to accept an explanation which cleared away ancient stories of the heathen gods, when it was transmitted on such excellent authority. Stringing together localities where the name of Zeus was prominent, Euhemerus composed for him a biography ; he was a prince who had conquered Syria and Cilicia, Crete and many other regions, ' and in those days when men lived in chaos and confusion, those who excelled in strength and ability not only became tyrants, but pretended to supernatural faculties and called themselves and were called by others divine.' (As were Alexander and

Julius Cæsar in much less remote ages.) Euhemerus could point out local names which testified to the particular centre in which each so-called god exercised his activities, there were even tombs associated with the memory of some members of that Pantheon which Homer and Hesiod had sorted out and regularized. Sometimes the gods were conquerors, sometimes men or women who had conferred some signal benefit on humanity, like Pallas the inventress of weaving, who had her first culture-centre at Lake Tritonis in Libya. So Pluto was a cruel and gloomy tyrant of the Molossians, who used to imprison travellers in a subterranean dungeon, and Apollo was a much-travelled physician and archer. To call a man the son of Zeus or Apollo merely emphasized in hyperbolical terms the fact that he was endowed with exceptional bodily or mental powers. This Euhemeran method was precisely that which was to be employed in the Middle Ages by certain chroniclers like Snorro Sturleson or Saxo Grammaticus, who, fascinated with ancient pagan legends about Odin, yet unable as Christians to grant him divinity, made him a human conqueror who came from Asgard and subdued all the North by his mysterious knowledge of languages, stratagem, machinery and thought-reading. Snorro, having duly buried Odin in his barrow by Upsala, was not quite certain that he or his spirit had not somehow survived. Hence his queer story of how King Olaf Tryggveson met the midnight mysterious visitor, in the midst of one of his fierce proselytizing tours, when he was forcing Christianity by the sword on all his subjects. To him, who sat late at night in a strange dwelling, there entered a venerable old man in ancient garb and with but one eye, who sat down before him and told him old-world tales, implying incredible knowledge of antiquity. The king was much intrigued by his presence, for no one knew who he was, or how he came there. Presently he was gone—having done nothing portentous, and apparently without having censured Olaf for his Christian zeal. The king thought, and so evidently did Snorro, that this was Odin come to say adieu, driven away by the Cross of Christ—the one eye was the distinguishing mark of the old god in all legends.

The later historians of the ancient world had at any rate some suspicion as to where myths ended and true chronology began, though they were a little tender to ancestral imaginings, when, unlike Euhemerus, they did not try to rationalize them, but merely reproduced them with a caution. They had some sense of the probable and the improbable. This faculty of criticism did not exist in the Middle Ages, when all pre-Christian annals were of much the same value, being for the most part transmitted at second hand through late Roman compendiums of general history such as that of Orosius, or collections of anecdotes. The chronicler had not before him any of the original Greek sources, Herodotus[1] or Thucydides or Xenophon or Polybius, which could not have been procured west of Constantinople. He had some late-Roman compendiums, a certain amount of the classical poets— Virgil was always treated as a historical authority— and of course the Bible, including the Apocrypha. The conception of ancient Greece was, I think, very

---

[1] The author of *Polychronicon* once or twice pretends to have information from ' Erodotus ', but evidently has not really read him.

meagre, and the names of its kings suggested little more than those of the kings of Persia or Egypt—they turned up occasionally in the Bible, like that famous he-goat—Alexander, to wit—in the vision of Daniel, who overthrows the equally mystic two-horned ram who figured the Medo-Persian Empire. And much concerning Greek tyrants could be got from the books of the Maccabees. There was a string of anecdotes about ancient Greek personages, notably Alexander the Great, Socrates, Diogenes the Cynic, Zaleucus, Plato, and Dionysius of Syracuse, drawn from Aulus Gellius, Valerius, or Isidore, or Cornelius Nepos. But the whole panorama was very vague ; a would-be historian like Geoffrey of Monmouth could produce in a fifth-century narrative, ' Epistrophius King of Græcia ', who turns up in the retinue of the equally fabulous Emperor Lucius Tiberius, to fight with King Arthur in Gaul, along with Alifantinam King of Spain and Teucer King of Phrygia. One wonders what precisely Greece meant to that fluent twelfth-century liar ; apparently a vassal monarchy under the Roman Empire. In romances of the later Middle Ages a King of Greece sometimes turns up among distressed sovereigns seeking for a champion—perhaps a blurred memory of some exiled emperor from Constantinople, like the young Alexius Angelus in 1204, or Baldwin II in 1261, or the much-travelled John Palæologus.

But Greek personages usually appear in anecdotic rather than in continuous narratives, to point a moral or adorn a tale—it must come as no surprise when in the *Eulogium Historiarum* Leonidas of Thermopylæ turns up as a King of the Athenians—the tale of self-devotion is inspiring whatever the King's nationality.

Undoubtedly the most famous and outstanding figure from ancient Greek history is Alexander the Great—something of him might be known from more respectable sources, but the masses of marvellous details concerning him appear to come in the main from the Pseudo-Callisthenes. There was a genuine Callisthenes, an unlucky philosopher, who came to disaster from crossing the ' Macedonian Madman ' when he was in one of his spasms of megalomania. He had actually written some account, as it appears, of his patron's earlier achievements before he fell a victim to Alexander's rage, but the Middle Ages knew his name as appended to a book of astonishing adventures, in which folk-tales and anecdotes, compiled perhaps at the Byzantine Court, but showing traces of Oriental as well as of Greek influence, were strung together as a coherent narrative on a very thin thread of real historical knowledge. The work was very well known in the West, first in a Latin form, and then translated into other languages, till in the shape of the *Romance of Alexander*, a version of it became the most popular book in Christendom. Chroniclers borrowed freely from it as a serious authority. It is touched with Christian as opposed to classical tradition in some sections. When Alexander reached the Caucasian Gates, the pass between the mountains and the Caspian Sea, he found hovering beyond them the descendants of the ten lost tribes of Israel, who petitioned for leave to journey back to Palestine. But on making inquiry from the high-priest Jaddua, whom he met at Jerusalem, concerning the history of these exiles, he was told of the heresy and wickedness which had led to the destruction of the Kingdom of Israel, wherefore he not only denied them passage, but built up the Caucasian Gates with a great wall of stone.   Oddly enough, the tradition of a great wall blocking out intruders from the North, got somehow confused in Western ideas with the Great Wall of China !   This extraordinary notion came from the fact that the fabulous history of Alexander took him much farther into the East than his real point of penetration, combined with the fact that the geography of Asia was very badly known.

Alexander's later exploits, outside the lands known to Western chroniclers, were extended into realms of pure fantasy.   He had dealings with Thalestris, queen of the Amazons, conversed with the talking trees of the Sun and Moon, who warned him against entering Babylon, and had his most famous adventure, immortalized in many mediæval pictures, in the land of the gryphons.   Having captured several of these winged monsters, he harnessed four of them to a car, and endeavoured to make a test flight.   He got up some distance into the air, but had a disastrous fall when the creatures took to jibbing, which nearly cost him his life.   There are scores of pictures of this incident in mediæval manuscripts.   Returning to Babylon, in defiance of the prophecy of the talking trees, Alexander perished, not—as in serious history—from fever and malaria, but from being given a draught of poison by his ambitious generals, Antipater and Cassander.

Only secondary to Alexander as a central figure for tales of the marvellous is his tutor, Aristotle, who appears in many tales as involved in his pupil's exploits.   He seems to have accompanied the Macedonian army not so much as the giver of philosophic advice as in the capacity of engineer and magician. The title of philosopher indeed in the Middle Ages had acquired a rather sinister meaning, philosophers were suspected of acquaintance with the Black Art— as indeed were all early scientists, and their successors even down to the sixteenth century. Aristotle and Socrates in the old world were suspected of nigromancy, even as Roger Bacon and Doctor Faustus were in later times. To find Socrates as a magician seems a little surprising to those who know him through the medium of Plato and Xenophon. But it must be remembered that he often spoke of his little δαιμόνιον, which warned him against ignoble acts or words— what we can see to have been conscience personified. To the mediæval chronicler this inhibitory monitor became that well-known phenomenon, a ' familiar spirit ', by aid of which Socrates accomplished marvels. For example, at the behest of Philip of Macedon, he put an end to two dragons who depopulated a region of Armenia by their poisonous breath, by means of an enormous observation pillar of glass. That Armenia was never in Philip's possession, and that Socrates was dead some years before the king was born, are matters of detail which would not have affected Albert of Stade, from whose *Universal History* the compiler of the *Gesta Romanorum* got the tale.

But Aristotle appears much more frequently than Socrates as an archimage, and has a whole cycle of adventures to his credit—or discredit. For while invaluable as a slayer of monsters and basilisks his moral character suffers sadly in romance. There is a weird tale of the indignities to which he was subjected by his mistress, of which occasional pictorial illustrations may be seen. Of his death several versions are given. The most popular, and the one for which comparatively early authority may be found, is that he plunged into the Euripus in a fit of rage, after discovering that he was unable to explain its curious double tide—a very unphilosophic end for a philosopher. This watery grave hardly fits in with another story to the effect that Aristotle had made provision for his interment, along with all his books of magic, in a tomb guarded by a spell which prevented any one from being able to approach its door. We are assured, however, that in some future age Antichrist will discover some way of opening the tomb, and by means of the compendium of Black Art contained in the library will work many miracles, and become Master of the World for a time. This curious legend is perhaps an echo of a genuine classical tradition, concerning Neleus of Scepsis, to whom Aristotle left his books : he was so jealous of them that he hid them underground for many years, so that they were much injured by damp before they were sold, several generations later, to a philosopher named Apellikon, from whom Sulla got them after the fall of Athens. This tale is vouched for by Strabo and Plutarch.

That wild legends could be attached in books of serious history to such definite personalities as Socrates, Alexander, and Aristotle, is easily to be explained by the fact that the mediæval chronicler was so familiar with marvellous tales belonging to much later ages, the saintly records of the early Christian centuries, that he saw no reason to reject similar wonders attributed to the old heathen times. Nor had he any dividing line between the early Greek and Roman mythological personages, and individuals from the centuries just before the Christian era. Æneas was just as real as Antiochus Epiphanes—though the former might come from Virgil and the latter from the books of the Maccabees ; Romulus was hardly more intangible than Julius Cæsar—strange tales were current about both of them. If St. George slew a dragon, which was certain, why should not Cadmus or Jason have done the same—or Socrates ? The ancient world, no doubt, was full of marvels—but so was the modern world—as witness all the semi-human creatures vouched for by Solinus—considered a most respectable geographer—or by the pseudo-Mandeville, who declared that he had seen some of them in his fourteenth-century travels. Do not the sea-serpent and the Loch Ness monster still crop up occasionally ? There was in the Middle Ages no reason to reject an ancient story merely because it was marvellous.

The main difficulty in dealing with classical annals was to see how they could be screwed into the accepted world-chronology dated by the genealogies in the Old Testament, and with Noah's deluge as a central stopping-point in 2340 B.C. Every one had to descend from one of Noah's three sons, unless indeed a compiler was bold enough, like one of the genealogists in the Anglo-Saxon Chronicle, to invent for the patriarch a fourth son, ' Sceaf born to Noah in the Ark ', from whom kings of Wessex could descend. What was to be done then with the personages of the early classical myths, for whom genealogies quite different from those of the accepted families of the house of Noah were existent? Taking the ancient Greek genealogies it was necessary to make synchronisms between them and the Biblical genealogies. It was worked out that Agamemnon and Achilles must have been contemporary with Ibzan, who judged Israel about A.M. 4026 or B.C. 1180. But what of their progenitors, of whose existence the mediæval chronicler had no more reason to doubt than he had to doubt of that of Alexander the Great? The authorities on whom he relied were of the same value for the earlier as for the later kings. There were serious difficulties in dealing with them—sometimes solved by taking a progenitor-god, after the manner of Euhemerus, as a glorified mortal. Higden is quite sure that Jupiter was a king of Crete, whose *floruit* was about the time of Joshua, i.e. somewhere near A.M. 3750, less than three hundred years before the sack of Troy, which the *Eulogium* fixes at A.M. 4003, when Jair was judge over Israel. Æneas did not get settled in Italy, apparently, till nearly twenty years later, when Abdon the Pirathonite was the dominating personage in Palestine.

There was a special snare set before the feet of English chronologers, in that they, almost without exception, swallowed the impudent invention of Geoffrey of Monmouth, and believed in a long series of British kings, descended from the Trojan Æneas, whose regnal years Geoffrey had carefully recorded. Brutus, the son of Silvius, and great-grandson of Æneas, had the misfortune to kill his father by chance while hunting ; he was expelled from Italy by his kinsfolk, and came to Britain after many adventures in A.M. 4084. This was while Eli was judge over

18

Israel. Brutus conquered Britain, then called Albion, and renamed it after himself. From him came generation after generation of fabulous kings, whose uncouth names are duly recorded by the *Eulogium* along with the contemporary rulers of Rome and of Palestine. Locrine, with his wife Gwendolen and his unlucky daughter Sabrina (of whom John Milton sang in ' Comus ') covered the time of King Saul. The foundation of Rome by Romulus and Remus fell in the reign of Ahaz, A.M. 4484, but taking the Christian reckoning in 753 B.C. which was just after the tragic fate of King Lear and his daughter Cordelia.

Continental chroniclers were not aware of the fact that, when we hear of the sack of Rome by the Gauls in 393 B.C., the invaders were not Gauls in the least, but Britons. Their chief Brennus was a British prince, expelled by his brother Belinus, who is best remembered from his having built Billingsgate in the City of London. Having gathered war-bands beyond the Alps, he not only sacked Rome but occupied all Northern Italy and set up the great Celtic settlement which the ancients called ' Cisalpine Gaul '—the first British colony !

The co-relations of Britain, Palestine, and the classic lands go on regularly—Xerxes and Aristides were about contemporaries of Molmutius Dunwallo, Britain's first legislator, King Lud (from whom Ludgate has its name) might have come into collision with Sulla, and Cassivellaunus (we come on a real person at last) was the prince who successfully beat off the invasion of Julius Cæsar. The chronicler could see no difference in authority between the career of Cassivellaunus and that of Lear or Locrine !

One of the results of this craving to conciliate classical and Biblical chronology, was a tendency to suppose that names had somehow got confused, and that a heathen ancestor was often a Biblical character misrepresented. In its wildest form this idea took the strangest developments—Serapis was a misconceived Joseph—and Æsculapius a rendering of Moses ! Perhaps the most startling narrative depending on this sort of conjecture is that concerning the foundation of Rome, which may be found in almost identical terms in the first chapter of the *Mirabilia Urbis Romæ* and the twenty-fifth of Higden's *Polychronicon*—the Chester monk obviously got it from the same source as the author of the *Mirabilia*, whom he calls ' Magister Gregorius '. This contains a fine mixture of items picked up from Virgil's *Æneid*, from the first chapter of Livy, from expanded Biblical tradition, and from malobservation of the ruins of ancient Rome by some archæologist of the Dark Ages.

' After the sons of Noah built the Tower of Confusion (Babel) Noah himself with some of his descendants entered into a ship and came to Italy. And close to where Rome now stands he founded a city called after his own name, where his travels and his life came to an end. Then his son Japheth and Janus his grandson, together with one Camisa, built the city of Janiculum. For Janus across the Tiber fortified the height where now stands the Church of St. John in Janiculo, though he had his kingly seat in the palace on the Palatine hill, where all the Cæsars and Emperors of after times dwelt. Moreover Nimrod, who is the same as that Saturn who was so shamefully maltreated by his son Jupiter, came to the realm of Janus, and built on the Capitoline Hill the settlement that is called Saturnia after him. And in those days Italus, with the Syracusans, coming to Janus and Saturn, built a city by the river Albula, and called it Italia after his name, and the river of Albula he renamed Tiber. This was before Hercules came into the realm of Janus with his Argives, or Evander the Arcadian with his men made their abode on the Palatine, as Virgil tells. After whom Roma, a daughter of Æneas, with a multitude of Trojans settled on the Palatine, and Silvius Aventinus, King of Alba, reared his abode and mausoleum on the Aventine mount. All this was before the day when, 433 years after the sack of Troy, Romulus, who was born of the blood of Priam, the last king of Troy, being in the twenty-second year of his life, encompassed all those old cities with a wall, and called the same Rome, after his own name, on the 15th day before the Calends of May, 753 years before the birth of Christ.

Oddly enough the one supernatural incident from early Roman Republican history which got reproduced again and again in mediæval books is the story of Marcus Curtius and his patriotic self-devotion in the yawning chasm of the ' Curtian Gulf '. But this tale got associated in the most astounding way with a statue then standing before the Lateran, though it is now placed on the summit of the Capitoline hill, in front of the Palazzo dei Conservatori. This is the fine bronze-gilt equestrian figure of the Emperor Marcus Aurelius, pacing slowly in triumph and extending his right hand. Higden in his *Polychronicon* very clearly says that it was known by several names—

some called it Constantine, some Theodoric, but clerks styled it Marcus Curtius.

The legend may be found both in Higden, in the *Eulogium Historiarum*, in the *Mirabilia Urbis Romæ*, and in the *Gesta Romanorum* in varying shapes. ' In the time of the Consuls and Senators ' Rome was besieged by a mighty king from Messina who had subdued all Italy not so much by force of arms as by Art of Magic. The Romans, after suffering much slaughter, shut themselves up inside their walls. A certain young man named Marcus, or Quintus (according to Higden), Curtius therefore offered the senate to deliver the city if he were promised 30,000 sesterces and an equestrian statue of bronze in case of his success. He had discovered that the tyrant was wont to go every night to the foot of a certain tree in the suburbs to renew his spells, also that his magic though it protected him from human hands was ineffective against animals. Wherefore he disguised himself as a camp servant or groom with a truss of hay across the crupper of his horse, and, coming out of the city by circuitous ways, rode round the edge of the hostile camp to the place where he knew that the king would be ' when the owlet hooted '. Passing through the escort which was waiting for the king, he made a sudden dash, though the lords in the escort shouted to him to go off to his business. But he came upon the king taken unawares, rode him down under the hoofs of his horse, and then snatched him up like a bundle, quite senseless, and galloped to the Lateran gate with his captive. Thereafter the Romans made a sally, raided the hostile camp, and dispersed the besieging army. The statue was duly erected as a memorial. Now the *Mirabilia* says that in front of Curtius there was a small quailing figure of a man in bonds under the horse's forefeet. It is possible that Marcus Aurelius in his original setting may have had a suppliant Sarmatian on his knees before him, as was not uncommon in Roman triumphal statues. If so, this figure had been removed when Paul III shifted the emperor from the Lateran to the Capitol in 1533. This is made the more likely by the fact that another account of the statue, in which it is given its alternative name of Constantine, also speaks of a minor figure before the horse. There is no trace of it on the present base.

The other form which the story of this bronze-gilt monument has taken, viz., that it represented the knight who sprang into the miraculous gulf in the Forum, may be found in that strange farrago the *Gesta Romanorum*. ' In the midst of Rome a chasm opened, which no human efforts could fill. The prophets, consulting the oracles, found that unless some man should voluntarily commit himself to the abyss, it would never close. Proclamation was made inviting a man to sacrifice himself for the weal of the State, but no candidate came forward till a certain knight, named Marcus Aurelius, said, ' If you will permit me to live as I please for the space of a whole year, I will cheerfully surrender myself at the end of it to this yawning chasm '. The senate assented, and Aurelius indulged for that year in every wish of his heart. ' Then mounting his war-horse he plunged into the abyss, which immediately closed its jaws.' The humour of this story is that the real Marcus Aurelius was a Stoic philosopher most indifferent to pleasures of all sorts. What a 'year off' would have meant to him is hard to guess. Considering his melancholy and introspective character, I can only conceive that it might have meant being let off for a year from the thankless job of being a highly responsible emperor.

With the approach of the end of the Roman Republic and of the commencement of the Christian Era, we find ourselves in a very curious stage of history, in which the usual anecdotes from Cornelius Nepos and such people get mixed with scraps from Josephus, and countless tales from the Apocryphal Gospels and the lives of the early saints. Pompey the Great, as we are assured, lost his good fortune for ever on the day on which he persisted in entering the Holy of Holies in the Temple of Jerusalem, despite of the warnings of the High Priest. A less well-known legend from this siege of Jerusalem, I happed upon at Florence, in a Renaissance picture by Ghirlandaio. Pompey's augur, one Fulvius, killed during the storm, is alleged to have prophesied that the tomb in which he was to be laid would one day be shared by a divinity.

> 'Ense cadens Solymo, Pompeii Fulvius augur
> Numen', ait, ' quae me contegit urna dabit.'

I cannot discover where this story had its origin. There are other legends about Pompey used as morals concerning fallen greatness and the chances of life. But about Julius Cæsar there is a whole cycle of tales— was he not one of the Seven Champions, and is there not even a 'Romance of Julius Cæsar', containing all the marvels of his real career, with many apochryphal ones added. Of course the gigantic phantom which forbade him to cross the Rubicon is not forgotten, but there are many incidents much more strange recorded. For example, after his murder in the Senate House, though he had been killed by more than twenty dagger thrusts, his body did not show the mark of one single wound when exposed for his funeral. It is surprising to learn that the Egyptian obelisk, which stands since 1586 in the Piazza in front of the Vatican, but which in the Middle Ages was before the Church of St. Andrea, contained Cæsar's ashes enclosed in a golden ball, on which was inscribed :

> Cæsar tantus eris quantus et orbis,
> Sed nunc in modico clauderis antro.

The verses, as their rhythm shows, suggest the eleventh century after Christ, rather than the first before him. William of Malmesbury has got them, but with a reference to a much later Cæsar, of Teutonic extraction.

The personality of Julius, incidentally, raised a great psychological problem to Renaissance thinkers. Was he to be considered the first legitimate Emperor of Rome, the starter of the great series of names which ran through Augustus and Charlemagne down to Louis of Bavaria, or Frederic of Hapsburg, or was he a military adventurer who had destroyed an ancient and venerable Republic ? The former view generally prevailed in the Middle Ages—the latter began to crop up in Republican Italy even before the Renaissance. Dante opted for the former view, being a consistent Ghibelline, and placed Brutus and Cassius, as ' traitors ' in the hottest place of his Inferno, along with Judas. But Italian tyrannicides who had to deal with Renaissance despots naturally took the opposite line, and the highest compliment that could be paid to the murderer of Alessandro de' Medici was to be called the ' Second Brutus '. Already Jacobin mentality was beginning to appear.

This ideological contrast, however, was of little importance before the fifteenth century while the existence of the Holy Roman Empire was obvious, and its origins were accepted as going back in some way to an original foundation by Cæsar and Augustus. A much more difficult problem was to combine respect for the immemorial and splendid imperial position with the thought that many of the early emperors were vicious persecutors of the infant Christian Church, not merely Nero, whom sacred and profane authors united in denouncing as a monster, but princes whom the heathen historians represented in a favourable light, such as Marcus Aurelius, Valerian, Decius, and even Diocletian. On the other hand we find Tiberius (of whom more hereafter) represented by the Christian writers in a rather sympathetic aspect—he is credited with some leanings towards reverence for Our Lord. Philip (the ungrateful murderer of young Gordian), receives in one story praises for having done public penance for his crime at the behest of St. Babylas, bishop of Antioch. And Domitian, at whom most modern writers look with the eyes of Juvenal, appears as a very wise and just prince who suffered no criminals to escape and ended his days in quiet ; while Maximinus also was ' a very gentle and peaceful emperor '.

Of course where the heathen and the Christian traditions clashed, the former had to be rejected. The

Gospel of Nicodemus was necessarily preferred to Tacitus. And this is why the narrative concerning the earlier emperors as presented by the mediæval chronicler contains so many surprises for us.

The history starts, of course, with Augustus, in whose reign Our Lord appeared. This great monarch was so named, according to Higden, because he was born in the month of August (!)—a strange inversion— or because he so much increased the size of the Empire (from the verb *augeo*). In his declining years he received a miraculous visit from the last authentic sibyl—the Tiburtine lady—who, while they were standing together on the western slope of the Capitoline Hill, showed him a vision of a Virgin and Child seated in a cloud-encircled halo of light upon an altar. The Emperor, much impressed, reared an altar on the spot, where the church of Ara Cœli now lies. At the same moment a certain ancient statue, which was to stand till the Lord of the World should come, fell to pieces, a circle of light was seen around the sun, and a fountain of oil sprang from the earth on the slope of Janiculum—not so impressive a phenomenon as the rest.

Incidentally, as falling at about the same date, we must mention that King Herod, being forced to journey to Rome in order to propitiate Augustus for his murderous doings, on his way burned the ships of the men of Tarsus, because they had given berths to the Three Magi, when they made their prudent escape from Bethlehem after the Nativity, instead of returning to Jerusalem to make their report to the king of what they had seen. This incident would destroy a subject familiar to all painters of all ages—the kings of the East making off on their camels. No other version that I know makes them depart on ship-board.

If Augustus was reigning at the time of the Nativity, the Crucifixion fell in the time of Tiberius, and around that monarch cluster a whole series of legends. We must cast away all our preconceived ideas drawn from Tacitus and Suetonius. Tiberius was the most wise and just monarch that Rome ever saw, according to the Gospel of Nicodemus, the primary authority used by mediæval chroniclers. But he was troubled (as Suetonius also relates) with an unpleasant disease of the skin which made his face unsightly. One result of this affliction was that on hearing that there was, in Judæa, a wonder-working healer, who could cure diseases by a word, he sent a courtier named Volusian to Pontius Pilate, ordering him to send the physician to Rome without delay. The unhappy Pilate had to confess to the imperial messenger that he had crucified the healer only a short time back, at the instigation of the Jews, who declared that Jesus had declared himself a king. Volusian therefore held an inquiry into the circumstances, came to the conclusion that Pilate had behaved abominably, arrested him, and took him off to Rome to face the emperor. But as the best thing connected with Christ that he could offer as evidence, he brought to Tiberius the linen cloth of St. Veronica, on which the face of our Lord had been impressed during his journey to Calvary, and the woman herself to vouch to its miraculous character. On receiving the ' Vernicle ' as the Middle Ages styled the holy cloth, Tiberius was at once healed of his loathsome disease. He acknow-

ledged the divinity of Christ on the spot, and turned
to punish Pilate, who was imprisoned and while under
sentence of death by torture slew himself with a knife.
His body was thrown into the Tiber, but all the evil
spirits of the air hovered around the bloated corpse,
with such lightnings, thunderings, disturbance of the
water by whirlpools, and foul stenches, that the emperor
ordered the body to be fished up and sent by boat to
the Rhone—surely an unpleasant voyage for the boat-
men ! But when Pilate was again ·plunged into that
river near Vienne, the same unpleasant phenomenon
followed, and a pestilence broke out in the town. The
citizens, therefore, again dredged up the putrid corpse,
and sent it over the hills to Losanna, in Helvetia—
but for Lausanne we must read Lucerne, for it was
certainly near the latter place that ' in a waste water
surrounded by steep hills where even to this day
horrible sounds and voices are heard ', i.e., under
' Mount Pilatus ', the wicked procurator found his
last resting place. Higden owns that the whole story
seems muddled in the Gospel of Nicodemus, as according to one version that he had seen Pilate was put
to death by Caius Cæsar, not by Tiberius, several
years after the Crucifixion of Our Lord. ' Sed potest
utraque historia sinc repugnantia salvari,' for Pilate
might have been brought twice to Rome—anyhow,
both Eusebius and Bede say that he slew himself.

But the Gospel of Nicodemus goes on to give us
some more very curious information about Tiberius.
He was so grateful for the miracle of healing wrought
by the ' Vernicle ' that after twenty months he got
himself baptized, and ordered the Senate to acknowledge the divinity of Christ, and to place his statue

above that of all other gods in the Pantheon. But when the Senate made strenuous objection, he grew so much provoked that he ordered several prominent senators to be executed, with various forms of punishment. And though up to this time he had been held a most merciful and moderate prince, now ' saevissime grassatus est in nobilitatem Romanam '. This is the reason why Pagan writers have maligned his general character, and represented him as drunken, profligate, and cruel. But his reign of terror did not last for long, for he died shortly after ; while walking by the temple of Isis on the river bank, he missed his footing, fell in, and was drowned. This, as we read with astonishment, was the incident from which the River Tiber got its name ! We are not informed as to its earlier appellation, or how it came to be that Virgil, Livy, and others persisted in calling it the Tiber, before this unfortunate drowning.

Nero, of course, was a favourite target for the mediæval historians, who ascribe to him not only his familiar atrocities—the deaths of his wife Octavia, his mother Agrippina, and his tutor Seneca, but some additional crimes. Of Seneca, incidentally, we may add that his name was ominous—*quia se necavit*—he committed suicide : also that he was a familiar friend of St. Paul, and attended his sermons in that ' hired house ' in Rome which is mentioned in the Acts of the Apostles. Eight letters in very barbarous Latin, supposed to have been written by Seneca to Paul, were current in the fifth century, a very early example of a pious fraud !

The queerest story of Nero, I think, is that of the frog, to which he attached an unholy origin, and which he kept in a secret underground chamber—on the spot afterwards called the Lateran—*a latente rana*, from the hidden frog. All through the Middle Ages the malevolent ghost of Nero was supposed to haunt the gardens outside the Porta del Popolo, and to bring ill-luck to all who met it. It may not generally be known, though the *Polychronicon* gives full details, that Nero was a great patron of Simon Magus, and that when the magician's aerial flight came to a disastrous end, through the ban of St. Peter, he was infuriated against the apostle. This is why Peter, instead of being executed in the ordinary fashion, was crucified upside down.

The short reigns of Galba, Otho, and Vitellius attracted little notice from the chroniclers, though they did not omit a mention of the gluttony of the last-named emperor, who had five meals a day, and once shared a dinner with his brother and his friends, at which two thousand fish and seven thousand birds were served up at table. His special delight was in a large silver dish, which he called ' Minerva's shield ', on which were laid out nothing but the tongues of pheasants and other delicate birds. These, of course, are all borrowings from Suetonius.

Vespasian was a favourite hero for legendary tales —primarily (no doubt) because he figures so largely in Josephus, whose Jewish histories were in every monastic library. But in addition to tales from that source, such as the sinister visions in the air and the cannibalism during the siege of Jerusalem, there are other and wilder stories current from less trustworthy authority. Though the parentage may seem surprising, Vespasian is alleged by the *Eulogium Historiarum* to have been the son not of a Sabine farmer but of a king of Galatia. His name was given him from a curious disease—he was always infested by wasps in his nose ! *Quoddam genus vermium naso insitum ab infantia gerebat, quæ vespæ sunt dictæ, et inde a vespis dictus est Vespasianus.* Being visited by a Christian named Albanus, who used the holy name as a spell against his disease, he was cured—the wasps fell from his nose and died. Becoming, as was natural, a baptized convert, he resolved to show his gratitude in some practical fashion, and resolved to punish the Jews. Having got leave from the Emperor (one version says from Tiberius, another from Nero), he raised an army and marched against Jerusalem. After this prologue to the legend, we come on screeds of perfectly sound history from Josephus, but a strange finish is reserved for the catastrophe. We must remember, however, that throughout his operations Vespasian is regarded as the conscious avenger of the crimes of Annas and Caiaphas, not as a mere Roman general. The astounding termination of the tale is that when, in the last stage of the siege of Jerusalem, the Romans burst through the temple wall, they found, bricked up in it, but quite alive, a venerable old man, who, when interrogated, declared that he was Joseph of Arimathæa, the disciple of Christ. The Sanhedrin had been so much incensed at the part that he took in the burial of Our Lord, that they had ordered him to be walled up without food or water, to die of starvation. But not only was his life preserved, but he was fed from time to time with heavenly food, and visited by flashes of celestial light for thirty-seven years. Nor was his bodily strength abated, for on being released, he preached the Gospel in Britain, and founded the original church in the Isle of Avalon, which men now call Glastonbury, and there planted his well-known thorn which blooms at Christmas. The dates here seem a little confusing, for in one chapter Joseph's mission to Britain is placed in the year A.D. 63, while the fall of Jerusalem certainly took place in A.D. 70. But such difficulties mattered little to the omnivorous compiler of the *Eulogium Historiarum* !

Trajan was the central figure of several famous legends. He was somewhat of a puzzle to the chroniclers—for the verdict of all the pagan historians was in his favour, yet undoubtedly there was a sharp persecution of Christians in his time. The author of the *Eulogium* compromises, by saying that he persecuted ' *non voluntate propria sed coactus* '. His letter to Pliny on the subject was known and quoted—from which it was deduced that he had no great wish to persecute, but was unable to break administrative rules, condemning those who refused to do sacrifice to the gods. And so it came to pass that, though his memory is saddled with the stories of the martyrdoms of St. Irenæus, of Simon Cleophas, Bishop of Jerusalem, and apparently of Pope Evaristus, the legends about him do not centre around acts of cruelty, but are rather favourable to his reputation. The most famous is that of ' Trajan's Justice ', connected with a famous sculpture of an emperor and a kneeling woman, which stood at the ' Arch of Piety ' and was much visited in the Middle Ages. Trajan, it is said, was mounted and setting forth on an expedition at the head of his army, when a widow woman threw herself before his horse, and cried for justice. He checked himself, looked down, and said that on his return she should have justice. ' But,' she said, ' peradventure thou mayest die and not return ? ' This considering, he lighted down and held a court then and there. The woman said, ' I had one only son and a man has slain him '. Upon this saying the emperor said, ' The murderer shall die and not live '. And he had the man apprehended and led out for execution, but seeing him about to perish, the widow relented, and asked that he might be spared, which Trajan granted, saying that he gave him over to the woman in return for the lost son : and then he went upon his way with all his army. The strange sequel to this story is that St. Gregory, five centuries after, looking upon the sculpture, was moved to pray that such a ruler, though a heathen, might be granted remission of the pains of hell, and in a vision received assurance that his petition was granted. Dante, in *Purgatorio*, x. 73, saw Trajan's shade among those who were to be redeemed in due course of time. It is probable that his name was better known than that of most emperors because of the marvellous works that he left behind him, not only the Column of which the *Mirabilia Urbis Roma* makes ample mention, but also the greater extension of his Forum, which were destroyed by Pope Paul V and other vandals of the sixteenth century.

One might go on for three centuries more giving further examples of the way in which the most hon-oured folk-tales of the general stock are fitted on to well-known Roman emperors from Hadrian to The-dosius, and made into a curious mosaic with broken scraps of Suetonius, the *Historia Augusta*, Orosius or Eusebius, and above all of the *Aurea Legenda* stories

19

of the saints. To suit the Church tradition, imperial characters sometimes take transformed shapes—Antoninus Pius commits an atrocity, Maximinus becomes a 'very gentle and peaceful emperor', Constantine a model personage, and Julian the Apostate is made to enact the whole appalling tragedy of Œdipus—which, as the Gospel of Nicodemus relates, had already been paralleled by that of Judas Iscariot.

In all these lurid centuries a problem keeps cropping up which puzzled the mediæval mind—what were the heathen gods ? Were they dumb idols such as the Jewish prophets used to denounce, or were they actual personalities—evil spirits : and if the latter was the case, what was their relation to Christian demonology ? Every reader of Dr. Garnett's extraordinary and amusing book on the *Twilight of the Gods* will remember how that whimsical archæologist dealt with this age-old difficulty in the *Poet of Panopolis*. Were heathen gods Christian devils, mere myrmidons of Satan, or were they supernatural beings of another sort ? There was good evidence in the lives of the saints for the view that the whole Greco-Roman pantheon were simply devils of greater or lesser degree. A fine illustrative story is that of St. Gregory Thaumaturgus and the oracle of Apollo. The saint, belated while travelling, took refuge for the night in a dark portico, which at morning light proved to be that of an oracular temple. He went on his way, but that day the oracle refused to perform at all : the priests discovered that a Christian had slept in the shrine, and sent after Gregory to beg him to take off the ban which he had unwittingly placed upon the utterances of their god. The saint did not—as might perhaps have been expected—refuse the petition, but, after warning the priests of the wickedness of their practices, wrote a short epistle and bade them place it upon the tripod. The words ran : ' Gregory to Satan—You may re-enter '. When the screed was placed upon the tripod the inspiration returned, and the machinery worked as usual. From this we can only conclude that Apollo was Satan—or at least a minor devil controlled by Satan.

The latter view is quite a conceivable hypothesis, for there is no doubt that Satan had many subordinate fiends in his employ. Though in the celebrated legend of Theophilus, which Eutychianus wrote and which Hroswitha dramatized, the despairing cleric made his bargain with the Devil himself, in others whole bevies of evil spirits appear. St. Anthony was tormented by a complete legion of them, and St. Guthlac by a good many. The Venus in the legend of the ring and the sorcerer Palumbus was certainly only a satellite of the master-fiend, who was compelled to order her to restore the ring. But the Venus of the Tannhäuser story, though sometimes conceived of as an emissary of Satan—*Teufelskind*—seems more properly to be counted as a personification of the old surviving nature-power of lust and luxury. That interesting writer Cæsarius of Heisterbach, who was a specialist in devils, and had come upon dozens of them, seems to deal sometimes with the supreme master of evil, much more often with less important sprites, who occasionally seem little better (or worse) than pucks or goblins. These were the sort of creatures whom wizards or witches could secure as ' familiar spirits ' by dreadful bargains with the infernal

19*

powers. And I suppose that the snake-like devil whom St. Philip casts out of the temple of Mars in so many fourteenth or fifteenth-century pictures was no more than a subordinate fiend, or the dragons who bore Simon Magus through the air before the admiring eyes of Nero. When the saints, therefore, healed persons ' possessed ', or chased away monsters, they were but dealing with Satan's petty militia, not with the Arch-fiend himself, who appears comparatively seldom as a dangerous and formidable adversary.

Leaving demonology and second-hand scandals about emperors aside, I feel that one ought not to quit the survey of mediæval conceptions of Roman history without a word on one great figure who was neither an emperor nor a saint, but pervades many legends—' Magister Virgilius ', not only poet but also magician. Why the author of the *Æneid* and the *Georgics* should have achieved such a pre-eminence in the mediæval tradition, it is not easy to discern. But he turns up everywhere ; not only did he accompany Dante in his awful visit to the underworld, but he appears in many lighter tales in a less majestic pose. Some think that the reverence for him as the one great surviving poet from the old world caused him to be treated with special respect, as Homer was by the Greeks. But this would not sufficiently account for the peculiar aspect which he assumes in mediæval tradition, not merely as poet but as a semi-supernatural personage. By an ingenious perversion of some famous passages he is made to foresee the Christian not the Augustan ' Golden Age ', and to herald the glories not of the young Marcellus but of the Messiah. Serious commentators have hazarded a guess that Virgil had taken a glimpse into Jewish Messianic prophecy.

But he is more often not a staid and almost saintly figure, but a freakish magician, given to strange and sometimes impish tricks of wizardry. The names of his mother and grandfather, Maia and Maius, were said to be corruptions of Maga and Magus, so that he might have been reared in a family addicted to the Black Art. The incantations described in the Eighth Eclogue were supposed to be serious affairs, drawn from personal knowledge—it could not, of course, be known in the Middle Ages that they were copied from Theocritus. But most certainly Virgil was a mighty enchanter and mechanician, even as Aristotle had been in an earlier age.

He fashioned for Augustus a group of images which were known as ' Salvatio Romæ '. They consisted of representations of each of the provinces of the Empire, holding bells in their hands. They were imbued with such mystic power that when any region was meditating insurrection, the figure representing it began to ring its bell, and did not stop till the priest in charge of the show had reported it to the emperor. Thus Augustus got warning of rebellion even before it had broken out, and was enabled to take preventitive measures betimes. The whole story has a slight adumbration of the idea of wireless telegraphy.

It is, chronologically speaking, more surprising to find that Virgil made for the Emperor Titus—he must have been a centenarian and more by A.D. 80— a machine even more useful than the figures of the ' Salvatio Romæ '—an image which, by the marvellous power instinct in it, communicated to the emperor

all crimes committed in secret. The illustrative anecdote concerning this figure in the *Gesta Romanorum*
shows that it would register even such slight offences
as working on a public holiday. So great was the
unpopularity of the image among habitual offenders of
all sorts, that Titus had to set a guard of soldiers over
it, or it would have been smashed on every night.
What an invaluable possession for the ruler of a
' policed ' state, such as those over which Hitler or
Stalin preside ! Instead of having to collect and
maintain an enormous system of informers, at vast
expense, the tyrant would be able, if only he possessed
a Virgil, to dispense with all fallible human reports
and to trust to machinery !

To find the poet-magician at work in the reign
of Titus is surprising—but how much more so is it
to discover in the sixty-sixth chapter of the *Eulogium
Historiarum* under the year 548, in the reign of Justinian,
' hoc anno Virgilius librum suum edidit, et Neapoli
sepelitur cum libro suo '. He must apparently have
survived for some six centuries, and like Aristotle
before him and Michael Scott in a later age, have been
buried with his book of spells. But his recorded
marvels, not only those cited above, but the wall of
glass, the bridge of air, and the golden leech which
devoured all other leeches, are all placed in the times
of the Early Empire.

Ancient history then, as visualized by the mediæval
mind, was a far more romantic record than it is to the
modern student. A glory has departed from it, and
we who ponder over the Minoan inscriptions, the
constitution of Cleisthenes, or the *proconsulare
imperium*, are debarred from feeling the thrills of the

fifteenth-century inquirer when he studied the curious dealings of the Emperor Claudius with the philosopher Socrates, shuddered at the dragon which Pope Silvester hunted out of the Colosseum, or marvelled at the strange visit of those two naked and austere sages Phidias and Praxiteles to the court of Tiberius, and at the revelations that they made to him. All these interesting scraps of history must have been familiar to Oxford graduates of the fifteenth century—now I fear that there is hardly any one but myself in the University who has ever heard of them ! But they may serve to raise a smile among those to whose notice they are now brought, for the first time.

ON GENERAL LESSONS AND MORALS

ALL that I have already put on record in the very miscellaneous gathering of my considered opinions on history may seem to some students mere occasional ' glimpses of the obvious '—to others paradoxical carping. Nevertheless I have to deliver my message to all who intend to make history the mistress of their life. The first conclusion is that ' the best ', the ideal, the vision of the infallible *magnum opus* which hovers before the mind of many a beginner, is the enemy of ' the good ', of the useful but comparatively unambitious book that he is really at the moment competent to write. Do not be led away by megalomania ; do not think that you can possibly produce a book without mistakes ; the man who imagines that he can do so will probably never write any book at all. The great Turenne once remarked that the general who has made no errors in strategy must have commanded in uncommonly few campaigns, and hinted that he did not believe that such a general had ever existed. It is the same with the writer of history : he must make up his mind that however hard he may strive to obtain accuracy of deduction from the material before him, it is certain that there will be errors of detail somewhere—perhaps errors of more than detail. A newly excavated inscription may prove that an accepted date is wrong—an unpublished letter of some statesman may reveal some unsuspected motive : a document in some public office may disprove figures which have passed through many a statistical summary. When the book has been published some meticulous critic will gloat over the fact that the writer did not know of some piece of evidence which at the time that he was at work was not yet available. But never, from fear of some possible error, shrink from production. I have known books hung up for years, and sometimes never issued, because the author had not the heart to confess himself possibly fallible. I can remember cases where a man who could have done good work died bookless, not because he was not capable of producing valuable work, but because he hated the idea of seeing his limitations revealed to the world by some captious critic. Such critics there are—generally people of the same type as the man who hates to commit his work to print. ' Oh that mine adversary had written a book,' exclaimed the patriarch Job ; since literary periodicals did not exist in his day, the Patriarch was not thinking of the joy of reviewing his enemy's work. But the modern critic feels that joy, when he has detected and made public misprints in the index, or when he can insert a mention of the fact that the ' author does not seem to have been aware of the private correspondence of X with Y ', recently published. But I must not fall into exposition of the ways of critics, anxious to show their own special knowledge of some minute point, rather than to give a general account of a new book.

The honest historian must not approach his life's work dominated by the pride which hates to acknowledge an occasional slip. Rather he must remember

that the competent labourer who refuses his co-opera-
tion in the great work of garnering the harvest of the
past is sinning against the light. The harvest is still
very great and the labourers are none too many. We
stand at present in a time when the raw material has
accumulated in such masses that there is a pressing
want of hands to sort and arrange it. To stand by
idle because some of the work looks like what Lord
Bolingbroke called 'drudgery', or because *amour
propre* revolts against the idea that some of one's
deductions may not be certain, and may be disproved,
is deplorable. By setting forth a hypothesis that may
turn out to be only half true, or by formulating a
thesis that requires indefinite modification, we may
serve the cause of history far better than by refusing
to put anything on paper that is not absolutely certain,
complete, and undeniable. It is only the most pur-
blind critic who condemns the pioneer in any line of
research for not having achieved absolute accuracy.
Columbus when discovering America wrongly believed
that he had reached the Indies : is his service to
geography to be ignored or derided because his
achievement was made while pursuing a hypothesis
that was erroneous ? The world greatly needs
Columbuses ; it has no great esteem for those who
gloried in exposing his error, after he had started the
great western quest. And if it be true that the path
of historical discovery, like the path of geographical
discovery, is strewn with wrecks of many expeditions,
it remains an undoubted fact that the expeditions were
made in good faith and bold initiative. The unpardonable thing is to follow the habit of those mediæval
chroniclers with whom I have been dealing of late,

who blindly accepted the existing record, and went on repeating it, without making any endeavour to test its accuracy or to enlarge its scope.

I would be far from denying that the critic has his uses. It is no doubt better to have set right in reviews even a dozen mistakes in other men's books, than to have written nothing at all. If one cannot be the pioneer, one can at least do unostentatious work, like the navvy who makes smooth the path which the pioneer has discovered, by removing stones or filling up quagmires. Only let the critic work in a reverent spirit, not denigrating but respecting the predecessor who found out the track on which he is now at work. It is only the meanest modernist who laughs, from his present pinnacle of knowledge, at Friar Bacon, Henry the Navigator, or Copernicus.

Different people with the historic urge upon them, may take up different lines of work—the important thing is that they should take up some line, and not confine themselves to meticulous criticism. The work undertaken may be small or great, ranging from a bibliography or the printing of the records of a mediæval borough up to the survey of centuries of civilization. But if one cannot write a large book one can write a little one. If even a small book is too much to ask, the printing or editing of some single forgotten record might have its worth. It may be an unremunerative piece of work, or an obscure piece of work, or even an uninteresting piece of work ; but it is incumbent on the individual to do what he can. Every trained specialist owes his ' stone to the cairn '. ' Research ' is not all that is needed—it may lead to the accumulation of knowledge in the researcher's brain, but unless its results are printed the accumulated knowledge will die with him. Rather what is required is zeal, insatiable curiosity, a dogged determination to work at all times and in all places, and *then* a stern resolve to print the results—even though they seem incomplete, and though there may be a danger of their being superseded on account of later discoveries.

Literary skill is desirable, but not indispensable, though a crabbed style is always to be deprecated. But it is rather less deplorable than the desire to shine at all costs, to let off fireworks, to write a historical ' thriller ', or to create a sensation by ' debunking ' some well-known national hero, or by whitewashing some notorious reprobate. Such work is done to attract attention to the writer's ingenuity, rather than to serve the cause of accurate historical truth. Above all things the guiding motive must be to strive for the increase of knowledge, not for the self-advertisement of the writer. A stoic resolve, perhaps, but stoicism means self-denial, without any regard for personal pride, and with much respect to one's ideals of right and wrong, which are, after all, the only things that matter to an honest man.

INDEX

Index